australia's SPORTING SUCCESS

J O H N   B L O O M F I E L D

australia's
SPORTING SUCCESS

the
INSIDE *story*

UNSW PRESS

A UNSW Press book

Published by
University of New South Wales Press Ltd
University of New South Wales
Sydney NSW 2052
AUSTRALIA
www.unswpress.com.au

National Library of Australia
Cataloguing-in-Publication entry:

    Bloomfield, John, 1932– .
    Australia's sporting success: the inside story.

    Includes index.
    ISBN 0 86840 582 5.

    1. Sports administration – Australia – History.
    2. Sports – Government policy – Australia – History.
    3. Sports and state – Australia – History.
    4. Sports – Australia – History. I. Title.

    796.0690994

Cover Brad McGee, Leon Mead/Newspix
Design Di Quick
Printer Everbest Printing, China

Contents

Dedication   viii

Acronyms and abbreviations   ix

Foreword   x

Acknowledgments   xii

Preface   xiv

Introduction   1

Chapter One   Australia — A sporting nation   3

Early social dynamics in Australian sport   3

  The 'currency'   3

  The British influence   5

  Nationalism   6

  Egalitarianism and social cohesion   9

  Tenacity   11

  Volunteering   13

Australia's sporting origins   14

  Early developments in sport   14

  Consolidation at home and forays into international sport 15

Sports development 1900–1972   23

  Domestic sport — before 1946   23

  International performances — before 1946   26

  Domestic sport — after World War II   27

  International performances — after World War II   30

  Australia falls behind   31

Chapter Two   Beginning a professional sports system   34

Pre-1973 sport developments   34

  National fitness councils   34

  Early calls for Ministries of Sport and Recreation   35

  Western Australia leads the way   37

The Whitlam era — 1972–75   38
  Frank Stewart's ministry   38
The Fraser years   43
  The early period — 1975–78   43
  Bob Ellicott's influence — 1979–83   54

Chapter Three Evolution of the sports system   69
The Hawke Labor Government — 1983–88   69
  The John Brown era   69

Chapter Four Consolidation of the sports system   91
The Hawke-Keating Labor Governments — 1988–96   91
  Graham Richardson's ministry   91
  After Graham Richardson   98

Chapter Five How governments assist sport   109
The role of various government agencies   109
  Specific sports services   109

Chapter Six Community support for sport   144
The role of non-government agencies   144
  Specific sports services   144

Chapter Seven A professional sports system in place   179
The Howard Government — 1996–   179
  The lead-up to Sydney 2000   179
  The Sydney 2000 Olympics   182
  The Sydney 2000 Paralympics   191
  Post-Games assessments   194

Australia's social ambience during the Games   195
Reflections   198

Chapter Eight The future — where to from here?   199
After the Sydney Olympics   199
  Avoiding a post-Olympic slump   199
  Post-Olympic performances   200
Problems ahead for Australian sport   209
  Threats from other countries   209
  Issues within Australia   213
Strategies for the future   217
  Current changes to the sports system   217
  Possible modifications for the future   218
  The way forward?   221

References and notes   222

Appendices   242
  Appendix A — Letter of request for a ministry   242
  Appendix B — Australia's sports performances in 1991–92   243
  Appendix C — Australia's sports performances in 1999   245
  Appendix D — Article by NSW Premier Bob Carr   247
  Appendix E — Article by Martin Stewart-Weeks   249
  Appendix F — Australia's sports performances in 2001   251
  Appendix G — Further references   253
  Appendix H — Photo credits   255

Index   256

Dedication

This book is dedicated to several individuals who have encouraged me, in my personal and professional life, to follow what has been both my profession and my enduring passion. They are:

PROFESSOR FRANK COTTON
who encouraged me to pursue my own sporting career
as a 16-year-old and who introduced me to sports science;

MR FORBES CARLILE
who assisted with my training as a young athlete, as well
as giving me an appreciation of the value of sports science;

PROFESSOR PETER SIGERSETH
my mentor and surrogate father for almost eight
years in the United States;

and

MRS NOELENE BLOOMFIELD
my wife for 44 years, who has been my best friend and
greatest supporter in all my endeavours.

Acronyms and abbreviations

AAESS   Australian Association for Exercise and Sports Science
ABC   Australian Broadcasting Commission
ACC   Australian Coaching Council
ACGA   Australian Commonwealth Games Association
AIS   Australian Institute of Sport
ANZAAS   Australian and New Zealand Association for the Advancement of Science
AOC   Australian Olympic Committee
ARU   Australian Rugby Union
ASC   Australian Sports Commission
ASDA   Australian Sports Drug Agency
ASMF   Australian Sports Medicine Federation
ASSH   Australian Society for Sports History
CAS   Confederation of Australian Sport
FIMS   Fédération Internationale Médicine Sportive
IOC   International Olympic Committee
LBII   'Life Be In It' Program
NASSH   National American Society for Sports History
NCAS   National Coaching Accreditation Scheme
NESC   National Elite Sports Council
NSIC   National Sports Information Centre
NSOs   National Sporting Organisations (formerly National Sports Associations or Federations)
NTCP   National Training Centre Program
OAP   Olympic Athlete Program
PGA   Professional Golfers' Association of Australia
SIA   Sports Industry Australia
SLSA   Surf Life Saving Australia
SMA   Sports Medicine Australia
SOCOG   Sydney Organising Committee for the Olympic Games
SSOs   State Sports Organisations

Foreword

When Sydney was selected in 1993 to host the 2000 Olympic Games, the President of the International Olympic Committee, Juan Antonio Samaranch, suggested to me that Australians would judge their success on the performance of the Australian team; and that our athletes must receive the necessary funding to ensure that success. His counsel became the catalyst for the injection of significant additional Australian Government and Olympic funding for Australia's elite Olympic and Paralympic athletes, who delivered well beyond the expectations of most.

Fortunately, the foundations for this success had already been laid in the 1970s. The poor performance of the Australian Olympic Team at the 1976 Montreal Games, combined with the Fraser Government's attempt to force the Australian Olympic Federation to boycott the 1980 Moscow Games, resulted in an outcry from the sporting public. In a placatory gesture, the Australian Government finally established the Australian Institute of Sport (AIS) in 1981.

The author of this book, Professor John Bloomfield, had long been at the forefront of calls to establish a modern sports system in Australia, including a National Institute of Sport. When the AIS was established, he was appointed the first deputy chairman and subsequently became its chairman. He is thus well qualified to chronicle the achievements of the AIS as well as the evolution of our sports system through to the Sydney Olympics. Indeed, such was John's remarkable involvement in the development of the Australian sports system that this aspect of our sporting history could well be his biography. The academic in him, however, resisted that temptation in favour of this most thoroughly researched and scholarly history.

John Bloomfield grew up on the south coast of New South Wales and was an Australian surf lifesaving representative, experiencing at first hand the development of that fine volunteer movement. While the performances of the Australian Olympic and Paralympic teams in Sydney ensured the support of a nation, it was the volunteers who helped to deliver the 'best ever' Games, and John is well qualified to assess this aspect of Australian society.

In this vibrant history he has objectively and critically analysed the evolution of the Australian sports system. I was particularly interested in the social dynamics of early sport in the colony and their effect on our evolution as a nation in general, and on our sportsmen and sportswomen in particular.

Finally, this book accurately identifies the reasons for Australia's sporting success thus far. Importantly, however, it also challenges any smugness that might be creeping into the system since the Sydney Olympics. While Australian sport is indebted to John Bloomfield for his key role in the development of the successful sports system we now enjoy, his early identification of some signs of complacency may become one of his greatest legacies. I hope so.

John D Coates
President
Australian Olympic Committee

Acknowledgments

This book would not have been possible without the invaluable advice and analysis so generously offered by the many people who expressed great interest in this project. Much of the basic material I have drawn from other sources — hence the 600-odd reference citations — but as well as that, I have interviewed 30 experienced professionals with a specialised knowledge of various aspects of Australian sport. In order to reach objective conclusions on several crucial issues, a structured interview technique was used with an additional 22 highly experienced individuals, so that a cohesive body of knowledge could be gathered on topics which were central to the evolution of the Australian sports system.

Many of those mentioned below participated in the above exercise, while others advised me on several specialised aspects of the book. I therefore wish to thank the following people for their assistance: Ron Alexander, Harvie Allison, Jock Anderson, Stephanie Beltrame, Colin Benjamin, Brian Blanksby, Alan Bloomfield, John Boultbee, Deirdre Boyd, Paul Brettell, John Brown, Ursula and Forbes Carlile, Sylvia Carr, Margaret Chalker, Renae Clement, Lauren Cowan, Perry Crosswhite, Jeff Crow, Bill Daley, John Daly, Wilson Da Silva, Graham Dempster, Wendy Deverson, John Devitt, Brian Dixon, Ralph Doubell, Ken Edwards, Mathew Eggins, Bob Ellicott, Bruce Elliott, Jack Evans, Ken Fitch, Wally Foreman, Daryl Foster, Donna Fox, Peter Fricker, Barrie Galton, Jason Gulbin, Allan Hahn, Phil Hamdorf, Pamela Harris, Greg Hartung, Jill Haynes, David Headon, Bob Hobson, Louisa Hubble, Adrian Hurley, Helen Irving, Don Jackson, Laksiri Jayasuriya, Rob Langer, Leanne Lind, Steve Lawrence, Karen McBrien, Ros McNamara, Roy Masters, Greg Nance, Mike Nunan, Pat O'Beirne, Peta Phillips, Helen Pru, Frank Pyke, James Rankin, Yvonne Rate, Jenny Rayner, Paul Ricketts, Maureen Roberts, Cheryl Robertson, Mark Robertson, Alan Robson, Ian Robilliard, Warren Robilliard, Louise Sauvage, Gene Schembri, Michael Scott, Saysana Sirimanotham, Wilma Shakespear, Barbara Smith, Kerry Smith, Greg Stewart, Leonie Stewart-Weeks, Graham Thompson, Mark Thornley, Charles Turner, Trevor Wallace, Margrit Walmsley, Alan Watson, Lance Watt, Willy Weerasekera, Bob Welch, Shirley Willis, Dale Wood and Laurie Woodman.

I also want to thank several other colleagues who carefully checked the accuracy of the manuscript as it evolved. John Coates, Jim Ferguson, John Graham, Alan Morton, Tony Parker, Mark Peters and Gordon Treble were particularly helpful, while Richard Cashman and Ed Jaggard assisted greatly by re-arranging or adding several topics. And Martin Stewart-Weeks carried out an extensive critique of the penultimate draft, which improved the final copy immeasurably. No book of this nature would be complete without appropriate photographs, and I am greatly indebted to Greg Blood and Don Gordon for their assistance. In addition, The University of Western Australia has assisted me with a publication grant and its photographic unit has also been most helpful. Last, but by no means least, has been the support of my publishers, UNSW Press, and in particular I wish to thank John Elliot, Mary Halbmeyer, Angela Handley, Greg Hunter and Di Quick.

Finally, my wife Noelene's many years of experience in academe were very helpful, as they have been on many occasions for my previous publications. Her assistance has always been freely given and gratefully received.

John Bloomfield

Preface

There are several tasks I hope to accomplish in this book. First, I want to analyse the extraordinary euphoria I experienced at the Sydney 2000 Olympics. The thrill of it all and the vibrant atmosphere went far beyond the winning of medals. It involved the magnificent crowds, the huge army of friendly, helpful volunteers, and the vast array of visitors from around the world. It was a stunning performance by a city, a state and a country still young by international standards and located at the end of the Earth for most of the world's population. How did Sydney in particular, and Australia in general, manage it so well? What is it about this nation that made such a feat not only possible, but so incredibly successful?

These were the questions I asked myself as I moved between the various Olympic sites via the efficient transport system, assisted by patient, smiling guides and drivers. Why did so many Australians, from such varied walks of life, participate so willingly in this event, so clearly convinced that it was important to do so? And what does such a spirit of co-operation and selflessness say about the very nature of what it means to be Australian? How could a nation that began only a little over two centuries ago as a struggling convict colony, with unpromising, unwilling and unskilled labour, organise such an undertaking so superbly? And how did Australian athletes manage to win 58 medals and achieve fourth place in the Olympic medal tally, as well as top the medal count in the Paralympics, against countries with much larger populations?

Being of 'original stock' myself, and having been involved in the development of sport in this country since the late 1960s, I felt I was better placed than many to identify at least some of the factors which made Sydney 2000 the triumph that it was. And I believe it is important now to attempt to answer the question many people asked as the Olympics drew to a close: 'How did we do it?'

I began by investigating our early history in an attempt to discover why Australians are so passionate about sport. It was also essential to identify those individuals and groups who have contributed to the formation of the Australian sports system and to examine the records of various governments in order to assess their impact on Australian sport. Both major political parties have played an important role in the introduction of radical changes to the management, financing, marketing and coaching of sport in this country. In fact, in a period of less than 30 years, sport in Australia has been transformed from a loosely structured amateur system into a highly organised one which is now the envy of many nations around the world.

I also hope to explain the link between these developments and the various social changes that have occurred since early colonial days. Politics, race, social status, gender, geographical location and climate have all had a strong effect on the development of sport in this country, just as sport has had a major influence on Australia's social evolution. And national, state and territory governments, universities, sporting associations, sport service groups and the commercial sector, as well as athletes, administrators, officials and coaches, have all played significant roles. In spite of, or perhaps because of, Australia's complex social environment and its diverse ethnic groups, this nation has somehow managed to produce a 'state of the art' sports system.

It is immediately obvious to those who visit this country that many Australians have an intense interest in sport. One only has to observe the widespread media coverage it receives and listen to conversations wherever people socialise to be aware of the important role sport plays in the lives of many Australians. In my attempt to explain the origins of this phenomenon, I have explored the development of sport in the fledgling British colony and the formation of amateur sports clubs and associations, as settlement spread from Sydney Cove throughout the country. Even in our early history Australian athletes produced some very good performances in international events, despite our geographical isolation and the fact that they mostly had to compete 'out of season' against opponents from the northern hemisphere.

As a result of extensive travel throughout Europe in the mid-1960s, I became aware that many European countries had already begun to professionalise their amateur sport programs soon after the Second World War. I realised that for Australian athletes and teams to compete on equal terms, they must be given better support, such as indoor and outdoor facilities, sport scholarships, talent identification programs and travel assistance to international competitions. By the late 1960s, I was in a position to begin working towards the training of more competent coaches, establishing more efficient sports science and medicine services and ensuring better management of the sports associations. By the mid-1990s, a modern sports system had evolved in this country – one that the rest of the world now views as efficient and cost-effective, especially for a comparatively small population spread over such a large geographical area.

At this point in our nation's history we need to assess what the future holds for Australian sport. We must determine the roles that future governments, sports associations, the Australian public, the private sector, the media and the athletes themselves will play in its future. If we are diligent, Australia's success story should continue. However, after such fine performances in the last decade, especially at the Sydney 2000 Olympics and Paralympics, as well as at the 2002 Manchester Commonwealth Games, we must guard against complacency. Several other countries are already adopting the Australian sports system model and luring away Australian coaches, sports scientists and administrators. If this trend continues, it will become more difficult for Australian sport to maintain its momentum and other countries are likely to move past us.

Finally, I have not attempted to write a comprehensive history of Australian sport, as other writers have already produced detailed chronicles of our sporting successes and failures. Instead I have focused on the way in which the sports system has developed. It is my hope that this book will act as a stimulus for social scientists to further investigate and critically analyse many of the issues that have been raised.

The Sydney 2000 Olympics and Paralympics demonstrated to the world that Australia's current sports system is one of this nation's greatest accomplishments. By the time you have read this book, I hope you will be closer to understanding how this phenomenal success was achieved.

Introduction

This book describes the role played by sport in the complex social dynamics that evolved in the early colony of New South Wales, as the young white native-born Australians regularly challenged the soldiers and new settlers to various sporting competitions. From this intense rivalry, various social characteristics such as nationalism, social cohesion and tenacity emerged, gradually becoming entrenched as Australia increased its range of sports and began to compete internationally.

The three decades from 1972 to the present time are then examined in detail, as this was the period in which the Australian sports system rapidly matured, with input from the voluntary sports organisations and the state and federal governments. During that time a sports infrastructure was put in place, enabling young sportsmen and sportswomen to develop their talent via well-defined pathways and giving them the opportunity to compete on equal terms with other elite athletes from around the world.

By the year 2000, this country had placed fourth on the Olympic medal tally and first in the Paralympics. Since Sydney 2000, Australian athletes have also been highly successful in world championships and in a large number of non-Olympic sports. In addition, our athletes won a record number of medals at the 2002 Manchester Commonwealth Games, against much stronger opposition than in previous Games.

Despite some recent concern about lower levels of sporting involvement, this country continues to have high sport participation rates. Currently 4.1 million Australians are members of the national sports organisations, while another 3.4 million regularly play informal recreational sport. The above figures indicate that approximately 39 per cent of the Australian public are active in sport at one level or another, and this compares very favourably with any of our international competitors.

Finally, this book seeks to explain the riddle of Australia's sporting prowess and to offer some suggestions on how to avoid possible problems in the future. This country's sports system is still efficient and effective, but some fine-tuning is currently needed. If this is done in the near future, it will better cater for those Australians who wish to enjoy the positive health and social outcomes emanating from sport, while still offering young Australians the opportunity to achieve international-level sports performances.

The 'Holey dollar' was used
as local currency in the
early days of the colony
of New South Wales.

Chapter One
Australia — a sporting nation

Early social dynamics in Australian sport

In exploring the story of Australia's sporting development, it is important to examine the way in which sport and society have interacted during this country's short history and to attempt to understand why Australians behave as they do, especially in highly competitive situations.

As most readers are aware, Australia began as a penal colony where brutality was commonplace, especially in the first 50 years of settlement. Oppression by the jailers bred a contempt for authority, encouraging the convicts to band together. Even after gaining their tickets-of-leave, they continued to be harassed and treated with disdain by both the military and the other colonists. However, the children of the convicts proudly proclaimed their birthright as the first generation of white native-born Australians and confidently asserted their right to live on equal terms with the free settlers.

The 'currency'

The early generations of white native-born youngsters were referred to in the new colony as the 'currency', or the 'currency lads and lasses'. This name is said to have been coined by a military paymaster who satirically identified the children of the convicts and emancipists with the crude currency that was used as legal tender in the colony of New South Wales. The local coinage was referred to facetiously as 'the Holey dollar',[1] as it was made by cutting the middle out of an old Spanish coin and stamping 'NSW' and its value on the outer ring. Molony says that 'the native-born were disparagingly referred to as the "currency" and those who arrived free as "sterling", denoting their respective value on the social scale',[2] as those born in the Mother Country were thought to be of superior breeding. The term 'cornstalks' was also used to describe white native-born Australians, because of their tanned skin, sun-bleached hair and strong, willowy bodies. By comparison, the new arrivals from Britain often looked pale, weedy and unhealthy.

For several decades the 'currency lads and lasses' were looked down upon, but because of their refusal to be bullied and their pluckiness and generally honourable behaviour, they slowly gained the respect, albeit grudging, of many of the free settlers and civil administrators. Hughes said of them that 'instead of growing up depraved, the "currency" showed the lowest crime rate of any group [in the colony]'.[3] Cunningham, who made four voyages to New South Wales as Surgeon Superintendent of Convict Transports, wrote: 'Our currency lads and lasses are a fine interesting race and do honour to the country whence they originated ... indeed, what more can be said in their favour than that they are little tainted with the vices so prominent amongst their parents?'[4] In fact, many children of the free settlers envied them, even attempting to acquire as a sign of status the distinctive cabbage tree hats which were the trademark of the 'currency'. Garvin wrote that 'to look like an old hand was to make you a less likely target of the raucous practical jokes practised upon any new chum who thought himself better than the locals'. Further, the 'currency' was fiercely proud of its native-born status, regularly challenging the new settlers to sporting contests, in which they frequently came out on top.[5]

At a later time, during the Gold Rush, the offspring of the 'currency' brought mateship, democracy, leadership and fair treatment to their fellow diggers, many of whom came from overseas. They also tended to work in teams of a dozen to 15, finding it more enjoyable and productive to dig for gold with their mates, voluntarily dividing up the labour and sharing the tasks and their finds with their friends. There was no place on the goldfields for snobbery or class distinction and everyone was expected to co-operate on an equal footing in order to survive and prosper. According to Garvin there was 'a rugged democracy at the diggings ... that meant a fair go for anyone who was willing to pitch in [and] pull their weight'.[6]

After the Gold Rush, when the land was settled in the western regions of the eastern states, similar co-operation was again common among the progeny of the 'currency lads and lasses'. Later still, in both World Wars, Australian soldiers were highly praised by the Allied commanders who fought with them. They were portrayed not only as courageous soldiers but as individuals concerned about the welfare of their peers, despite their distinct lack of conventional British army discipline.[7]

A 'currency lad': the name facetiously referred to this group's second-class status in comparison to the highly prized English 'sterling'.

The British influence

In the introduction to Elford's article entitled 'Sport In Australian Society: A Perspective', Jacques and Pavia suggest that 'sport developed so rapidly in the Australian colonies because it reinforced the type of social values that the community wanted to endorse. Prominent individuals in the community lent their patronage to the development of games, realising that they were helping to inculcate in the community virtues they hoped Australian society would pursue. The legacy is still with us in that even now it is widely assumed that sport builds character and nobility.'[8]

The growth of sport in Australia followed closely behind its development in England, and it rapidly became established as an important feature of Australian life. Australia's favourable climate, abundant food and limited availability of alternative recreations were other important factors. Elford suggests that the popular book by Thomas Hughes, *Tom Brown's School Days,* may have had an influence on society's concept of 'manliness' and on the role of sport in promoting character-building. He cites the first advertisement for a cricket match in South Australia in November 1838, calling for the support of 'this old English and manly game.'[9]

A well-known cricketer, yachtsman, politician and judge in South Australia, W.H. Bundey, presented a lecture to a large audience in Adelaide some time later, entitled 'Manly Sports, Exercises, and Recreation'. He stated his firm belief that sport not only promoted equality, but also co-operation, teamwork and comradeship. Bundey maintained that sporting pursuits taught self-reliance, loyalty and pride, and included volunteering as a positive outcome.[10] He added Australian (rules) football to his list of manly sports and Wills and Harrison, the founders of the code, believed it developed that 'key virtue of the Anglo-Saxon race — downright bulldog pluck'. Australia's rapid acceptance of the traditional British organised sports and games was a positive means of socialisation, being 'a product of the widely held belief that sport created better people and hence a better community'.[11]

Various economic and historical events, such as the Great Depression of the early 1930s and the Second World War, also affected the evolution of Australian sport. The development of sport in any society, especially in a Western democracy, has an effect on its social development. This is especially true of a relatively new country like Australia, where sport has been, and still is, an important facet of the nation's social history. According to Molony, 'the native-born were forced to make their own mark and stake a claim to equality' in the early days of the colony. This came about in part 'as a result of the prowess of the lads on the playing fields of Hyde Park ...' He goes on to comment on the 'considerable interest ... shown by the inhabitants of Sydney and Parramatta in a wide variety of sports congenial to the temper and to the spirit of Englishmen'. These sports included foot races, wheelbarrow and horse racing, trotting, prize and cock-fighting, kangaroo hunting, sailing, wrestling, rowing, as well as cricket and an early version of soccer.[12]

It is therefore well worth reviewing the past so as to examine the origin of the traits which Australians currently exhibit. Some writers insist that the sports brought to Australia in the 19th and early 20th centuries have had a positive effect on the social evolution of this country, and Elford states that Australia 'was not the growth of a new society but was, more accurately, the growth of a fragment of British life', without its worst features of class, privilege and tradition.[13] Snyder and Spreitzer maintain that 'sport has long been considered good preparation for the larger game of life' and that 'sport is commonly viewed as a microcosm or mirror of the larger society. The assertion that the Battle of Waterloo was won on the playing fields of Eton comes down to us as a verity and not as satire.'[14]

The predominantly British sports and games, as historians have labelled them, emanated from a democratic political system and as the rules and codes of conduct evolved, the notion of 'fair play' was central in their development. The recent success of the Sydney 2000 Olympics and Paralympics demonstrated the many positive aspects of the sporting tradition that has evolved in this country over the last two centuries.

Nationalism

Because Australia developed mainly as a penal colony, the administrators, the military and the free settlers who arrived in the early years often harassed the offspring of the emancipists about their convict origins. The free settlers still had strong links with England and thought of themselves as Englishmen and women currently resident in New South Wales, whereas the 'currencies' saw the colony in which they were born as their home and had little or no affinity with England.

Certainly the 'currency lads' singled themselves out from the new arrivals from Britain in the early 1800s by their strength and physical agility, becoming the first Australian sportsmen to play cricket and to compete in athletics, rowing, sailing, horse-racing, boxing and wrestling. Garvin describes a cricket match held in Hyde Park, reported in *The Sydney Gazette* in February 1830, in which a 'currency lad' cricket team played the 57th Regiment team. The report of the match observed: 'It seemed at first as though the locals had no chance, but as they began to take control, word spread throughout the city and by the time the might of the British Empire had fallen, an enthusiastic throng of currencies were there to share the victory.' The rematch, which occurred a month later, was the talk of Sydney and heavy betting took place. When the local boys won again, emotional scenes ensued and the euphoric supporters took to the streets to celebrate.

Garvin also gives other examples in which the 'currency' teams or single individuals openly challenged the members of the military garrison or the British free settlers. This was done through their newspaper, known in Sydney as *The*

A 'currency' cricket match, played outside the Hyde Park Military Barracks in Sydney in 1845. This was the first field set aside for public recreation in Sydney in 1810. (By permission of the National Library of Australia — see Appendix H for photo credits.)

Currency Lad. The first example relates to the cricket matches reported in *The Sydney Gazette.* The challenge proclaimed: 'Any sum of twenty pounds to one hundred pounds will be deposited at the meeting room of the Australian club ... against any eleven of the 57th Regiment or any eleven civilians who think they're better than the Currency Lads.'

Two other examples: 'A fight will take place on Monday morning for ten pounds a side between Lane, native-born and Scot, a Londoner. The Bowerbell boy seems pretty confident of success, but the Currency Lad may chance to humble his prowess'; and 'Some of the gentlemen who rode [in] the steeplechase appear to have lost their mettle very suddenly since our Mr Isaac Nicholls' challenge. We suspect that they do not like to chance their necks against a Currency Lad through his native bush ... [in] a steeple race, for twenty pounds ...'[15] This was a foretaste of the type of nationalistic aggression Australians demonstrated throughout the 19th century and continued well into the 20th, especially when competing against English teams or individuals.

More than any other sport, the game of cricket caught the imagination of the early colonists. Mandle, in a celebrated article entitled 'Cricket and Australian Nationalism in the Nineteenth Century', traces the growth of the sport from its beginnings to the late 1870s, when Australia began to seriously challenge England for supremacy. He states: 'There is a case for arguing that Australian nationalism and self-confidence was first and most clearly manifested in the late 1870s because of the feats of its sportsmen and particularly of its cricketers.'[16] Mandle also quotes the *Bulletin*, one of the most influential newspapers of the day, thus: 'This ruthless rout of English cricket will do — and has done — more to enhance the cause of nationality than could ever be achieved by miles of erudite essays and impassioned appeal.'[17]

Several other academics and social commentators believe that the first strong nationalistic feelings in Australia were displayed through sport in the 19th century. Helen Irving, one of Australia's foremost Federation scholars and formerly the Director of the *1901 Centre* in Sydney, argues that 'sporting pursuits, much more than military engagement, brought the colonies together and that the effect was working as early as the 1860s. Early cricket matches against the British united the colonies well before Federation.' Irving goes on to claim that 'sport brings us together because it unites us as a community, affects all classes and social groups, whether as participants or spectators, and combines high achievement with ordinariness. Perhaps the same could be said about war. And perhaps that's why Australian icons are invariably sports stars or diggers.'[18]

David Headon, a respected cultural historian, agrees, stating that 'sport was the most important factor in the development of this country's nationalism until the First World War'; and further, that 'war, then sport, were the most significant factors in the development of Australian nationalism in the 20th century'.[19]

There would be few social commentators better qualified to provide a third opinion than David Malouf. In the Century of Federation Commemoration supplement in *The Australian* newspaper on 1 January 2001, he made the point that federations do not work well if 'they come together out of economic convenience or need for security'. He suggests that what might be called a 'federation of feeling' is a better basis for a federated nation and that Australia already had this in the 1870s and 1880s as a result of sport, especially the nation-to-nation contests with England in cricket. Malouf goes further, arguing that 'sport has continued to be the place where we are most aware of ourselves as a people; and when we consider the alternatives there can be few healthier or more benign, more civilised ways in which a nation might discover a sense of itself than *at play*, at competitive play with friends and neighbours'.[20]

This nationalistic attitude, which was created by Australia's early athletes and the press, has continued for almost 200 years, with the pinnacle of national fervour being reached at the Sydney Olympics in 2000.

Egalitarianism and social cohesion

In many respects, the colony of New South Wales was in a parlous state very soon after the First Fleet landed. There was little fertile soil in the Sydney region and because the first crop was very poor, food was scarce. These problems were only partially alleviated by the second crop planted at Rose Hill (renamed Parramatta in 1791) and the supplies which came from further convict fleets in June 1790 and July 1791. However, it wasn't until 1792, when the drought broke, that the situation improved — not only for the convicts, but for the entire population of Sydney Town.[21]

As well as food, the colonists also needed shelter and the entire group, regardless of their class, had to struggle to survive. In some ways this was a good start, at least from the point of view of promoting equality and social cohesion, because during this period enterprise was needed and those who showed it were accepted regardless of their social status, albeit somewhat grudgingly.

The early naval governors and the first military governor, Lachlan Macquarie, were very much aware of the fragile nature of the new colony and worked hard to neutralise the sources of conflict. They basically felt that a successful society should be compatible and that harmony could be achieved by striving for a homogeneous population. Given the deeply entrenched prejudice among the military, the civil administrators and many of the free settlers against those of convict origin, it was a very difficult social environment. Nevertheless, there was a growing awareness that the various classes simply had to co-operate for the colony to prosper and the lower classes began to receive more equal opportunities. John Dunmore Lang, an influential minister of religion and later a politician, was a supporter of a 'fair field for all and no favour' policy, strongly promoting the notion that a good society should be harmonious.[22] Lang was known to have strong republican leanings and did not hesitate to appeal to the white native-born for their support with his various causes. In return he supported them in their pursuit of equality.[23]

As the colony grew there emerged a strong sense of mateship and social cohesion. Baker pointed out that there was a preponderance of males in the new colony; therefore men were forced together for amusement and companionship. He suggested that mateship was about more than just friendship, because there was a mutual dependence, whether in immediate hardship or later in war. This interdependence appears to have carried over to other aspects of life, including team sports.[24]

As stated earlier, in Victorian England the concepts of manliness, good character, loyalty and patriotism were often linked with sport and were sometimes raised by prominent leaders of the day. Bill Bundey, previously mentioned in the section dealing with the British influence on Australian sport, believed that sport led to 'natural democracy' and claimed that it fostered equality among those who played it.[25] Similar statements were also being made by newspapers such as *Bell's*

Life in Sydney and the *Sporting Times* in the late 1840s, and by leaders in some of the other colonies in the second half of the 19th century.[26][27]

By the end of that century, Australian sportsmen, especially its cricketers, were becoming openly critical of the class divisions that were very obvious in the English teams. Australians felt their opponents lacked social cohesion because of the amateur-professional schism, which mitigated against harmony and team spirit. The *Bulletin* claimed as early as 1895 that Australian cricket was more egalitarian and lacked the snobbishness of English cricket; and Mandle comments on the differences in the treatment of the English gentlemen amateurs and the paid professional players, who used different dressing rooms and separate gates to enter and leave the field. They also lunched separately, and the professionals were rarely consulted on team tactics. It was as if they were cricket mercenaries, not integral parts of the team. Mandle points out that J.H. Phillips, the manager of the 1899 Australian team, attributed Australia's success to its freedom from snobbery, its team cohesion and a democratic approach to leadership. Mandle quotes Phillips as follows: 'Surely if a man is good enough to play on the same side, he is good enough to dress in the same dressing room. It is there [that] the most useful hints and ideas are exchanged when a game is in progress, which cannot be done so well on the field.'[28]

Another probable factor in the development of egalitarianism and social cohesion is the fact that Australia has always suffered from the 'tyranny of distance'. This was especially evident before the automobile was invented, as many communities were relatively small and isolated. In the early days of the colonies, the centres of population were not as large nor as close to each other as the majority of the communities in England and, in order to field a cricket or other sporting team, traditional class barriers often had to be waived. Records show that there may have been only half a dozen professionals from the middle class in many towns or new suburbs; therefore the rest of the players would have come from the lower middle class. Thousands of teams developed a social mix out of such necessity, and this has been a very desirable state of affairs for many decades, with positive ramifications for a developing democracy such as Australia.

Various commentators have remarked that Australian people have also generally welcomed others from abroad and, by and large, social cohesion is alive and well, as long as the newcomers conform to the already established mores and customs of the country. Garvin raises another interesting point of view in the following statement: 'We are supposed to be a multicultural society and, while it is true that we have welcomed people from all over the globe, it is remarkable how homogenous we are. In other countries such as America ... the North and South are like different worlds, or England, where a mere fifty kilometres can separate two quite different accents. A sample of any hundred people from Cairns, to Hobart, to Geraldton, to Sydney, to Melbourne will reveal attitudes to authority, to politicians, to home ownership and the like, that are strikingly similar.'[29]

Tenacity

There is no doubt that Australians have always competed with great tenacity. During a visit to Australia, D.H. Lawrence, the celebrated English author, stated that they 'played their sport as if their lives depended on it'.[30]

Social historians, sociologists and journalists have given various reasons for the determination of so many Australians to do well in sport. It has been suggested that perhaps because of a sense of inferiority stemming from their convict origins, many young Australians are driven to succeed in sport to prove to the world that they are as good as anyone else. Waters expresses this well in his article on 'The Patterns of Australian Culture' when he says: 'Possibly the aggressive egalitarianism which many Australians believe to be a distinctive feature of the national character may help to explain the origins of the emphasis on competitive games. At the beginning of the nineteenth century the playing of organised sport was a pastime of "gentlemen" more often than of workers. The native-born Australian worker of the time does seem to have been very much inclined to assert that he was as good as any English officer and gentleman, if not better. Sport was one of the forms of upper-class culture which lower-class Australians could readily adopt and in which they could hope to prove themselves as good as or better than men of superior social standing.'[31]

Others have speculated that the 'currency' wanted to show the colonial administrators and the military that they were not going to be cowed by them. With people who needed assistance they were co-operative and helpful, but they strongly resisted officious discipline by demonstrating that they were tough, unbending and at times rather bumptious. Dunstan presents John Daly's thesis, which suggested that a 'distinctive Australian "type" developed during the nineteenth century, who greatly influenced the social attitudes of the early colonists.[32] Their rugged, tough, independent and never-give-in attitude created a role model that was reinforced by Australian newspapers, poetry and early literature.

A very good example of this determination was displayed by the Australian cricket team which toured England in 1882, when Fred Spofforth, sometimes facetiously known as the 'demon bowler', was used very effectively. Mandle observed that, unlike bowlers before him who had used a round-arm action, Spofforth delivered the ball from a position high above the shoulder.[33] Because he was tall and fast, the batsmen of the day had great difficulty playing him, especially on the rough wickets in use at that time. Garvin caustically describes the situation as follows: 'It was rumoured Spofforth was as interested in demobilising the English gentlemen cricketers as in getting them out. It had its effect. They were so terrified that they surrendered four wickets for two runs in his last eleven overs, ten of which were maidens. The shock of defeat set the English stiff upper lip aquiver.'

Garvin then quotes the famous mock death notice which appeared in the *English Sporting Times* the following day:[34]

'In affectionate remembrance of

English cricket

which died at The Oval

on

29th August 1882.

Deeply lamented by a large circle of sorrowing friends

and acquaintances

R.I.P.

N.B.— the body will be cremated and the ashes taken to Australia.'

Fred Spofforth was called the 'demon bowler' because he was the first cricketer to bowl at high speed, which he did by delivering the ball from a vertical position high above his shoulder. (By courtesy of the Melbourne Cricket Club.)

Gradually various prominent citizens, some native-born as well as English migrants, infused middle-class values relating to manliness, patriotism and self-discipline into Australian society. Such characteristics were to emerge when Australia went to war in support of the 'Old Country' at the end of the 19th and in the early 20th centuries. This tenacity appears to have been passed on through generations of Australian sportsmen and women, whose toughness is legendary among their opponents. Their resolute attitude has surfaced not only in cricket, but also in rowing, swimming, tennis, athletics, rugby league and more recently in rugby union.

Dunstan quotes the actions of several captains, coaches and individual sportsmen and women renowned for their tenacious attitude, such as Stuart Mackenzie in sculling, Warwick Armstrong and Don Bradman in cricket, Dawn Fraser in swimming, Ron Barassi in Australian football, Harry Hopman and Rod Laver in tennis, and Percy Cerutty and Herb Elliott in athletics.[35] Numerous other names could be added to this list, among them Ian Chappell and Steve Waugh in cricket, Don Talbot in swimming, Heather MacKay in squash, David Parkin in Australian football, Tony ('Slaggy') Miller in rugby union, Jack Gibson in rugby league and Ric Charlesworth in hockey.

Volunteering

Sport from its earliest times has always been competitive and played to a set of rules, even if they were originally very basic ones. From the beginning, some form of umpiring or judging was necessary, and therefore the first officials were either captains of both teams or members of one team or the other. As sport became more sophisticated and competitive, teams needed neutral umpires or referees and so the system of volunteer officials was born.

As rules, equipment, tactics and facilities developed, more volunteers were needed to officiate, judge, coach, or organise the clubs which the teams represented, as well as to take responsibility for the equipment and facilities. Because the cost of paying individuals to carry out these functions was too high, a volunteer system steadily evolved.

Britain, the early developer of sports and games, was more responsible than any other single nation for the evolution of the volunteer system, and Australia soon followed suit. A gradual growth of volunteers in this country accompanied the steady development of amateur sport, until the Great Depression, when for reasons stated later, there was a rapid increase in participants as well as officials, administrators and coaches. The same thing happened after the Second World War, when sports associations experienced another period of steady growth. However, as a modern sports system began to evolve in the late 1970s and early 1980s, it became apparent that many people assisting sport had not had the opportunity to undergo any formal training. It was at this time that brief courses were set up for coaches, officials and administrators, first at the state level but later funded by the Federal Government, enabling those individuals to carry out their duties with more expertise.

The Sport 2000 Task Force, which reported to the Australian Government at the end of 1999, stated that there were then approximately 1.7 million Australians (8.9 per cent of the population) involved with clubs or sports associations, acting as volunteer administrators, officials, coaches or in associated roles.[36] It has been conservatively estimated that these volunteers, who are a major resource for Australian sport, contribute at least $1.6 billion worth of expertise, allowing the sports system to operate cheaply and efficiently.[37] These figures are impressive for a country with a small population, but even more so was the response to the call for volunteers for the Sydney 2000 Olympics. A record number of 47 000 Australians volunteered their time to assist in the running of the Games and many were on duty for long hours, often seeing little or nothing of the events. Nevertheless, they completed their tasks with good humour and dedication and provided one of the most striking features of the games.[38] It is not well known that an additional 8000 people volunteered to assist with other essential services required in Sydney during the period of the Games, with another 15 000 volunteering for the Paralympics. The *Sydney Morning Herald* produced a Volunteers' Souvenir Edition on 6 October 2000, in which it was estimated that the Olympic volunteers 'contributed a total of 7 million hours worth $140 million if calculated at the rate of $20 per hour.'[39]

To examine how and why the above-mentioned characteristics have evolved, it is necessary to trace them in the context of the history of competitive sport in Australia, a subject addressed in the following section.

Australia's sporting origins

Early developments in sport

For obvious reasons, Australians directly inherited the British sports and games that had been slowly developing in the United Kingdom since the late 1600s. Sport emanating from simple games was poorly organised at first, but gradually became more refined. Between 1830 and 1850, several sports were well enough organised to be played competitively in Britain and in other parts of the British Empire.

The earliest competitive sport held in the colony of New South Wales was very informal, but there are reports of the army playing cricket from approximately 1803,[40] a race meeting in 1810,[41] a sailing regatta in 1827[42] and professional foot races by the early 1830s.[43] And a rowing regatta was held in 1838 with whale-boats competing, as part of Australia's 50th anniversary of settlement.[44] Public holidays were used for the various competitions, as was the case in Britain, but later the more privileged individuals in the colony were able to play sport on Saturday afternoons.

The earliest competitions in rowing, boxing, wrestling, running, cricket and football tended to be unstructured affairs, with simple rules, poor facilities and substandard equipment. The inner suburbs in Sydney and the nearby country towns formed 'pick-up' teams, playing against other local teams; gradually more clubs were formed and loosely structured competitions evolved. This pattern was followed in every area of settlement.

By the 1850s, regular low-level sport competitions were in operation in New South Wales, followed by Victoria and Queensland, but it wasn't until the late 1860s and 70s that they evolved in the other colonies. The most notable sports were those which had already developed a reasonably high degree of sophistication in Britain, cricket being the main one. Various types of football were also played, but football rules had not been standardised by that time, except for Australian (rules) football, which had developed quite rapidly in Melbourne in the late 1850s.[45]

Other popular sports which were reasonably well organised by the 1870s and early 80s were horse racing, rowing, bowls, rugby, soccer, cycling and athletics.[46] Towards the latter part of the 19th century, tennis, golf and later swimming became more popular, especially amongst the middle classes.[47] As more sports developed, local clubs were formed in the new suburban districts and country towns, and by the time of Federation in 1901 many colonial associations had already been established.

Consolidation at home and forays into international sport

As sophisticated sport slowly evolved, Australians became confident enough to compete in *cricket* by the 1860s against England. By that time her population was approximately 20 million, while Australia had barely two million people. The English teams were superior at first, but by the 1873–74 tour, led by W.G. Grace, the local teams were becoming much more competitive. However, it was not until the 1876–77 English tour that Australia defeated James Lillywhite's team in what was to become the first 'Test' between the two countries.[48] This win was attributed to the home advantage and the fact that England had not sent its best side. Therefore the following year, when an Australian touring team defeated an MCC team at Lords, the spiritual home of English cricket, the local crowd found this especially hard to swallow. And to make matters worse, the trend was to continue over the next 25 years.[49]

England tended to be seen as 'the enemy' by many Australians — not only in cricket, but also in other sports such as *rowing*. Fitzsimons quotes part of an article from the *Sydney Morning Herald* in 1876, when describing Edward Trickett's defeat of the Englishman, Joseph Sadler, in the World Sculling Championships held on the Thames. The reporter wrote: 'It seemed almost incredible that a man born and bred in New South Wales should go home to

Edward Trickett defeating Joseph
Sadler in the world sculling
championship on the River Thames
on 27 June 1876. (By permission of
the National Library of Australia —
see Appendix H for photo credits.)

England and beat the champion of the Thames.'[50] In the same article Fitzsimons
reports the delight Australians took in defeating England or her athletes: 'Oh,
and there was another thing we Australians found we loved, nay lived for,
when it came to sport ... Having one of our own, born and bred beneath the
Southern Cross, taking it right up to the ... Poms and whipping them
motherless.'[51]

Rowing had also been growing rapidly in the 1870s and 80s in both Sydney
and Melbourne, and Australian competitors were prominent in international
regattas. In fact, the oarsmen Edward Trickett, Bill Beach, Peter Kemp, Henry
Searle, Jim Stanbury, John McLean and George Towns won the world sculling
title on 22 of the 32 occasions on which it was held between 1876 and 1908.[52]

Boxing, probably one of the oldest sports, was also popular from 1788
onwards. At first it was bare-knuckled pugilism, which lasted for almost 100
years before the rules were changed in Australia. Fighters were brought mainly
from England and some from the United States, while lesser-ranked nationals
from other countries turned up in ships' crews and were willing to fight for
small purses. By the 1870s, fighters such as Larry Foley and Sandy Ross were
well known, taking on all comers from overseas and performing very well

THE 'OARSOME' OARSMAN

James Tomkins is without doubt the greatest Australian oarsman of the modern era, continuing the tradition established by our rowers as far back as the 1870s. James began international rowing in 1985 and by 2000 had won two Olympic gold medals in Barcelona and Atlanta and a bronze in Sydney. Over the 16-year period he also won seven world championships in coxed pairs, coxed fours and coxless fours.

A powerful man, 199 centimetres tall and weighing 95 kilograms, James has traditionally been the 'engine' of the boats in which he has rowed. He and his team-mates were dubbed 'the oarsome foursome' after their outstanding success at the 1992 Barcelona Olympics, retaining that name until 1998 after winning two Olympic gold medals and two world championships.

After an unfortunate back injury forced his team-mate, Drew Ginn, to withdraw, Tomkins teamed up with Matthew Long in the run-up to the Sydney 2000 Olympics, where they won a bronze medal. James Tomkins OAM is a Victorian Institute of Sport scholarship holder who rows for the famous Mercantile Rowing Club in Melbourne. He has very wide sporting interests, participating in surfing, skiing, golf and tennis when not in training or working as a merchant banker.[53]

against them.[54] In 1890 'Young Griffo' became the first Australian to win a world boxing championship by defeating Billy Murphy, a New Zealander.[55] As fights with gloves and more stringent rules were staged in the latter part of the 19th and early 20th centuries, other famous boxers appeared, the best known being Les Darcy.[56]

While *horse racing* was not a part of the traditional amateur sports system, it is important to include it in this section because of the huge impact it has had on Australia's social history. Horses were brought to New South Wales in the late 18th and early 19th centuries and were bred in the new colony from that time on. The first horses had come with the army officers of the NSW Regiment and others arrived with some high-level civil administrators and new settlers.

It is not surprising that this old English sport did not take long to establish itself in the new colony. The first official race meeting was held in October 1810 in Hyde Park in Sydney, organised by the officers of the 73rd Regiment. From that date on there was steady development of the sport and Molony states: 'From the 1820s horse racing became widespread and the clubs were formed (Sydney Turf Club 1825, Australian Racing and Jockey Club 1827) and the sport was widely followed among all classes, especially after a course was opened at

An 1857 wood engraving of the Homebush racecourse, which was built on land owned by the Wentworth family in 1840. The Sydney Olympic Games complex is situated on this site. (By permission of the National Library of Australia — see Appendix H for photo credits.)

Randwick in 1833.'[57] The second racecourse was built on land owned by the Wentworth family in 1840 at Homebush — the site where the main Sydney 2000 Olympic venues were erected.[58]

Racing spread quickly in Australia after the 1850s, especially in Melbourne. By that time, elimination heats were no longer used and more standardised rules had been developed, similar to those of today. The Melbourne Cup began in 1861 and the first race was a rather chaotic event in which two horses fell and had to be destroyed, but it gradually became Australia's most famous racing event, developing an international profile.[59] Mandle comments on its significance thus: 'The race broke with the British tradition of weight for age or age-grouped races. It was a handicap, a lottery, with big fields and unlikely winners. It catered for the developing Australian attitude to life.'[60]

As well as conventional horse racing on the track, cross-country races were being held in the early 1800s, with the 'currency' regularly challenging the new settlers.[61] Later in the 19th century polo developed in Australia and inter-colonial events were held during the 1880s.[62] Show jumping became another popular

The Sydney 2000 Olympic Equestrian Centre, showing Andrew Hoy of the Australian team about to clinch the gold medal in the three-day equestrian team event.

equine sport and still continues at various shows throughout the country. However, the main emphasis during the last 50 years has moved to the equestrian events and Australian riders have performed with distinction internationally over the last 40 years.[63]

One of the most exciting sports in the last two decades of the 19th century was *professional running*. Many country towns, especially in the goldfields, had 'gifts' or purses and the place-getters were well rewarded. The majority were handicap races, which sometimes brought allegations of race fixing and at times, when the fans felt that the handicaps were rigged or that some runners 'ran dead', a furore broke out. The Stawell Gift, contested since 1878, became the best-known event.[64]

An Australian football match played
in Yarra Park on 24 July 1874,
probably between Melbourne and
Carlton. (By permission of the
National Library of Australia —
see Appendix H for photo credits.)

The most famous professional runner competing at the beginning of the 20th century, Jack Donaldson, known as the 'Blue Streak', held six world records over distances of 100 to 400 yards. Several of his records were not broken in either professional or amateur running until 30 years after they were set.[65] However, it was not until the end of the 19th century that amateur athletics became popular in Australia. Edwin Flack, the sole Australian representative at the first Olympic Games of the modern era, held in Athens in 1896, increased that popularity when he won the 800- and 1500-metre races. Amateur athletics in Australia steadily developed from that point.[66]

Although *Australian (rules) football* is not an international sport, it certainly deserves a mention because of its rapid development and popularity first in Melbourne, then throughout the state of Victoria, the southern states and finally across the nation. Thomas Wills is credited with devising some simple rules and supervising the inaugural Australian (rules) football game between Scotch College and the Church of England Grammar School, which was played on 7 August 1858 on Richmond Paddock, close to the site of the Melbourne Cricket Club. Wills, with his cousin Henry Harrison and several of their middle-class friends, formed a team in early 1859 and standardised the rules (which have since changed very little). It was said that Australian football was not a 'dirty' game but rather a manly one, as it did not have the rough rucking and mauling of some of the early varieties of rugby being played in England. From the early days of its development, Australian (rules) football has attracted massive crowds and continues to do so.[67] [68]

While informal games of *rugby union* were played at Sydney University from 1863, the Sydney University Football Club (SUFC) was not formally constituted until 1865, becoming the first official rugby club in Australia. On 19 August of that year, a match was played by the SUFC against the Sydney Football Club and was described on 21 August 1865 in the *Sydney Morning Herald*. The game was very rugged, with only a few basic rules relating to scrummaging, tackling, rucking and mauling.[69] Moreover, players were obliged to play 'on-side', or behind the advantage line at all times, in quite a different style of game to those in vogue at the time. In fact, rugby union and later its breakaway relative, rugby league, are the only two completely 'on-side' field games in existence. In the early days rugby union was an upper-class game played mainly by private school boys, university students and graduates. By the 1880s and 90s, New South Wales, Queensland and an Australia XV were playing both England and New Zealand[70] and in 1908 at the London Olympic Games, Australia won the rugby union gold medal.

Soccer was the third football code to come to Australia, with the Wanderers' Club being formed in Sydney in 1880.[71] The game grew slowly until the post-World War II migration scheme brought a large number of Europeans to Australia. Since that time it has expanded rapidly, with approximately 320 000 registered players by 2000 in Australia, and standards have steadily risen, especially at the junior level.[72] Unfortunately, many of the game's elite young players are attracted overseas. By 2001 approximately 120 of Australia's top soccer players were playing professionally, mainly in Europe.

The last football code to develop in Australia was *rugby league*. It broke away from rugby union in northern England in 1895 and soon became well established there as a professional game. It was not until 1907 that James Giltinan, along with Victor Trumper, the great Australian batsman, masterminded the establishment of the NSW Rugby Football League in Sydney. In 1908 several clubs were formed, Newtown being the first, and a nine-team competition commenced in Sydney. Several top rugby union players, including the great Herbert 'Dally' Messenger, joined the league and it soon became the rugby code preferred by the working man.[73]

Rugby league grew rapidly, first in New South Wales, then in Queensland, and by 1975 had become the second-largest football code in Australia with approximately 375 000 players.[74] In the early part of the 20th century this country did not fare well against England, but after World War II Australia improved rapidly to become the world's premier rugby league nation, a position it has retained for the past three decades.

One middle-class game that came to Australia quite early was *golf*. It was first played in Tasmania in the late 1820s on a course laid out by Alexander Reid on his property near Bothwell. The first club was started in Melbourne by James Graham in 1847 and the next in 1869 in Adelaide by the Governor of South Australia, Sir James Ferguson. The late 1880s and the 1890s saw golf's steady development in both Sydney and Melbourne, but this was still mainly amongst the professional classes. The game became more popular in the early years of the 20th century as it started to spread into the country areas, particularly in the eastern states.[75]

The modern game of *tennis* came to this country soon after it developed in England in the mid-1870s. Like golf, it was a middle-class game, but its growth was partially hampered by inadequate playing surfaces. As the 'antbed', grass and asphalt hard-court surfaces improved and tennis equipment became more sophisticated during the early 20th century, the game was poised for rapid development after World War I.[76]

Competitive *swimming* was a sport in which Australia was to excel very early in its development. However, it did not begin in an organised form until 1892 with the establishment of the NSW Amateur Swimming Association. The first recorded swimming championship was contested in 1846 at Robinson's Baths in the Sydney Domain. The top performer of the carnival was W. Redman, who swam the 440 yards in 8 minutes 54 seconds, probably using sidestroke.[77]

The first swimmers to rise to national and then international prominence were the Cavill brothers. Dick Cavill used an overarm stroke to win 18 national championships and in 1902 became the first man to break 60 seconds for 100 yards freestyle, using what was to become known as the 'Australian crawl'. This was a crawl stroke action with a two-beat flutter kick which had earlier been demonstrated in 1898 by a young Solomon Islander named Alick Wickam at Bronte Baths in the eastern suburbs of Sydney.[78] During this period, Cecil Healy is believed to have developed side breathing, an important refinement in the stroke for the Australian swimmers who followed him. After the Cavills and Healy, Freddie Lane, Barney Kieran, Fanny Durack and Mina Wylie also placed Australia's name on the international swimming map by the end of the late 19th and early 20th centuries.[79] [80]

By the late 1890s, as swimming standards improved in Australia, many people were enticed to swim at the beautiful Sydney beaches. The problem was that a local government ordinance prevented public bathing 'in waters exposed to [public] view from any wharf, street, public place or dwelling house, between the hours of 6.00 am and 8.00 pm.' This ordinance was becoming increasingly difficult for the police to enforce in the last few years of the century, and it took a memorable act of defiance to bring it to an abrupt halt. W.H. Gocher, the editor of a Manly newspaper, advertised in his paper that he intended to bathe publicly within the proscribed hours. At noon on Sunday, 1 September 1902, he entered the water at the Manly ocean beach, swam without hindrance, and continued to do so from that day on. Others soon joined him and it was not long before more beaches close to the city became regular bathing spots.

A wood engraving of the first cycling race held on the Melbourne Cricket Ground, circa 1869. (By permission of the National Library of Australia — see Appendix H for photo credits.)

It was at this time that the sport of surfing began in Australia, leading to the development of the internationally acclaimed *surf lifesaving* movement, which will be described in detail in Chapter Six.[81] [82]

Sports development 1900–1972

Domestic sport — before 1946

Around the turn of the 20th century, clubs all over Australia were steadily growing and many colonial sports associations had already been formed. The sports which had regular inter-colonial contests, or virtual Australian championships before 1900, were cricket, rowing, Australian (rules) football, bowls, rugby, soccer, cycling and athletics. Many of these already had national associations.[83] After Federation in 1901, several more national associations were established, initially in the Olympic and smaller sports. Naturally, sport became de-emphasised during World War I, when a large number of adventurous young men volunteered to fight overseas. It wasn't until the early 1920s that it began to grow again, especially in country areas.

The late 1920s and 30s saw a steady increase in sports participation, as well as some changes in the class structures within various sports. More people joined country tennis and golf clubs as memberships were gradually opened to include other social classes. Rugby union was still mainly played in the private schools of Sydney and Brisbane and many of these young men joined community rugby clubs when they left school. Rugby league, often referred to as 'the working-class game', was played in country high schools and in Roman Catholic colleges in both the city and country areas.[84] This led to its rapid development in the wider community, until it became the major football code in Queensland and New South Wales in the post-World War II period. Australian (rules) football, when first established in Melbourne, was mostly played by young middle-class men from cricket clubs during the off-season. It soon spread to the Victorian goldfields, where miners who had played some form of football in Britain or Ireland became enthusiastic participants. As a result it became a classless sport, played by young men of varied backgrounds who were keen to take part in a skilful contact game.[85]

Athletics, mainly supported by former private school boys, began to change its social mix in the eastern states with the development of the state high schools during the latter part of the 1930s and 1940s. These schools initiated annual athletic carnivals as part of their sports program, as did other high schools in the less populated states, and gradually team-oriented interschool athletic carnivals were developed. At these competitions prospective young athletes identified themselves, some of whom joined district athletics clubs upon leaving school. By the end of the 1930s and into the 1940s athletics was on the way to becoming a classless sport, in contrast to the situation in Europe and the United States, where only those who had attended private schools and universities were able to compete.[86]

THE EFFECT OF THE GREAT DEPRESSION

The Great Depression of the early 1930s influenced both the growth of sport in Australia and its social mix. With substantial numbers of young men out of work, the local sports clubs became places for them to gather. Some who lived near the coast and were reasonable swimmers joined surf lifesaving clubs, mainly in New South Wales and Queensland. Other sports clubs where Australian (rules) football, rugby league, cricket and rugby union were played also became popular meeting places for unemployed young men. It was during this time that many of the desirable social outcomes fostered by sport, which had evolved over the previous 100 years in Australian society, were reinforced. Egalitarianism, volunteerism and social cohesion developed from a social environment in which people experienced a degree of shared hardship while having a common goal to strive for within the sport of their choice. A lot of Australians in this period had time on their hands, some actively participating while others did rudimentary coaching or perhaps some sports administration. In fact, this was the beginning of what became known as the 'kitchen table administration' era, as the club's committee meeting was often held at the president or secretary's home around the kitchen table. Club minute books from this time usually reveal primitive records of these often rather informal meetings.[87]

Australian sport also benefited in two additional ways during and just after the Depression. First, there was an increase in spectator numbers, which had always been reasonably high for a country with a small population. This certainly took place in Australian (rules) football and rugby league, but the biggest increases occurred in cricket, probably stimulated by the great Don Bradman and the renowned 'Bodyline' series against England. Cricket had always been popular, but in this period its appeal increased markedly. Crowd levels surged not only at the international level, as even state and district games drew larger followings.[88] [89]

The other positive development was the building of outdoor sport and recreation facilities in the outer city suburbs and larger country towns. Towards the end of the Depression, governments around Australia invested in civil construction projects and one aspect of this program was the building of parks, outdoor sports fields and courts. There are many municipal sports facilities still in use today which were originally built in the 1930s. Of course, most of these have been renovated and other facilities added in the meantime, but undoubtedly this period was very important in the development of basic sport and recreation facilities in Australia. There were many negative aspects of the Great Depression for a large number of Australians, but one positive outcome was the steady development of sport and outdoor sporting facilities during that period.[90]

WORLD WAR II — ITS EFFECT ON SPORT DEVELOPMENT

As many young men had experienced some type of sport during the 1930s, albeit in a rather rudimentary form, the period of the Second World War saw a continuation of sports participation. All the Australian armed services promoted sport during times of rest and recreation, with team games such as cricket and the various football codes being the most popular.[91] Sport was also played in prison camps[92] and ships' crews often formed cricket and football teams to play other teams while in port. The football codes played by the ships' crews were often related to the locations from which the men had been recruited; therefore there were usually two, or perhaps even three, codes of football played by the crews of the larger ships. Boxing was another sport fostered by the armed services, and the odd athletic carnival was held, with running and jumping events and perhaps a team tug-of-war. Towards the end of the war, teams representing the various services competed in inter-service contests and the standard was often quite high. For example, the Australian services cricket team, which included several first-class cricketers, played in the Victory Test series in England at the end of the war.[93]

Finally, the community service aspect of the surf lifesaving movement continued during the war. Beaches in the Middle East, the Pacific Ocean and even

Britain were patrolled by surf lifesavers wherever Australian troops were stationed. Australians also trained hundreds of men to become qualified lifesavers during the war period, as well as holding several surf competitions at a reasonable distance from the war zones.[94]

International performances — before 1946

Although Australia's international representatives had become heroes to many Australians, their performances were not particularly good against the top sporting nations in the early part of the 20th century. The big powers in sport at that time were the United States, Great Britain, France and Germany; and the Scandinavian countries also did well considering their small populations. However, Australia's performances were reasonably good against the other Commonwealth nations at that time.[95]

Cricket, which was mainly played against England, was the most popular game at the international level in the 1920s and 1930s in this country. Intense rivalry began after World War I, when Australia won eight Test matches in a row. The beginning of the 1930s was also a period in which Australia dominated her traditional rival, with Don Bradman scoring prodigiously. In three successive innings he scored 254, 334 and 232 in the 1930 series in England. However, in the 'Bodyline' series held in Australia in 1932–33, the English team took home the Ashes after allegations of unfair play had been made against the captain, Douglas Jardine, and the series became so heated that it almost caused a diplomatic incident between the two countries. Before Bradman, Victor Trumper had been the outstanding Australian batsman. Players of the calibre of Stan McCabe, Bill Ponsford, Bert Oldfield and Clarrie Grimmett were to follow, teaming up with Bradman and the great leg-spinner Bill O'Reilly to ensure Australia's dominance in world cricket at that time.[96] [97]

Tennis was the other sport in which Australians were very prominent internationally. Norman Brookes made an international name for himself as an outstanding player from 1905 to the beginning of World War I. He was also a gifted administrator, and was largely responsible for setting up a very functional tennis system in Australia after his retirement from competition.[98] [99] Other outstanding Australian players in the first half of the 20th century were Gerald Patterson, J.O. Anderson, Jack Crawford, Harry Hopman, Adrian Quist and John Bromwich.[100]

Australia also had considerable success internationally in *golf*. Joe Kirkwood was the best performer in the 1920s, while Jim Ferrier, Billy Bolger and Norman Von Nida won several international tournaments in the late 30s and 40s. Australians always had the disadvantage of a long boat trip to Europe or the USA, as it was not possible to practise while on board ship (except by hitting into a net, which was of little value to the professionals). Players were therefore obliged to stay overseas for long periods in order to prepare themselves before competition. This was often not financially viable, as prize money was quite insignificant at the time.[101]

In the *Olympic sports*, Fanny Durack, Mina Wylie, Claire Dennis, Alecia ('Bonnie') Mealing, Freddie Lane, Frank Beaurepaire and Andrew ('Boy') Charlton were all fine performers in *swimming*, winning many Olympic medals between them, while Dick Eve won the platform (high) *diving* event at the 1924 Olympics.[102] 'Bobby' Pearce scored gold medals in both the 1928 and 1932 Olympic Games in *sculling* and Edgar Gray won the 1000 metre *cycling* sprint event in 1932.[103] In addition, Hubert Opperman was a very successful cyclist at the international level in the pre-war era, becoming the outstanding road racer of that time.

In the first half of the 20th century, Australians also performed well internationally in several sports which were often referred to as 'minor' in this country, despite being considered major ones in Europe and North America — for example, Eddie Scarf in *wrestling*, Reg (Snowy) Baker in *boxing* and Walter Lindrum, who held the world record in *billiards* for 20 years.[104]

Domestic sport — after World War II

At the end of the Second World War, men returning from military service abroad often found it difficult to adjust and were rather restless. As they slowly returned to their jobs or retrained for other vocations or professions under the Commonwealth Government's training scheme, many joined sporting clubs seeking the camaraderie they had experienced during the war. By the mid-1950s, Australia had a high sport participation rate, and this was bolstered by the postwar migration program. Migrants stimulated the growth of soccer, water polo, basketball, table tennis, skiing, fencing, gymnastics and ice-hockey, and brought with them sports such as volleyball, handball and bocce.[105] Furthermore, the social mix in several sports, in which white-collar workers had been the main participants, steadily changed after the war. More blue-collar workers took up tennis, surf lifesaving, field hockey, lawn bowls and later golf. It was also a period in which municipal governments provided more outdoor facilities and numerous courts, fields and Olympic-sized outdoor swimming pools were constructed. In the late 1950s and 1960s, additional public golf courses were also built, allowing people to play the game cheaply without being obliged to join a private golf club. In addition to the growth of the sporting associations and facilities, the numbers of spectators stayed at a high level in the major football codes and cricket after the war. However, the late 50s and 60s saw a decline in spectators in several of the major sports, possibly because the so-called minor sports were becoming more popular both to watch and play.[106] [107]

On the global sports scene, Australia was able to recover from the Second World War more rapidly than Britain and the continental European countries, many of which had been devastated between 1939 and 1945. Without such rapid postwar development, Australia could not have made a great success of staging the Olympic Games in Melbourne in 1956.

CRICKET LEADERS CARRY ON THE TRADITION

Since the late 1870s Australian cricketers have been known for their resolute style of play, especially against England. That tradition has been carried on by our current cricketers, who are officially world champions and generally considered the best team in the world. Profiles of three outstanding leaders who epitomise the characteristics displayed by former Australian players appear below.

AN OUTSTANDING TEST CAPTAIN

Steve Waugh, who first represented his country in the 1985-1986 season, is one of Australia's sporting greats. In his early career, Steve was a middle-order batsman and an aggressive medium-pace bowler. However, a back injury limited his bowling and he was forced to specialise. Waugh has scored 21 485 runs at an average of 51.89 in first-class cricket, and more than 10 000 at an average of 49.91 in Test cricket.

However, he will be best remembered for his astute captaincy. 'Tough, competitive and highly skilled — as well as ruthless out on the field — Steve Waugh is the very essence of Australian cricket', according to John Polack in his player profile. Waugh is also a fine leader of men, as his record as both a Test and one-day captain has demonstrated.

Steve Waugh was Wisden Cricketer of the Year in 1989 and again in 2000 and 2001, as well as the recipient of the Alan Border Medal in 2001. Steve sometimes gives the impression of being a taciturn captain both on and off the field, but he is playing the game to win, which is what the nation expects of him. His compassion for the underprivileged is widely known and he must be applauded for his generosity.[108]

AUSTRALIA'S ONE-DAY CAPTAIN

Ricky Ponting is one of Australian cricket's outstanding batsmen and arguably its best fieldsman. Ricky had shown exceptional promise when only 12 years of age and by 1986 was chosen to play for the Tasmanian northern region's U13 team. He caused quite a stir in that cricket carnival by hitting four successive centuries and being dismissed only once. He was immediately promoted to the U16 team and promptly notched another century. On the strength of these performances, Ponting was offered a Kookaburra bat sponsorship, becoming the youngest person to receive such a contract in the history of the game. Ricky was playing first grade cricket by 14 years of age and attended the AIS Cricket Academy for a two-week coaching clinic at age 17. He was immediately offered a two-year scholarship by Rod Marsh, then head coach of this prestigious unit.

Ricky Ponting made his first appearance for Australia in 1995 and his record of over 4500 runs at an average of 49.5 in Test cricket, with 15 centuries, places him among the elite. In 2002 he was appointed as Australia's one-day captain. If this outstanding cricketer is chosen to succeed Steve Waugh as Australia's next Test captain, he will handle the role with distinction.[109] [110]

THE WICKETKEEPING BATSMAN

Adam Gilchrist, Australia's vice-captain, is one of the world's most exciting cricketers as well as one of Australia's greatest ambassadors. Born in the country town of Bellingen in northern New South Wales, Adam's potential was obvious from his junior days. He gained a scholarship to the AIS Cricket Academy in Adelaide in 1991 and began his first-class career with New South Wales a year later. He moved to Western Australia in 1994, becoming captain of the Western Warriors in 1996 and vice-captain of the Australian team in 2000.

There is no doubt that Adam Gilchrist is a world-class wicketkeeper. He currently holds the world record for the greatest number of dismissals by a keeper in a Test innings, a total of six, set during the 1999–2000 Australian tour of South Africa. As a batsman he has been a phenomenon in international cricket, his Test average of 58.5 ranking him second in the world. An explosive left-hand opener in one-day games and an extremely punishing middle-order Test batsman, Gilchrist is regarded by most pundits as the greatest wicketkeeper-batsman of all time.

In addition to his cricketing skills, the ACB web site states that 'his talent and general cricketing acumen have also seen him come to occupy a position among Australia's core of group leaders over recent years'. There is a firm body of opinion that despite being a wicketkeeper, Adam would also make a fine Australian captain in the future. It is also heartening to see the man who was named Wisden Cricketer of the Year in 2002 acting as a role model for our youth. Adam Gilchrist is both a fine cricketer and a positive young man who represents his country with distinction.[111]

Steve Waugh, Australia's most successful cricket captain, playing in the one-day tournament at the 1998 Commonwealth Games in Kuala Lumpur. (Newspix.)

International performances — after World War II

The period of Australia's international success immediately following the Second World War began with the Australian cricket team's outstanding performances against England in the 1946-47 and 1948 seasons.[112] The team included some of the top pre-war players, with the addition of Keith Miller, Sid Barnes, Arthur Morris, Neil Harvey and Ray Lindwall. Australia's performances in recent years have been equally impressive, and three modern cricketers are profiled in the previous pages.

In the 1948 Olympic Games Australia won two gold medals, six silver and five bronze, in seven different sports. This was Australia's best performance in any Olympic games to that date; and in 1952 at Helsinki, six gold medals, two silver and three bronze were won. Several young performers were on the rise, with the Australian junior swimmers recording excellent times, athletic performances improving rapidly and several very fine young tennis players on the way up. By 1956, this nation's sporting performances had reached a level where Australian athletes were highly competitive against the rest of the world.[113]

The Melbourne Olympics held in 1956 yielded a total of 35 medals for Australia in six different sports, with 13 gold, eight silver and 14 bronze — by far the best Olympic performance recorded by Australia to that point. The home advantage probably played a part — experts rate the degree of advantage at 15 per cent in terms of medal returns at a home Olympics. Thus Australia should still have won about 30 medals had the Games been held elsewhere, compared with 11 at the 1952 Olympics and 13 in 1948. The swimmers and athletes performed exceptionally well, and such names as Betty Cuthbert, Shirley de la Hunty Strickland, Murray Rose, Jon Hendricks, Dawn Fraser and Lorraine Crapp are still revered for their outstanding performances.[114]

In the latter part of the 50s and early 60s, Australian *swimmers* continued their dominance in international events, as did the *tennis* players, led by Lew Hoad, Ken Rosewall and then Rod Laver.[115] *Golfers* such as Ossie Pickworth, Norman von Nida, Peter Thompson and Kel Nagle performed with distinction, both at home and abroad. In team sports, Australia also did well; and by 1960 Australian sport across the board was at an all-time high.

It was then that the celebrated American sportswriter Herbert Warren Wind visited Australia to observe at first hand the Australian 'sports machine'. Wind was a senior journalist for the internationally renowned US magazine *Sports Illustrated*. At that time, Australia held the Davis Cup for tennis, the Eisenhower Cup for amateur golf, the Canada Cup for professional golf, and the Ashes for cricket. Australians already held many individual world titles and records and Wind stated early in his article that this was a land 'inundated with athletes'. He summarised his reasons for their successes thus: 'A fine climate, plenty of room, plenty of time, an inbred love of sports and the wish to excel at them, the lack of competing fields of interest, the worship of the physical which is part of a young country, the right pitch of support from one's family and friends, the splendid natural facilities, the relatively inexpensive cost of sport, the early orientation in school, the opportunity to develop in highly organised competition, and added to these good food for growing bodies and the natural desire of the people of a small nation to do famously in fields which command world attention and respect — these in combination are the amalgam which has made Australia the most vigorous sporting country of all time. It doesn't explain, though, the emergence of its super athletes. If you add two other factors on which Australia places strong emphasis it does. They are: able coaching and plain hard work.'[116]

During the early 1960s, performances in a wide range of non-Olympic sports were similar to those of the late 50s. However, Australia's Olympic team at Rome in 1960 brought home only 22 medals. This was realistically a reduction of about eight in comparison to the Melbourne Olympics, taking the home advantage into consideration. Officials attributed the result to a small number of team members who did not achieve their personal best performances. However, there was another factor of which Australian sports officials were not aware at that time: the gradual emergence of the professional sports systems of Europe and the United States. Close scrutiny of Australia's performances in general reveals that they were still quite good during the 60s, but were gradually declining by the latter part of the decade. At the Olympic Games, Australia won 18 medals at Tokyo in 1964, 17 at Mexico City in 1968 and 17 at Munich in 1972.[117] However, very few people in Australia forecast that the bubble would burst so dramatically at the 1976 Montreal Olympics.

Australia falls behind

The slow decline in Australia's international performances had not been obvious at first, and the majority of sports-loving Australians appeared to expect the status quo to continue. This was a reasonable assumption, as Australia still had high participation rates and it was presumed that the cream would rise to the top automatically. However, there was a continuing problem with Australia's isolation, as international air travel was expensive and still in its infancy in the late 1950s and 60s. In addition, Australian athletes had to compete out of season in the northern hemisphere and without year-round facilities for training at home, they were at a grave disadvantage when competing overseas. The major problem, however, was that the Australian sports system was still basically an amateur one, with virtually no financial assistance from either the state or federal governments. This was in stark contrast to the government support being provided for sport in Eastern and Western Europe.

SPORTS SYSTEM DEVELOPMENTS IN NORTH AMERICA AND EUROPE

During the 1920s and 1930s, the United States had been slowly developing a very different sports system to those of the Western democracies of Europe, as sport was not centred around community sports clubs, but based in the high schools and universities. Throughout the country, high schools had developed athletic departments with many well-trained coaches, the majority of whom were employed not only to teach physical education but to coach various sports teams as a condition of their employment. The university sector had done a similar thing, but in a much bigger way. By the 1960s American high school and university sport had evolved into a dynamic system and professional sport was making rapid strides in American football, basketball, baseball, tennis and golf. Canada too had reasonably strong school and university sport programs, as well as the club or association system modelled on the British one. Canada had been quick to observe Europe's developments and by the late 1960s and early 1970s had plans to professionalise its basically amateur sports system.[118]

It was Eastern Europe, however, led by Russia in the late 1940s and very closely followed by Poland, Czechoslovakia, Romania, Bulgaria, Yugoslavia, East Germany and finally Hungary, who determined that if participation and elite performances were to improve, national governments must become much more involved in sport. This approach was very radical, as sport in Europe before 1945 had been strictly amateur in every respect. Developments such as professionally managed multi-sports clubs and sports associations, talent identification programs, state-funded training facilities, sports institutes, international travel assistance, sports scholarships, highly trained coaches and sports science and medicine assistance were previously unheard of. In addition, national sports institutes, provincial centres of excellence and sports schools were being set up in geographically strategic areas to carry out many of the above programs.[119] There was a high degree of secrecy in regard to sports science and medicine research, as superior training techniques were being developed and research on performance-enhancing drugs was being conducted – a development the Western world was not to discover until at least a decade later.

By the mid to late-1950s, the Eastern European satellite countries had developed the majority of their centrally controlled systems. It was only half a decade later that several Western European democracies, with the exception of Great Britain, followed suit. Italy, France, West Germany, Holland and Belgium, as well as the Scandinavian countries to a lesser extent, had partially copied the Eastern European model, but their budgets were much less generous and their programs not as highly developed.[120] [121] Furthermore, by the early to mid-1960s, the European countries had largely recovered from the ravages of World War II and this meant they had completed most of their postwar reconstruction programs, allowing them to concentrate more on sport and recreation developments. It is important to emphasise that the Eastern and

Western European sports systems did not just cater for the elite Olympic sports, but also attempted to increase the overall levels of sport participation and to foster physical and health education through their education ministries.[122]

During the 1960s the writer spent eight years away from Australia, studying and coaching in the United States and lecturing in Eastern and Western Europe. It was therefore possible to observe at first hand a large number of the sophisticated programs and facilities already established, or being developed, in 13 European countries. It was clear that the amateur sports system in Australia would sooner or later be swamped by the highly professional approach of North America and Europe. It was to happen even sooner than expected, as will be explained fully in Chapter Two.

Chapter Two
Beginning a professional sports system

Pre-1973 sport developments

In the latter part of Chapter One it was pointed out that Australia entered the 1970s with an outmoded sports system and found itself competing against highly sophisticated systems from the United States and Europe. Rees noted in 1972 that more than 20 Ministries of Sport and/or Recreation had been set up in other countries since the Second World War, whereas Australian sport still had a pre-World War II amateur system, with no direct government support.[1] These overseas ministries not only developed elite athletes but also attempted to increase the levels of sport participation in the wider community. At the same time, physical fitness programs were being fostered in liaison with their Ministries of Health and Education within the schools and the community.

National fitness councils

The advent of the Second World War caused the Australian Government to set up the Commonwealth Council for National Fitness and six State Councils in 1941, under the Commonwealth National Fitness Act. It was thought that these councils would be able to foster higher levels of physical fitness, particularly in young males, many of whom were found to have low fitness levels when they enlisted in the armed forces. It was also believed that all Australian citizens needed to be fitter during wartime and mass exercise sessions were mounted for the public at several locations around Australia. Whether or not the objectives of the National Fitness movement were ever fully achieved is open to question, but at least a structure was in place on to which some additional recreational functions could be grafted after the war years.[2]

By the early 1970s, both the Commonwealth and state National Fitness Councils had grown to the point where they had modest budgets, which mainly financed staff in Canberra and the state capitals. By 1972, the then Federal Treasurer, Billy Snedden, had increased the Commonwealth National Fitness budget to $800 000,[3] which was minuscule in comparison to the spending of other Western democracies similar to Australia. However, no state had yet established sophisticated sport and recreation programs, nor was there any regular liaison between the states. By the late 50s and early 60s, both the Commonwealth and the states had gradually moved away from fitness-oriented programs towards physical recreation. At a later time, some of the State Councils began to give minimal support to selected sport programs. This was because the National Fitness Council of Western Australia had already set a precedent by establishing an Associated Sporting Committee as early as 1950 to assist the major sports associations in that state.[4]

Early calls for Ministries of Sport and Recreation

THE STATES

The first serious discussions about the formation of a state Ministry of Recreation in Australia occurred in Western Australia in late September 1969. Both Herb Graham, the then Deputy Leader of the Labor Opposition, and the writer were vocal in their calls for the government of the day to establish a ministry. Sir David Brand, Premier of Western Australia at that time, responded with the following statement: 'I would be loath to make another department. There is no real justification because the time is not ripe. We are mindful of the trends and we do encourage leaders in our community, but I feel it is wrong to pass it all to the Government. We have the facilities and we should encourage more voluntary efforts and get people to organise themselves.'[5]

Many of the volunteers integrally involved with sport in the state were unhappy with that statement, feeling that the government was abrogating its responsibilities. However, they were obliged to wait until the Western Australian Labor Government came to office in 1972 before their repeated requests were heeded and a ministry was established.[6]

Although it never really functioned, plans for a Ministry of Sport in New South Wales had been announced on 26 January 1971 by Bob Askin, Premier of New South Wales. The impetus for this development had come from Dick Healey, the Liberal member for Davidson, who had previously held discussions with the writer about a proposed ministry.[7] In a letter to Bloomfield dated 19 February 1971, Healey stated that a Ministry of Sport in New South Wales would be able to cater for the areas covered by national fitness, youth affairs and physical recreation and could be broadened at a later time.[8] Unfortunately, for reasons which are still not clear, the proposed body did not develop, remaining a ministry in name only.

THE COMMONWEALTH

The earliest calls for the appointment of a Commonwealth Minister for Sport were made by Senator Geoff McLaren (ALP, South Australia) in mid-September 1971. He asked Sir Kenneth Anderson, the then Leader of the Coalition Government in the Senate, to use his influence to establish a ministry. Anderson declined, stating: 'I do not know that the creation of a new portfolio is warranted. Such a matter would have to be considered by the Prime Minister and the Government.

I think a more likely proposition is that sport is in some ways included in the responsibilities of other portfolios.'[9]

Senator Anderson then referred Senator McLaren's request to the Prime Minister of the day, William McMahon, who rejected the proposal, saying: 'The Commonwealth Government's involvement in sport and physical recreation in Australia is a financial one.' He outlined what these finances covered and asserted that 'a separate Ministry would not be warranted'.[10]

One year later, in 1972, Senator McLaren again raised the matter in the Senate. This time it was prompted by the then Manager of the Australian Olympic Team and Secretary-General of the Australian Olympic Federation, Julius ('Judy') Patching, who called on the Federal Coalition Government to appoint a Minister for Sport. Again the government refused, Senator Drake-Brockman declaring that 'if the Olympic authorities believe they have a case they should put it to the Prime Minister for his consideration'.[11]

Just prior to McLaren's second call, the writer had delivered an address at a National Conference on the Human Consequences of Technological Change, held at the University of Sydney on 25 August 1972. In a paper entitled 'The Conservation of Man', the Australian Government was urged to set up a Federal Ministry of Recreation, similar to the Ministries of Sport and Recreation which existed in Europe. The request was well received by those individuals and politicians in the eastern states who had been pressing for a federal ministry, and considerable discussion ensued. The paper was forwarded to Gough Whitlam, Leader of the Labor Opposition, and to Barry Cohen, the Member for Robertson in the Opposition, who had contacted the writer for further discussions.[12]

In fact, Barry Cohen was largely responsible for the establishment of the first Federal Ministry for Tourism and Recreation when Labor came to office late in 1972. He had formulated a Caucus paper on the future development of sport and recreation in Australia which had been accepted as the ALP sport and recreation platform for the December 1972 elections. In early September he announced details of his plan, which was to prove crucial in modernising the Australian sports system over the next 24 years. In his policy speech to the Caucus, he proposed that if Labor were elected to office:

- a Ministry of Sport would be established;

- one hundred indoor pools and gymnasiums would be built in Australia in the first three years of office;

- matching grants would be made to national sporting associations;

- matching grants would be allocated to local government for the provision of playing fields and other sporting facilities;

- an Institute of Sport would be established;

- a National Sports Council would be created to advise the Minister on priorities for sport development.[13]

These policies were well ahead of their time in Australia and Barry Cohen showed considerable foresight and tenacity in having them accepted as the Labor Opposition's sport and recreation policy. Both Senator Ron McAuliffe and Senator Geoff McLaren played a significant role in supporting the proposals.

During this period the writer was President of the Australian Sports Medicine Federation (ASMF). At the Annual General Meeting held in Adelaide in October 1972, a motion was moved from the Chair to lobby all federal politicians to support the establishment of a Ministry of Recreation and Sport. A letter co-signed by the ASMF's secretary at that time, Dr Ken Fitch, and the writer was sent to all members of the Federal House of Representatives and the Senate, asking them to support the establishment of a Ministry of Recreation and Sport. This document can be found in Appendix A.[14]

Of the 36 responses, 27 were from Labor members and nine from members of the Coalition Government. Fortunately, 15 positive replies came from those Labor Party Opposition members who became Cabinet Ministers when the Labor Government took office shortly afterwards in December 1972. This strong display of support for a Ministry of Recreation was a resounding endorsement for Barry Cohen's efforts in the six-month lead-up to the election.[15]

Western Australia leads the way

Following an appeal by the writer at an ANZAAS Conference in Perth in late June 1972, the newly elected State Labor Government in Western Australia[16] decided to establish the first functioning Ministry of Recreation in Australia on 4 July 1972.[17]

The first Minister for Recreation in Western Australia was Tom Evans. However, it was Herb Graham, the newly-elected Deputy Premier, who was largely responsible for guiding the new policy through the Cabinet, as he had been very supportive of the concept for several years. The Labor Government of the day amalgamated the National Fitness Council and the Youth Council, forming the Community Recreation Council of Western Australia in the latter part of 1972.

The first chairman was Harry Dettman, the former Director-General of Education in the state; the writer became the deputy chairman and Bill English was appointed as the new director. However, English was unable to continue in the position for health reasons and John Graham was appointed acting director early in 1973, becoming the director at the end of the year. The council took on a very wide focus and was responsible for the development of recreation, sport and youth affairs until 1978, when it became the Department of Youth, Sport and Recreation under John Graham's inspiring leadership.[18] During the Tonkin Labor Government's term of office, a vibrant state sport and recreation system rapidly evolved. Programs were developed in sports management, sports coaching and recreation leadership, as well as in sports science and sports medicine, and improved indoor and outdoor sport and recreation facilities were planned for the near future.

The Whitlam era – 1972-75

Frank Stewart's ministry

Some members of the sporting community were disappointed when the new federal ministry was named the 'Ministry for Tourism and Recreation', as they had expected it to be entitled 'Sport and Recreation'. Unfortunately, Barry Cohen was not elected to the Cabinet by the Labor Caucus, which meant that he was not in a position to hold this new portfolio despite having done the majority of the groundwork to develop it. The Minister chosen was Frank Stewart, who had been the Shadow Minister for Minerals and Energy while in Opposition. As well as serving in the Australian army in the Pacific during World War II, Stewart had been an A-grade tennis player and an outstanding first-grade rugby league footballer in Sydney for several years with the Canterbury-Bankstown Club. There is no doubt that his sporting record gave him a high profile as Australia's first Minister for Sport, but he also had a keen interest in a wide range of sports.[19]

Frank Stewart was the Minister with a responsibility for sport in the Whitlam Government. During his three-year term he began the development of a modern sports system in Australia. (By permission of the National Library of Australia — see Appendix H for photo credits.)

Because the Labor Party's election platform had been very comprehensive and it had been out of office for 23 years, there was a flurry of activity when Labor came to power in late 1972. The first 100 days of office were 'counted down' by members of the press, who reported various policy announcements day by day. Tourism and recreation received some media coverage, but Frank Stewart at first steadily appraised the current state of each of the areas for which he was responsible. This proved to be a wise move; as a result, policy was not made on the run. Lloyd Bott became the secretary of the new Department of Tourism and Recreation and his role appeared to be that of a general overseer for both areas of the new department. Graham Dempster, a young Commonwealth public servant who had been the Commonwealth National Fitness Officer under the previous government, was appointed as Director of Recreation. His knowledge of the current status of sport in Australia and his vision for its future development were to prove invaluable within the new portfolio. Even though the new Minister had only a small and youthful team to support him in the recreation and sport section, they served him well, giving judicious advice in the early stages of the ministry.[20]

THE BLOOMFIELD REPORT — 1973

The first major action of the new Recreation Division was to commission the writer to prepare a white paper on the current status and future development of sport and recreation in Australia. The terms of reference were brief but the report was expected to be wide-ranging. Seventy-eight professionals in the fields of sport, recreation and physical education were interviewed throughout Australia and many of their suggestions were included in the final report. The major recommendations were:

- that programs be developed to improve physical fitness levels both in the schools and the community;

- that the existing amateur sport and recreation system be professionalised;

- that matching grants for programs and facilities be established between the Australian and state governments;

- that multiple use of school and community sporting facilities be fostered;

- that programs be developed in the following areas: sports management, sports coaching, sports officiating, sports scholarships, overseas travel, talent identification and sports science and medicine services;

- that a National Institute of Sport be established.

The report was generally well received, and a meeting was held in Canberra between the federal Minister and the state Ministers responsible for sport and recreation to co-ordinate its implementation. There were some minor disputes, due more to party ideologies than the content of the report, but the state

Ministers agreed with it in principle and the general feeling was that the recommendations should steadily be implemented. This report was tabled in the Federal Parliament in mid-1973 and became government policy for the future development of sport and recreation in Australia.[21]

EARLY DEVELOPMENTS IN THE NEW DEPARTMENT

It became obvious during the early months of the existence of the department that the major emphasis was being placed on tourism. This was initially the case not only because tourism was seen to be a future revenue earner, but because promoting it seemed less complex than coming to grips with the loosely co-ordinated areas of sport and recreation. Attention also had to be paid to the individuals and organisations who, in their lobbying for the establishment of a ministry, had stressed the preventive medical and recreational benefits for the Australian community.[22 23]

Naturally, the sports lobby groups were also impatient to see more rapid improvements to the sports system and it took some time for the various priorities to be established. In hindsight, there was probably some benefit gained from the relatively slow pace of development of sport and recreation in the first year of the new ministry, because it gave the Minister and his advisers time to think through the various issues confronting them.

FEDERAL GRANTS

The first substantial government grants in the history of sport in Australia were initially organised to assist athletes' travel, coaching and sports management, and later to boost sports facility development. Planning began in mid-1973 and the programs commenced in 1974. The following is a brief overview of the sport and recreation initiatives that were undertaken for the first time in Australia:[24]

- *Travel subsidies* for Australian competitors and officials became available for attendance at national and international championships, and assistance was also provided to state officials to attend their national associations' annual meetings. In addition, national associations received assistance to send their delegates overseas to represent them at annual meetings of their international bodies. One of the most popular subsidies was for the *transport of competitors' equipment* for national and international championships.

- *Coaching subsidies* were provided for the appointment of national coaches, often on a full-time basis. Previously only a few national associations had full-time coaches, whereas the smaller ones had only part-time or unpaid national coaches. *National coaching seminars* were introduced and from 1974 onwards, overseas coaches were invited to lecture in Australia with most of their expenses paid by the Australian Government.

- *Sports management subsidies* were granted for national associations to appoint professional managers, enabling several associations to finally emerge from the 'kitchen table administration' era. The administrative costs of running national and international-level championships were also subsidised; and associations for the first time were able to mount spectacles to attract spectators, increasing their revenue base.

After the Bloomfield Report had been accepted by the Federal Government in mid-1973, various states applied pressure on Canberra for assistance to develop modern *sports facilities*, because almost all of the facilities throughout the country at that time were substandard by comparison to those in Europe and the United States. The Labor Government initiated grants for sporting facilities by allocating $6 million in 1975. This was the biggest single initiative that had ever taken place in government sports development in Australia, and it set the stage for two and a half decades of sport facility growth, eventually leading up to the Sydney 2000 Olympics.

FEDERAL–STATE GOVERNMENT CO-OPERATION

The Whitlam Labor Government, although strongly centralist, expected the states to match the federal grants from within their own fledgling sports systems. Victoria had developed a Department of Youth, Sport and Recreation in 1973, with Brian Dixon as the first Minister. He had established a small but highly competent department under the guidance of Bert Keddie. Dixon was a positive and effective Minister who had a comprehensive knowledge of sport *(see accompanying profile)*. Despite some disagreements with the Labor Government in Canberra, in private Dixon felt that it was doing a good job and his department was well enough developed to match the federal grants. Western Australia's Ministry of Recreation's functional arm was the Community Recreation Council of Western Australia, which catered well for both sport and recreation; and because of its flexible structure and the level of its development, it too was able to interface well with Canberra. When the other states became aware that matching grants were on offer, they gradually began to organise their embryonic sports systems, but the Federal Labor Government was removed from office on 11 November 1975 before they could avail themselves of many of the grants offered by the federal ministry.[25]

THE AUSTRALIAN SPORTS COUNCIL

Following Barry Cohen's recommendation in September 1972 to the Labor Opposition, Frank Stewart had established an Australian Sports Council in early 1974. This was an advisory body with a high level of expertise among its members. Each state was represented and several specialised individuals were appointed by the Labor Government. However, like most Commonwealth advisory bodies, it did not have a great deal of impact on policy development. In fact, just as it was becoming a reasonably cohesive and effective group, the Federal Government was dismissed in late 1975 and the council went into limbo. It was not convened by the new Coalition Government until well after the Montreal Olympic Games debacle, which will be discussed later in this chapter.

THE FOOTBALLER-POLITICIAN

The Hon Brian Dixon's contribution to sport and recreation, both in Australia in general and Victoria in particular, has been enormous. Brian was very well known in his home state as an Australian (rules) footballer before being elected to parliament in Victoria, having played 258 games for Melbourne and 11 for the VFL. In 1973 he became the Minister for Youth, Sport and Recreation, a portfolio he held for nine years. He initiated numerous programs, many of which are still in operation today.

During his term of office Brian Dixon had a very high profile. It has even been suggested that he was better known than the two Premiers, Dick Hamer and Lindsay Thompson, under whom he worked. Dixon balanced the three responsibilities of youth, sport and recreation very well. While Assistant Minister for Education, he established physical education as a requirement in Victorian state schools and developed a Community Recreation Officers' Scheme which operated through local government, promoting sport and recreation at the grassroots level. He also established a policy of using school facilities for recreation and was the first Minister to support the building of larger state-level facilities for sport. Dixon initiated several major reports which firmly established a sports system in Victoria, as well as being responsible for the highly successful 'Life Be In It' program.

Brian has not rested on his laurels since retiring from Parliament, continuing his interests in sport both within Victoria and internationally. He is currently the President of the Melbourne Football Club and is integrally linked to a movement to spread our national football game into the international arena.[26]

THE COLES REPORT — 1974

In late September 1974 the Federal Minister for Tourism and Recreation had appointed a committee to report on the feasibility of establishing a national Institute of Sport, which had been previously recommended in the 1973 Bloomfield Report. This committee was chaired by Dr Allan Coles, then a senior academic in human movement from the University of Queensland. It was a wide-ranging yet in-depth report which established a rationale for the development of an institute. Its major recommendations were:[27]

- that a National Institute for Sport be established in Canberra with branches located in the states;

- that a comprehensive national coaching system be developed;

- that courses for sports administrators and officials be established by the institute in conjunction with national sports associations;

- that sports science and sports medicine education be encouraged by the institute;

- that technical services relating to sports facilities and equipment be developed.

Many of the recommendations related to support services for elite sport, and this was in contrast to the high performance-oriented Australian Institute of Sport model which was eventually set in place by the Fraser Government in 1981. Unfortunately, the Coles Report was not tabled in Parliament before the Whitlam Government's dismissal; thus its recommendations could not be implemented and it was pigeon-holed by the incoming Fraser Government. However, some of the recommendations were later included when the Australian Institute of Sport established support services for elite sport; and the Australian Sports Commission included several others among its own initiatives when it was established in 1985.

THE LABOR GOVERNMENT'S ACHIEVEMENTS — 1972-75

When evaluating this period it is important to acknowledge that a significant first step had been taken by the Whitlam Labor Government and, in particular, by the first Australian Minister for Recreation, Frank Stewart. They created the foundation upon which a modern sports system could be established, and when one compares what was in place before 1973 with what had been accomplished by November 1975, two conclusions are obvious. Not only had many basic initiatives been put in place, but more importantly, members of the Australian sporting community had developed an expectation in regard to government assistance. They had experienced at first hand how valuable well-directed sports funding could be, and were determined to keep the pressure on future governments for more of the same. However, the new Fraser Government placed sport and recreation very low on its priority list and consequently it was strongly criticised by the sporting community for its inaction in the latter part of the 1970s.

The Fraser years

The early period — 1975-78

Progress towards the development of a more sophisticated sports system floundered when the Fraser Coalition Government came to office in late 1975. The first casualty was the Department of Tourism and Recreation, which was disbanded by the new government, placing at risk funding for the programs already initiated. Not only were the federal programs jeopardised, but the recently established joint programs between national associations and the states were also threatened. To be fair to the new government, several programs already in place were continued, often with reduced funding, with the result that most of them survived only until the joint state-federal agreements expired.[28] The states of Victoria and Western Australia already had reasonably well developed sports systems by that time, so the withdrawal of federal funds did not affect them as severely as it did in the other states.

Apart from funding cuts, the other problem was one of identity. There was no longer an obvious portfolio directly related to sport and recreation, as these areas were placed under various other portfolios during the next seven years. Moreover, a rapid turnover of Ministers did not instill confidence within the Australian sporting community. The first Coalition Minister responsible for sport was Ivor Greenwood, who unfortunately died shortly after taking over the portfolios of the environment, housing and community development, within which sport and recreation had been included as a minor section. The second Minister was Kevin Newman, who carried on the new government's policy to introduce a new structure and to drastically reduce the public service.

Fortunately, Graham Dempster continued to head up the new sport unit, assisted by Paul Brettell. These two enthusiastic young officers were largely responsible for keeping sport and recreation alive during this period, through their dedication and firm belief in the intrinsic value of their chosen profession, which had originally been physical education. They tried to enthuse their political masters over the next three years, but this proved a difficult task because of the rapid turnover of Ministers and the low priority assigned to sport and recreation. The new Coalition Government only had a general sport and recreation policy and played a reactive, rather than a pro-active, role with the national sports associations and the state governments during their first six months in office.[29] It took Australia's very poor performance in July 1976 at the Olympic Games in Montreal to draw the nation's attention to the sorry plight of Australian sport at that time. This was to be reinforced two years later by an equally disappointing performance at the 1978 Commonwealth Games in Edmonton, where Australia finished third behind Canada and England in the medal tally.

THE MONTREAL OLYMPICS — JULY 1976

Australia's failure to win even one gold medal at the Montreal Games shocked the Australian public as much as it did the competitors and coaches. Only five medals were won overall, and outraged protests were heard both in Montreal and back in Australia. Like the previous Coalition Governments which had been in power for 23 years before Labor's three-year term, the Fraser Government had been largely ignoring sport and recreation and stubbornly opposing any proposed changes. Despite the positive initiatives during its short term in office, Labor had not had sufficient time in government to make a significant impact at the elite level. Concurrently, the build-up of the various sports systems in Europe and the growth of university sport in the United States had created a significant performance improvement from those quarters. Meanwhile, Australia and the majority of the Commonwealth countries had retained their amateur systems, dropping well behind their European and American rivals.

With its meagre five medals of the total of 613 awarded, Australia could only manage a 32nd placing in the final medal standing.[30] This low ranking insulted national pride.[31] The press reflected Australians' shattered expectations with headlines such as: 'AUSTRALIA'S GOLDEN DAYS HAVE GONE';[32] 'OUR OLYMPIC FLOPS WILL CONTINUE UNLESS...';[33] 'ANGRY ATHLETES TELL PM TO BE MORE LIBERAL';[34] 'ONLY MANDRAKE CAN HELP US';[35] and 'CANADIANS TURN TABLES ON US'.[36] The reaction from the United Kingdom was swift and cutting, with an article by Ronald Kaye from *The Guardian* expressing England's gleeful reaction to Australia's sporting slump. Kaye observed that Australia was 'like a middle-aged athlete gone flabby', and that the country had stumbled into a national identity crisis, stricken by self-doubt and torn by bitter recrimination over real or imagined failings. He went on to say that 'the crisis had been brought on by the sudden collapse of Australia's greatest claim to world esteem – their athletes, who were turning in their worst Olympic performance in 40 years'. Finally, Kaye said the debacle had 'created a crisis for the Government and set off a strong debate over how the nation can regain its lost athletic potency'.[37]

The Prime Minister, Malcolm Fraser, was accosted by a vocal contingent of indignant Australian athletes towards the end of the Montreal Games. He made a positive statement, promising more government assistance for sport and declaring that he would order an official inquiry to be held in Australia after the Olympic Games had finished.[38] At the same time, however, he decried the scramble for gold medals as a wrong-spirited approach to the Olympics, and asserted that athletes should not be regimented into military style win-at-all-costs academies.[39] Just one day later in Canberra, the Minister responsible for sport, Kevin Newman, stated that the government had 'an important role in developing Australian sport', but that it should not adopt the all-encompassing Eastern European approach because Australian people would find this unacceptable.[40]

These statements brought an angry response from both the media and the sporting public. Athletes, coaches and sports scientists complained that the Prime Minister and several members of his government did not fully understand the handicaps Australian athletes had to overcome when competing in the international arena.[41] Dr John Daly, whose profile appears in the accompanying box, was a respected academic and head coach of the Australian track and field team at the Montreal Olympics. He expressed the athletes' frustrations succinctly in an open letter to *The Australian* newspaper, entitled 'Courageous Amateurs Must Fail',[42] comprehensively defining the problems they faced when competing against the rest of the world.

THE ACADEMIC-COACH

Professor John Daly was head coach of the Australian Olympic track and field team when he wrote an open letter entitled 'Courageous Amateurs Must Fail' to the Australian sporting public in 1976, following Australia's dismal performance at the Montreal Games. He was concerned that criticism about the lack of sporting success at those Games was being unfairly directed at the athletes and coaches, whereas it was Australia's antiquated sports system that was at fault. The letter caused considerable controversy throughout Australia, unleashing a movement which was to last until 1980, as various individuals and sports organisations consistently harassed the Coalition Government.

The then Prime Minister, Malcolm Fraser, had promised the sporting public an inquiry into 'amateur sport and the Government's role in its development'. However, it was to take another four years, and Australia's divisive involvement in the 1980 Moscow Games, before the Australian Institute of Sport was opened in January 1981.

John Daly was appointed to the inaugural board of the AIS and continued his role with the Australian track and field team until the early 90s. He was the personal coach of Glynis Nunn, who won a gold medal in the heptathlon at the 1984 Olympic Games in Los Angeles, as well as head coach of Australia's track and field team at several world championships and five Olympics (Montreal, Moscow, Los Angeles, Seoul and Barcelona). A sport historian at the University of South Australia, Professor Daly has written numerous articles on Australian sport and eight books, including *The Quest For Excellence: The Australian Institute Of Sport*.

As well, Daly has taken up several appointments to government committees on sport development in Australia. He helped establish the highly acclaimed Australian Coaching Council and was partly responsible for the influential paper 'Junior Sport Policy', which was to radically change junior sport in this country.

John Daly was awarded the medal of the Order of Australia in 1991 for his outstanding services to Australian sport. [43]

The newspaper article with perhaps the most impact in relation to the government's promises appeared in *The Australian* just after the 1976 Games.[44] David O'Reilly warned that the Federal Government had no intention of pouring big money into sport, despite the apparently sympathetic hearing it had given to 'our athletic prophets of doom in Montreal'. He stated: 'Time will show that the emotional pleas for aid to revive our flagging international sports reputation have already fallen on deaf ears. Political leaders know only too well that the chances of large-scale funding for amateur sport are remote ... They are convinced that public concern over our dismal Olympics performance will be short-lived.' He claimed that government sources had admitted privately that the injection of significant funds into sport would go against every economic principle expressed by the Coalition Government. As one government spokesman caustically commented: 'Montreal is over — the football semi-finals will soon be here. And after all, the Moscow Olympics don't come around for another four years — if indeed they are held at all.' This seemed a cynical statement, but David O'Reilly was soon proven correct, as very little tangible assistance was granted until a great deal more pressure had been brought to bear on the government by journalists, sports administrators and Opposition members over the next few years.[45]

As expected, the Labor Opposition was also very critical of the Fraser Government. Tom Uren, the then Deputy Leader, accused the government of misrepresenting the current budget figures for sport and recreation.[46] He claimed that the 1975-76 financial year projected budget allocation made by Labor had been $2.8 million, but that this had been reduced by 60 per cent by the Coalition Government during their first year of office. Finally, the Gallup Poll asked the Australian public if sport should be given more financial support by the government. The response was overwhelming, with 70 per cent of Australians indicating that more government aid was necessary if Australian sportsmen and sportswomen were to compete with the rest of the world on an equal footing.[47]

MORE FEDERAL GOVERNMENT INACTION

It has already been mentioned that the Prime Minister had publicly pledged to mount an inquiry over Australia's poor showing in the Olympic Games.[48] However, eight months after the Prime Minister's promise, Kevin Newman, the Minister responsible for sport, still had not called the Australian Sports Council together to initiate such an inquiry. The Fraser Government may have believed that the council's members were biased towards the Labor Party, which had appointed them, but this was not the case; the members were highly professional and had good credentials for the positions they held.

When the council eventually did meet, little of substance emerged and the Minister continued to make announcements about future funding possibilities which came to nothing. For example, his proposal to establish a national lottery to support sport[49] was not a viable option at that time, as the states strongly objected to any such lotteries being mounted by the Federal Government.[50]

CRITICISM BY SPORTING OFFICIALS AND THE PRESS

THE OLYMPIC FOUNDATION AND THE CONFEDERATION OF AUSTRALIAN SPORT

The first concrete step taken by sporting officials in early September 1976 was to form a lobby group to pressure the government into increasing funding for sport. Under the chairmanship of David McKenzie, an Australian member of the International Olympic Committee, the Olympic Foundation was formed. The founding president was Sir Arthur George, who was at that time also President of the Australian Soccer Federation. In a speech at Anzac House in Sydney on government support for sport, McKenzie outlined the various ways in which the needs of sport could be met. However, he was very critical of the Fraser Government, accusing it of having very little interest in the development of the sports system.

Following the formation of the Olympic Foundation, a considerable amount of pressure was applied to the government, and in mid-February 1977 $3.75 million was allocated to Australian sport to assist with preparations for the 1980 Olympic Games in Moscow.[52] In April 1977 Greg Hartung, a journalist with *The Australian* newspaper, commenced a series of articles in which he strongly pressed the case for systematic sport development in Australia by the Federal Government.

The Confederation of Australian Sport (CAS) had also been formed in November 1976 under the chairmanship of Wayne Reid, a respected sports administrator.[53] The confederation represented 67 national sporting associations with a combined membership of over 5.5 million sports people, giving it considerable muscle. One of its first actions was to prepare a report on the financial problems facing Australian sport[54] with information gathered from its affiliated national sports organisations. The report demonstrated that elite sport in particular was in dire straits. Requests were made for increased funding for international-level facilities, for high-level coaching, for increasing the opportunities to compete internationally, and to upgrade national-level competitions. Backed up by Greg Hartung's hard-hitting articles, whose evocative headlines read: 'THOUSAND TO ONE — SPORT IS THE POOR RELATION';[55] 'NO MONEY, NO MEDALS, SPORTS PEOPLE TELL GOVERNMENT';[56] 'SPORT IN CRITICAL POSITION PM TOLD',[57] CAS proved to be an effective lobby group for sport for several years and in August 1977, mainly as a result of the above pressure, the Treasurer, Phillip Lynch, announced a $3 million grant for sport for the next three years.[58] In fact, this was less than half the amount of the first major budget allocation made by Labor four years beforehand, and would prove to be only of limited assistance to Australian sport because most of the momentum had already been lost in the meantime. It was too little too late, so the lobby groups kept up their pressure.

SPORT AND RECREATION INITIATIVES IN THE LATE 1970s

THE NATIONAL SPORTS ADVISORY COUNCIL

In late 1977 the federal Minister formed an Advisory Sports Council chaired by the well-known sports administrator, Jim Barry, to replace the Australian Sports Council established by the Whitlam Labor Government. The formation of this body was a gesture by the government to try to heal the rift between itself and sport, and it included several very competent members. Like many advisory groups however, it lacked teeth, but it was able to distribute grant monies on behalf of the government and was also in a position to advise the Minister with regard to sport policy. However, it was apparent that the Minister was not listening, as very little changed and resentment continued to build up within the sports lobby towards the Fraser Government.[59]

AUSTRALIAN COACHING COUNCIL (ACC)

The current highly acclaimed coaching accreditation program was originally developed by the National Fitness Council of Western Australia, under the direction of the writer and John Graham, the then deputy director of the council. The first course was held in mid-1969 in the newly established Department of Physical Education at The University of Western Australia. After its formation in 1972, the Community Recreation Council of Western Australia continued to conduct these courses until 1978, when they were taken over by the Federal Government. This followed a meeting in Perth between the states of Western Australia, Victoria and South Australia and the Confederation of Australian Sport, at which broad guidelines were developed for the scheme, to be modelled on the Western Australian program. In May 1978 the Recreation Ministers' Council approved this new program, which from then on was known as the National Coaching Accreditation Scheme, to be administered from Canberra under the Australian Coaching Council. The new council consisted of government officers and representatives from various sports organisations with an interest in coaching. This council, whose development will be covered later in this book, was to become an essential part of the Australian sports system as it steadily evolved.[60]

PHYSICAL FITNESS PROGRAMS
The Life Be In It program (LBII)

In 1975 Brian Dixon, the Minister for Sport in Victoria, had initiated a survey to assess people's attitudes to physical fitness. The study found that only 20 per cent of the public in Victoria had positive attitudes about the value of physical fitness, 20 per cent were ambivalent, and the remaining 60 per cent were unconvinced of a need to engage in fitness activities.

A fitness campaign was designed with a 'soft sell' approach, entitled the '*Life Be In It*' program, with the main target being the latter group. A five-year plan was prepared (1975-80) and a cartoon character named 'Norm' became the 'anti-hero'. The campaign was well planned and professionally launched, with high-quality support. There was also a range of new initiatives which were released as the impetus of the program slowed down. Two evaluations were later carried out, the first in 1977 to determine people's awareness of the program and its message; and the second in 1979, a comprehensive evaluation of its outcomes. The first survey was already positive, but the final one indicated that the program had been even more successful than anticipated.

However, after the initial five-year period was completed and the program had been universally recognised throughout Australia and overseas, it was dealt a crushing blow in 1981 by the Fraser Government's 'Razor Gang', who withdrew

Norm was the larger than life
'anti-hero' of the Life Be In It
program. (By courtesy of Life
Be In It.)

Commonwealth Government support for it. The State Government of Victoria formed a *Life Be In It* company, but the program gradually lost much of its momentum and Australia forfeited the only really successful nation-wide physical fitness campaign ever mounted in this country.

LBII International Pty Ltd still operates today and runs a significant number of recreation and lifestyle programs, but if it is to have the impact it once had, it needs considerable Federal Government assistance.[61]

Competitive recreation

During the period from 1976 to 1980, as the LBII campaign was gathering momentum, Earth Games, or Family Games as they were later called, became popular. This period also saw the beginning of corporate cups, fun runs and half or full marathons. The Big M marathon in Melbourne, sponsored by the Victorian Milk Board, was the first mass participation run in Australia and following its success, the Sydney and Perth City To Surf Fun Runs were some of the first to be held outside Victoria. Similar competitions, particularly swimming events in open water, have since spread all over Australia, steadily increasing in popularity. During the same period, walkathons and jogathons attracted increasing numbers of competitors and were often associated with raising money for charity. Multi-sport competitions like triathlons, as well as ironman and ironwoman events, were also very popular with thousands of competitors around the country.[62]

FACILITY DEVELOPMENT − 1975-80

As previously mentioned, the Whitlam Government had realised early in its term of office that Australia's sporting facilities at all levels were sub-standard and towards the end of its term had begun to co-operate with the states in a matching grants program. Under the Fraser Government a national-level committee was eventually formed, consisting of senior officers of each state sport and recreation organisation. Its report was submitted to the Recreation Ministers' Council, which asked the states to develop a priority list as part of a national plan to allow some co-ordination of the major facilities to be developed around the country.[63]

The Coalition Government was still reluctant to fund what it considered to be 'extravagant claims' by the states. However, it was eventually obliged to assume responsibility for some of the larger facilities throughout the country. The most successful type of facility development that took place during and following this period was the establishment of local Community Recreation Centres, which had been strongly recommended to the Commonwealth Government in the 1973 Bloomfield Report on sport and recreation. In many cases matching grants from federal, state and municipal government sources supplied the funding and some state education departments also shared in the cost, on condition that the centres were made available for school usage during the day. Once constructed, management of the centres was taken over by local governments and these facilities have enabled local areas to establish more varied sport and recreation programs, as well as to use the centres for physical fitness activities. This has turned out to be the best approach, as rather than being a 'top-down' program, it has become a 'bottom-up' development, with the local level being catered for first. There is no doubt that the Community Recreation Centres, and the fields and courts which were usually located nearby, are now regarded as the backbone of Australia's sport and recreation programs at the local level.[64]

The Joondalup Arena. This
complex is a good example of a
community sport and recreation
centre in Western Australia.

Facilities for the 1982 Commonwealth Games

In contrast to the situation in the section outlined above, the major facility
developments that took place in Brisbane towards the end of the 1970s and in the
early 1980s were exceptional. In 1976 Brisbane had bid for the 1982
Commonwealth Games, defeating Birmingham in the voting. This forced the
Fraser Government to allocate federal funds and when these were combined with
state government monies, excellent international facilities were constructed in
Brisbane.[65] These were the first of the high-level facilities to be built in Australia
and this trend continued around the country until Sydney 2000. As a result,
Australia now boasts some of the best sporting facilities in the world.

FURTHER PRESSURE ON THE FRASER GOVERNMENT

The Fraser Government gradually began to realise, as the press and others
continued to harass it, that various individuals and lobby groups were most

dissatisfied with its funding of sport and recreation. In late 1977 Syd Grange, the newly appointed President of the Australian Olympic Federation, had warned the Federal Government 'that without big injections of money ... Australia would slip further behind'.[66] The then Chairman of the Confederation of Australian Sport, Wayne Reid, stated in a letter to the Prime Minister in 1978 that the last Australian Budget had allocated '$1.86 per head of population for the arts and only 9 cents a head for sport'. He also pointed out that 'Canada provides $1.46 per head of population for sport, and Great Britain 47 cents per head'.[67] This letter was followed by a hard-hitting statement by Brian Dixon, the Liberal Minister for Sport in Victoria, who accused the Federal Coalition Government of a complete lack of interest in sport and recreation in Australia. He went on to say that 'he was bitterly disappointed and disturbed at Canberra's stand against aid of any consequence' and told the Minister for the Environment, Housing and Community Development, Ray Groom, 'that the Federal budget provision of $1.3 million was only "token" acknowledgment of insistent demands for help at the national level'. Dixon also stated that the Federal Government's stand was receiving 'widespread and understandable public condemnation'.[68]

IMPACT OF THE 1978 AND 1980 SPORT REPORTS

With a considerable amount of development occurring in Victoria and Western Australia and some early initiatives in South Australia, both New South Wales and Queensland observed the situation with interest. During this time there was increasing interchange between the states, and ideas and actions were being discussed nationwide. Two reports were circulating at that time and these are discussed below.

The Bloomfield Report (WA Government) — 1978

Late in 1977, the Western Australian Government had commissioned a report on the future development of sport, to be produced by the Community Recreation Council of Western Australia under the chairmanship of the writer. This report was adopted by the Western Australian Government in late 1978 as the policy for the development of sport and recreation in the state for the next decade. Its major recommendations were:

- that a modern sports system be developed;

- that sport in the state be administered by a Department of Youth, Sport and Recreation;

- that programs in sports management, sports coaching, sports science and sports medicine be established, and that grants to sports associations and sports service bodies be provided;

- that national-level training and competition facilities be provided for all sports and that a State Sports Centre be erected;

- that a State Institute of Sport be established.

As this was the first state government report of its type, the other states were keen to receive it and many of the above recommendations appeared in similar documents over the next ten years around the country.[69]

The master plan for sport — 1980

The Confederation of Australian Sport decided in early 1979 to prepare a report to the Fraser Government so that its repeated requests for more assistance to sport would be taken seriously, and this was submitted in March 1980. It included a series of well-supported recommendations and a schedule for their implementation, as the confederation had held a series of seminars around the country on the needs of sport in Australia involving 1474 interested individuals.

The impressive introductory statement, which appeared ahead of the various rationales supporting the recommendations, read: 'Sport is probably Australia's most under-valued social service. Its contributions to our physical, mental and social health are enormous; its savings to our national health and social welfare bills are incalculable.' The major recommendations of this plan were:

- that a Ministry of Sport be created;

- that an Institute of Sport be established;

- that talent identification and elite athlete development programs be commenced;

- that coaching standards be improved;

- that sports facilities at all levels be upgraded;

- that a Sports Aid Foundation be established.

The above recommendations received good press when presented to the Coalition Government, but there was very little positive response from the Fraser Government. Fortunately, several of the major recommendations of the 1980 master plan later appeared in the Labor Opposition's sport and recreation policy, and were implemented when Labor came to office in 1983.[70]

Bob Ellicott's influence — 1979-83

After years of frustration for all those interested in Australia's sporting resurgence, a Minister finally arrived on the scene with the necessary resolve to steer Australia back to its former sporting glory. Robert Ellicott QC had been elected to the Federal Parliament in 1970 after earning an enviable reputation in the law in Sydney. When the Fraser Government came to power in 1975, he became Attorney-General, a position he held until 1977. Because of the Federal Government's adverse publicity following Australia's poor performance in the Montreal Olympics and the looming political problems of the Moscow Olympic Games, an astute politician was needed to take the heat out of the sport debate. In late 1978, the Prime Minister invited Bob Ellicott to take over the Home Affairs and Environment portfolio, of which sport was a part. Instead of viewing sport as an encumbrance, as his colleagues had done before him, Ellicott decided that it was an important facet of Australian life and fostered its development. The new Minister was not only an able politician; he also had a deep love of sport and a vibrant enthusiasm for it which was to infect everyone with whom he worked.

THE AUSTRALIAN INSTITUTE OF SPORT

Bob Ellicott, who was already Minister for Home Affairs and Capital Territories, took over the sport portfolio towards the end of 1978 and in 1979 he visited China, where he saw a sports institute in operation. On his return, Ellicott's staff made him aware of the Bloomfield[71] and Coles[72] reports, both of which had recommended the development of an Institute of Sport. The Minister, on the advice of Graham Dempster and Paul Brettell, decided to focus on something tangible rather than tackle sport development across the board, as the Whitlam Labor Government had done. As Daly stated, 'Bob Ellicott favoured the emulation model rather than community recreation centres – the creation of national heroes and heroines who could inspire others to imitate them.' In addition, Daly claimed

Bob Ellicott was the Minister with responsibility for sport in the Fraser Government. It was his initiative which led to the establishment of the Australian Institute of Sport. (By courtesy of the Australian Sports Commission.)

that Ellicott argued for a sports institute in Canberra which would aim to 'reverse Australia's sporting talent drain, acknowledge the significance of sport in Australia and produce new sports stars who would ... do Australia proud in international sport'.[73] In hindsight, Ellicott's decision was a good one, but it was certainly not without its critics.

This criticism came from academics, several sports administrators and some former international-level athletes who did not believe in what they called 'professionalism'. It was not only the elite nature of the proposed institute that upset some people, but the fact that it was to be placed in Canberra. Since Federation in 1901, the centralism versus federalism debate had reverberated around the country. In this case it continued until 1984, when the institute began its decentralisation program.[74]

The establishment of the Australian Institute of Sport (AIS) was announced in late January 1980. In early February of the same year, the Minister and the writer met Prime Minister Fraser privately for a detailed briefing on the essential nature of the proposed institute and its value to Australian sport. It was decided that it must be an institution in which many of Australia's best sportsmen and women could be trained in order to give them the opportunity to reach their full potential. The Prime Minster was initially non-committal, but because of Ellicott's previous record with the government and his enthusiasm for this project, he agreed that it would be a useful development for Australia in general and for sport in particular.[75]

A steering committee of prominent ex-athletes, sport administrators and the Minister's advisers, Dempster and Brettell, met in Canberra and Sydney to plan the institute; this committee then became the interim board of management. During this time the Minister was very active in discussions with the planning group and his staff, addressing target groups and even writing personal letters to invite several of Australia's top athletes to take up scholarships. Furthermore, he personally conducted several site visits to Bruce, a suburb of Canberra, where the National Training Centre was in its infancy, to show key people where the institute would be located. On one occasion in early February 1980, the writer recalls the Minister enthusiastically drawing a plan with a stick on the bare earth, showing the proposed placement of future institute buildings.[76]

THE MOSCOW GAMES DEBATE

In the lead-up to the 1980 Olympic Games, to be held in Moscow in late July, there was a great deal of political manoeuvring involving trade embargoes and cultural exchanges. The United States and several other Western democracies called for sanctions in response to the USSR's decision to sent troops into Afghanistan.

As a result, several nations decided to boycott the Games and the Fraser Coalition Government wanted the Australian athletes to follow suit. However, the Australian Olympic Federation decided that the team would go, despite the withdrawal of several individuals and some teams. This decision was strongly criticised and the Australian team left without wearing their official blazers. At the Olympic Opening Ceremony they marched behind the Olympic rather than the Australian flag.[77]

The team's performance, winning nine medals, was only marginally better than at Montreal, when one considers that the United States, West Germany, Japan and several smaller but strong sporting nations did not compete. The confusing issue was that previous Coalition Governments had always separated sport from politics, yet suddenly sport and federal politics had been brought together for the first time in Australia's history.[78]

Bob Ellicott handled the whole affair well and was not sidetracked from his major objective, which was to open the institute in early 1981. On Australia Day, 26 January 1981, the Prime Minister, Malcolm Fraser, officially opened the Australian Institute of Sport. Daly records that in his opening address Fraser declared that we were 'no longer going to let the rest of the world pass us by' and that 'the new centre will bring together Australia's most talented youngsters, guided by the best coaches that can be found. Young men and women will be given opportunities that are second to none in any country anywhere.' This was certainly a radical policy change by the Prime Minister, but he kept his word until his government lost office in March 1983.[79]

One hundred and fifty-three scholarships were awarded from among the 800 applications and eight sports were initially included in the program. These were basketball, gymnastics, netball, soccer, swimming, tennis, track and field and weight-lifting.[80] Not surprisingly, there had been a good deal of jockeying during 1980 with regard to the selection of the sports. Some were chosen by the Minister, while others were the result of intense lobbying from powerful sporting administrators such as Jim Barry (gymnastics) and Les Martin (weight-lifting).[81]

EARLY DAYS AT THE INSTITUTE

The board of management was appointed in late 1980 and Kevan Gosper, a former Olympic track athlete and high-profile businessman with the Shell Company, became the first chairman, while the writer was appointed as deputy chairman. In order for operations to commence in early 1981, the institute was initially incorporated under the Australian Capital Territory Companies' Ordinance.[82] Under normal circumstances, it would have commenced as a statutory body, but there was not enough time to formulate the appropriate Act and steer it through the normal legislative process. Certainly the initial structure of a public company limited by guarantee gave the institute more freedom to operate without a bureaucracy constantly looking over its shoulder. In addition, it was able to interact more independently with the corporate sector, as this status avoided too close a tie with the government. That loose early linkage also enabled it to obtain sponsorship more easily from the private sector. The above arrangement appeared to suit everyone except the Canberra public servants, who were uneasy with such a flexible structure. So as to exert more control, they placed strict staff ceilings on the institute to prevent expansion occurring too rapidly.[83]

'Gymnasts',
sculpted by John
Robinson, was
unveiled at the
opening of the
Australian
Institute of Sport
on 26 January
1981.

Don Talbot takes over

Don Talbot, the first executive director, had an enviable record as a swimming coach, having mentored more than 30 Olympic medallists and world record-holders. He had been in Canada and the United States for eight years, and during that time had experienced high-level international competition. His appointment was a popular one with those people who understood what must be done to raise the performance levels of Australia's elite athletes. They knew that Talbot had a thorough understanding of what was needed and that he also possessed the determination and toughness to achieve it.[84]

The coaches selected for the eight sports were mainly resident in Australia, except for the head swimming coach, Dennis Pursley, and the head track and field coach, Kelvin Giles. The majority of the other senior coaches, namely Wilma Shakespear (netball), Adrian Hurley (basketball), Bill Sweetenham (swimming), Ray Ruffles (tennis), Jimmy Shoulder (soccer), Lyn Jones (weight-lifting) and Kazuya Honda (gymnastics) were already well known, but were to gain much higher profiles as a result of their later successes. One who was representative of this high-level group was Dr Adrian Hurley, whose profile appears below.

A small sport science unit was also established, staffed by Dr Dick Telford, an exercise physiologist, with some sports medicine sessions covered by Dr Peter Fricker. Peter Bowman, a highly regarded sports administrator, was in charge of a small but dedicated administrative staff of seven.[85]

Scholarship holders begin

The institute had only two facilities at that time, and thus some of the incoming scholarship holders had to travel to other venues in Canberra for their training. Until the athletes' residences were completed, they could not live on-site, so many of them were billeted with families or lived in the residential colleges of the Australian National University and the Canberra College of Advanced Education.[86] The travel to training was time-consuming and unsettling for both athletes and coaches, but they doggedly pursued their goals, as this was the opportunity both groups had been waiting for. Some outstanding senior international athletes were the first scholarship holders, but the majority were at the international youth level. Selection of the scholarship holders was difficult for the coaches, but after some trial and error during the first year, most sports found that a mix of a few mature international-level performers and a larger group of up-and-coming younger athletes was the best way to achieve a balance in each squad.[87]

THE FIRST YEAR AT THE AIS

The board and the executive director were aware that if athletes trained day in and day out, there might be problems if they had no qualifications or training to lead them into employment at the end of their sporting careers. Athletes were therefore expected to undergo some form of part-time education or vocational training. The Canberra College of Advanced Education set up a sports studies

THE EDUCATOR-COACH

When Dr Adrian Hurley became the coach of the Illawarra Hawks in the fledgling National Basketball League in 1980, Australian basketball was second-rate by world standards. When he left coaching in 1996, this nation's standards and achievements in basketball had improved immeasurably, and much of the credit for such a spectacular turnaround must be attributed to Dr Hurley.

Adrian Hurley began his professional career in New South Wales as a teacher. He was a state player and captain before winning an academic scholarship to the University of Oregon in 1972. While in the United States, he gained a Doctor of Philosophy degree and concurrently became immersed in the very competitive United States College basketball system, which was to stand him in good stead for more than 20 years of coaching back in Australia.

In 1981, when Dr Hurley became the inaugural coach of the AIS basketball program, he immediately began to develop a wealth of talent which later became the nucleus of the Australian men's and then women's basketball teams in the late 1980s and 1990s. As coach of the Boomers from 1984 to 1992, he took Australia to fourth place in the 1988 Olympic Games and to several final rounds in the world championships. While coach of the Perth Wildcats from 1993 to 1996, his team reached the final play-offs every year, winning the triple crown in 1995.

In addition to his fine coaching record, Adrian Hurley has played a vital role in developing the cream of men's and women's basketball in Australia. He had previously coached nine members of the Australian Opals team, who won the silver medal at the Sydney 2000 Olympics, as well as 12 players from the Australian Boomers, who were placed fourth in the men's competition.

During his long career as a coach, Adrian never lost sight of the fact that he was primarily an educator. His contribution to youth development squads, clinics, seminars and educational material was outstanding. For his meritorious service to Australian sport, Dr Hurley was awarded an Order of Australia medal in 1991 — a fitting tribute to a life devoted to the development of young Australians.[88]

Adrian Hurley, one of the inaugural coaches at the Australian Institute of Sport, demonstrates to the men's basketball squad. (By courtesy of the Australian Sports Commission.)

course under the guidance of Dr Frank Pyke, a well-known sports scientist and a former state-level Australian (rules) footballer. If the scholarship holders had already completed their education, they were encouraged to work part-time and some of them did so.

The other initiative developed by the executive director and the coaches was a code of ethics. This related to the athletes' general behaviour and the way they conducted themselves during both training and competition. They also signed an agreement within the code relating to the non-use of performance-enhancing drugs and agreed to undergo random drug testing if required.[89]

Towards the end of the first year of operations, various groups, either supportive or critical of the AIS, felt obliged to pass some opinion as to its efficacy. Generally, strong support for the institute came from those sporting associations whose athletes were already scholarship holders. However, there were some sectional interests within those sports who were unhappy about their athletes being centralised in Canberra. This discontent was expressed by several coaches and strong clubs, as well as by some state swimming, basketball, netball and gymnastics sports associations. However, the sports that were lobbying for their associations to be admitted in the near future were strongly supportive of the institute.

Overall, the athletes who had gained scholarships to Canberra were satisfied, as they had experienced high-quality coaching — in some instances for the first time. Because the AIS coaches interfaced well with them, a certain amount of their expertise was passed back to their associations, several of which were considering the possibility of creating professional coaching positions, either as national coaches or directors of coaching.[90] As well, the AIS squads who travelled overseas to compete against national or second-string national teams performed very well. In fact, at the end of the first year of operation, the AIS swimming squad had a head to head meet against the Canadian national team in 1981, winning the point score and 60 per cent of the first places.[91] Don Talbot stated that the AIS athletes had experienced a good year of competition both at home and abroad, but warned all those interested in the development of the institute that it would still take five or six years before any really significant improvements were made.

As always, there were some critics. Several journalists insisted that the money should be spread around more equitably, but had difficulty proposing an alternative plan. They had few, if any, helpful suggestions for Australian sport, but played the devil's advocate, sometimes in an entirely negative way. They were backed up by the more geographically distant states of Western Australia, South Australia and Tasmania and a few of the smaller associations whose sports had little chance of gaining admittance to the institute. These groups needed to be appeased, and steps were already being taken to help them become part of the institute by establishing decentralised AIS units in the states and a National Training Centre for the smaller associations in Canberra.[92]

AIS FACILITY DEVELOPMENT

The facilities for a National Training Centre were already being developed in the ACT and it was Bob Ellicott's aim to utilise them as part of the AIS. By the time the institute opened in early 1981, the track and field stadium had been ready for some time and the indoor stadium had just been completed. Both facilities were to be used by the institute in conjunction with other venues in the Canberra area.

Since announcing the establishment of the institute, the Minister had been working on plans to add other facilities to the complex. So that the sport budget could be used mainly to fund the programs, he persuaded his parliamentary colleagues to build the remaining facilities with funding from the National Capital Development Commission's budget.[93] This action enabled eight additional indoor and five more outdoor facilities to be built with non-sport monies. Because the precedent had been established, the Hawke Labor Government continued the same policy when it came to power in 1983.

BOB ELLICOTT RESIGNS

In early 1981, Bob Ellicott resigned from Parliament after a little over two years as the Minister responsible for sport. This was not a long term in office, but in that period he had made a very important contribution to Australian sport, first by establishing the AIS and second by building its facilities from non-sport funds. That beginning, together with the later assistance provided by the Hawke Labor Government, was the foundation which would give Australia an institute which today ranks among the best in the world. Furthermore, Ellicott's foresight in establishing a central hub around which high-performance sport could develop ranks him among Australia's finest Ministers for Sport.

AFTER BOB ELLICOTT

There was considerable disappointment among the sports fraternity when Ellicott resigned. Fortunately, however, he had developed a momentum which did not slow down, as he had ensured that budget monies had been committed well in advance and the next two Fraser Government Ministers, Ian Wilson and Tom McVeigh, continued the steady development of the AIS and the sports system in general. This appeased any potential critics, who would have been up in arms if the Coalition Government had reverted to its former policy in relation to sports funding.

THE SECOND YEAR AT THE AIS

Nineteen-eighty-two was a test year for the institute, as the Commonwealth Games were to be held in Brisbane in October. The press, looking for controversy, questioned whether the existence of the AIS would result in improved Australian performances. This put some pressure on AIS athletes and coaches, but they took it in their stride and performed well. Australia topped the Commonwealth Games medal count and of the 107 medals won by Australians, institute athletes won 26. The press suggested that the AIS had contributed greatly to this result, but Don

Talbot was quick to point out that the home advantage had helped and that it would still take some time before the real impact of the institute would be felt in international sport.[94]

Many people did not realise that the only athletes from the AIS to compete in the Brisbane Commonwealth Games were swimmers, track and field athletes and weight-lifters. This was not widely publicised and people generally were not yet aware of which sports had actually been included in the institute program. Hence the AIS received more kudos than it possibly merited at that time.[95]

There were also outstanding results during 1982 in the non-Commonwealth Games sports of basketball, netball, tennis and, to a lesser extent, gymnastics, which further helped the AIS to gain recognition in the second year of its existence. These teams toured in 1982, mainly in Europe, posting excellent results when matched against athletes of a similar level. It augured well for future international-level performances, as many of the competitors were still only in the early stages of their sporting careers.[96]

From the day of his arrival in Canberra, Don Talbot had continually stressed the importance of high coach/athlete ratios at the elite level. In the first year that ratio was low, but he was determined to improve it in his second year, insisting upon more and better-qualified coaches. The coaching staff doubled during 1982, with some high-quality assistant coaches joining the institute staff. In addition, men's and women's squads were established. The staff increase was only accomplished by Talbot's determination and the strong support of the executive of the board, while some of the constraints that had been placed on the institute by the public service were amended.[97]

The National Training Centre Program (NTCP)

In late 1982, the Coalition Minister with a responsibility for sport, Tom McVeigh, announced that a new program would be established in early 1983. This was to be known as the National Training Centre Program and was a welcome development for the national sports organisations that had not been included in the original eight sports.

The centre commenced in February 1983, with selected athletes from various sports visiting the institute for short periods of time. Those included in the first year were rugby, water polo, canoeing, squash, baseball, rowing, volleyball, cycling and pistol shooting. Each athlete in these sports received airfares, accommodation, coaching, use of the AIS facilities and access to the sports science and medicine services. Of this group, water polo, squash, canoeing, rowing and cycling were admitted to the institute on a full-time basis over the next four years.

The opportunity to take part in the centre's programs enabled the national sporting organisations to experience the AIS at first hand and at the same time, the institute was able to become acquainted with other prospective full-time sports. This program proved to be popular with the participating sports and later became known as the *National Sports Program* by the early 1990s.[98] It has been one of the most successful initiatives embarked upon in Australian sport, greatly improving its services since the early days and leading to more co-operation between the sporting associations and the government. It has also given a large number of athletes, particularly those from the small associations, the opportunity to experience national-level coaching, sports science and sports medicine assistance.[99]

Early calls for decentralisation

There had been complaints from those states located furthest from Canberra on two fronts. They criticised the location of the institute, asserting that few of the country's better athletes would be willing to leave their homes to take up residence; and they maintained that there should be a plan for decentralisation of the AIS into the states. The first complaint was being partially addressed, because more senior athletes moved to Canberra than was at first expected. The second one had also been discussed, but it was not possible to act on it until the budget built up as the institute grew. In fact the writer had discussed a decentralisation policy in early 1980 with the Minister and his staff and Bob Ellicott presented a possible future plan to the Recreation Minister's Council in Darwin in mid-1980. This proved to be a popular recommendation, but unfortunately, because of other pressing items and some personnel changes, it did not eventuate until 1983. By then South Australia had already established its own state institute, while Western Australia was planning one.[100]

STATE DEVELOPMENTS – LATER YEARS OF THE FRASER GOVERNMENT

The state governments of Western Australia, Victoria and, to a lesser extent, South Australia had led the way in overall sport and recreation development during the Fraser Government's seven and a half years in office. Up to that time, Queensland, New South Wales and Tasmania had not professionalised their state sports systems, other than to establish a sports grants program. Western Australia had already acted on the recommendations of the 1978 Bloomfield Report, establishing a Department for Youth, Sport and Recreation in the same year. In the early 1980s an embryonic State Institute of Sport was established, but it was not till the Burke Labor Government came to power in 1983 in Western Australia that a true institute came into operation.[101]

Earlier in this chapter, the dynamic leadership of Brian Dixon in Victoria was mentioned, especially his enthusiasm for the *Life Be In It* campaign. During his ministry he also supported sport development, and by the late 1970s had decided to commission a report so that several new initiatives could be undertaken in Victoria.

A Green Paper on 'The Development of Sport in Victoria' was commissioned in late 1980. The then Associate Professor Brian Blanksby, of The University of Western Australia, was appointed as the project co-ordinator and Graham

The Western Australian
Institute of Sport is housed
at the Western Australian
Sports Centre, also known
as Challenge Stadium. (By
courtesy of the Western
Australian Institute of Sport.)

Thompson acted as the project manager, with the assistance of members of the State Sports Council and professional officers of the Victorian Department of Youth, Sport and Recreation. This preliminary paper comprehensively covered sports administration, coaching, officiating, facility development and ways in which sport should be integrated with the school system. It also considered how the government could assist various special groups such as veterans' sport, women in sport, sport for the disabled, children's sport and sport for elite performers. Furthermore, it demonstrated how various service groups, such as sports science and sports medicine, might benefit mainstream sport.[102] Two months later a smaller Green Paper by the same authors was released, its main thrust being a proposal for the establishment of a Victorian Sports Assembly and a Sports House.[103]

Following consultation with all the groups that were part of the Victorian sports system, a White Paper entitled 'New Directions in Sport — A Structure and Context for the Development of Sport in Victoria' was launched by Dixon in January 1982. This wide-ranging document, authored by Thompson, provided a framework for a state sport program to cover the entire spectrum of sport from low to high performance levels. It also acted as a model for other state government developments as they refined their sports systems in the mid to late-1980s.[104] The gradual interfacing of the state systems with that of the Commonwealth was to be a vital factor in the eventual development of the Australian sports system during the mid-1990s, and will be covered more fully later in this book.

THE FIRST STATE INSTITUTES OF SPORT

South Australia was the first state to establish a fully functioning Institute of Sport, which opened in 1982 *(see Table 2.1 below)*. The driving force behind its development was Mike Nunan, who had previously been an outstanding Australian (rules) footballer in Adelaide. Nunan had visited institutes in Eastern and Western Europe in 1978, gaining an appreciation of their value in a sports system. However, it wasn't until the South Australian Coalition Government came into office in 1981 that the institute became more than just a concept. Entitled the South Australian Sports Institute, it was set up on the Underdale Campus of the South Australian College of Advanced Education and offered scholarships for athletes and disabled sports people in 22 sports. It had a sports science centre and athletes had access to specialist sports medicine doctors. In addition, it had a well-stocked Sports Resource Centre, which was one of the earlier developments of its kind in Australia.[105] [106]

The second state institute was established in Western Australia soon after the 1983 Bloomfield Report[107] had been adopted as the sport policy of the newly elected Burke Labor Government. It commenced operation in 1984, with Wally Foreman being appointed as director shortly afterwards. Foreman had been an ABC journalist in Adelaide and returned to his home state to pioneer the new state institute. During his 17 years as director, he developed it into a highly effective institution which led the way at the state level in Australia for several years, producing many fine elite-level athletes in a state with a small population.[108]

Table 2.1
Establishment years of institutes/academies

Institute/Academy	Year
Australian Institute of Sport (AIS)	1981
South Australian Sports Institute (SASI)	1982
Western Australian Institute of Sport (WAIS)	1984
Tasmanian Institute of Sport (TIS)	1985
Australian Capital Territory Academy of Sport (ACTAS)	1989
Victorian Institute of Sport (VIS)	1990
Queensland Academy of Sport (QAS)	1991
New South Wales Institute of Sport (NSWIS)	1996
Northern Territory Institute of Sport (NTIS)	1996

THE FRASER YEARS IN RETROSPECT

When the Fraser Government came to office in late 1975, it was made clear to the electorate that drastic budget cuts would have to be made because of the overspending of the Whitlam Government. Budget reductions were imposed in several areas including sport, and in 1976 various programs received cuts or were allowed to run down. This coincided with Australia's poor performance at the 1976 Montreal Olympics, with the result that both the Prime Minister and the Minister responsible for sport, Kevin Newman, were severely criticised by the athletes, the public and the press. Despite repeated assurances by both of the above, little was initially done to improve the situation.

It was not until Bob Ellicott's arrival in the portfolio of Community Development in late 1978 that any positive action occurred. The new Minister introduced several initiatives, markedly raising the stocks of the Fraser Government during his term in office. In fact, it is ironic that after such a poor start, it was the Fraser Government which played such a crucial role in the establishment of the highly successful Australian Institute of Sport.

It was fortunate during this period for the states of Victoria and Western Australia that they had already begun to develop their own sport and recreation systems before 1976 and, as a result, were not greatly affected by the early inaction of the Federal Coalition Government. However, when the Hawke Labor Government took office in March 1983, Australia was to experience the greatest sustained development of its federal sports system, under the leadership of John Brown. Over the next five years, Brown succeeded in making an enormous contribution to sports development in this country.

Chapter Three
Evolution of the sports system

The Hawke Labor Government — 1983-88

The John Brown era

In the year before the 1983 March elections, John Brown, the Shadow Minister for Sport and Tourism, had been carefully observing the performance of the Fraser Government in his areas of interest. When the Hawke Government took office, Brown entered the scene as the best-informed Minister to hold the portfolio of sport and tourism. He came to office as a successful businessman and a keen sportsman, having been both a surf lifesaver and a rugby league player in his youth, as well as an above average golfer. Brown was a colourful individual who was popular with his political colleagues, although his well-chosen quips sometimes made the Opposition squirm.

EARLY YEARS OF THE HAWKE GOVERNMENT

The new Minister knew exactly what he wanted to do with the tourism, sport and recreation portfolio. His first action was to establish a separate entity which included all three of the above, putting a direct focus on these three areas of the ministry. This was in contrast to the Coalition Government's policy of placing them in a multi-purpose portfolio where none of them even rated a mention. Because the sport program, except for the Australian Institute of Sport, had been doing little more than marking time, John Brown concentrated first on making a case for a very substantial increase in the 1983-84 budget[1] and despite the difficult budgetary climate, a total of $22.5 million was allocated for sport and recreation. Of this amount, $6.4 million was earmarked for specific sport programs, representing an 81 per cent increase on the previous government's funding.

While the budget was being prepared, the new Minister was also working on his strategy for the remainder of his term of office. This was in the form of a comprehensive statement which first examined the current state of sport and recreation in Australia and then outlined the initiatives he would take to improve it. The document was entitled 'Sport and Recreation: Australia on the Move'. Its main points are summarised below:[2]

- The new Hawke Government had a fundamental commitment to revitalise the quality and direction of national leadership in many fields in Australia. It was also stated that the government needed to use the fields of sport and recreation as mediums to assist in unifying the nation. This was the first occasion on which any Australian Government had declared that sport was not just an end in itself, but that it could be used as a vehicle for nation building.

- The new Labor Government favoured a balanced approach to sport and recreation, whereas the Whitlam Government had been more disposed towards physical recreation. In contrast, the Fraser Government had favoured sport more than physical recreation, and from 1980 the majority of its budget had been spent on elite sport. In order to achieve its national development objectives, the Hawke Government decided that a balanced program was essential.

- *The sport development program*, which was seen as a cornerstone of the new system, received a budget rise of 75 per cent ($5.59 million). Monies for junior sport, coaching, administration, travel to competitions and the National Athlete Award Scheme, as well as a significant increase in funding for general sport development, were all part of this program. The latter initiative was aimed at improving the efficiency of club sport and attracting more people to participate at the grassroots level.

- *The Australian Institute of Sport* had been growing steadily under the Fraser Government and Labor's plan was to continue this development at a similar level to pre-March 1983. The budget increase of almost 20 per cent allowed some decentralisation to occur; additional sports joined the National Training Centre Program and athletes from other Commonwealth countries were invited to the AIS as part of Australia's foreign aid program. As well, $10 million was allocated through the National Capital Development Commission for capital works at the AIS. John Brown followed Bob Ellicott's initiative of funding the AIS facilities from a separate budget not connected to sport, which had proven to be such a good policy.

- *International sport facilities funding* had been given a low priority under the Coalition Government, except for assistance to Queensland for the 1982 Commonwealth Games. John Brown accelerated this program and $8 million was committed on a shared basis with the states and territories. The Hawke Government realised that such funding was essential if Australia wanted to host international championships, and that these events attracted tourists. Further, Australia's 1988 Bicentennial celebrations were to be held in four and a half years and Australia had already applied for several world championship events to be staged at that time. If these were to be successful, international facilities would be required.

- *Community recreation centres* were in great demand, with many municipal authorities requesting assistance. The new government stated that matching grants would be allocated for these centres at the local level. Wherever possible, they were to be constructed adjacent to existing school sites and would be owned and managed by local government for the benefit of the whole community. Within a year, this program was well underway and developed steadily.

The above 'big-ticket' items were the basis of a functional sports system. However, there were several smaller programs which also needed funding. These were:

- *National Elite Award Scheme*: funds were provided for potential and world-ranking athletes, for training and competition expenses.

- *Olympic Games*: additional money was granted for the Australian Olympic Federation to help athletes prepare for the 1984 Olympic Games.

- *Proposed Australia Games*: funds were made available to organise and run the first Australia Games in Melbourne in 1985.

- *Assistance to lifesaving organisations*: substantial monies were made available for both the Royal and the Surf Lifesaving Associations of Australia.

- *National Coaching Accreditation Scheme*: funds were allocated to encourage coaches to improve their qualifications.

- *National recreation organisations*: funding was provided to national recreation bodies to upgrade their administration and to encourage more participation in recreational activities.

- *Projects with the states*: shared funding arrangements for sport and recreation programs were organised with the states.

- *Research in sports science and medicine*: funds for improved co-ordination and co-operation in sports science and sports medicine research were initiated.

- *Sport and recreation for special groups*: funding was allocated to encourage physical activity and sport for special groups, namely the disabled, the elderly, ethnic groups, indigenous Australians and women.

- *The Australian Sports Commission*: an allocation of funds was made and an interim committee appointed to report on the role, functions and structure of the proposed Australian Sports Commission. The major reason John Brown gave for the establishment of the commission was that sport should have a direct voice in its own controlling body, thereby eliminating political interference as much as possible. This was an enlightened move and demonstrated that, rather than wishing to control his highest executive body, the Minister was happy to accept their informed decisions.[3]

Undoubtedly Brown made a flying start with his first budget. His strategic statement[4] was well received by the sporting fraternity because he produced a balanced program with 'something for everyone'. However, his term of office was just beginning and there were some potholes in the road ahead, especially at the AIS.

THE AUSTRALIAN INSTITUTE OF SPORT

The first two years of the operation of the institute, although at times a little frenetic, had been quite smooth, as there was a close-knit group and an atmosphere of camaraderie. Everyone there, including the athletes, coaches and administrators, felt that this was their big chance to succeed, and initially it seemed that no obstacle was too great to overcome.

John Brown's arrival in the portfolio was welcomed by the institute staff and for the five years he was in office he was generally a popular Minister. On several occasions there were major eruptions not of his making, but he handled the problems in a calm and efficient way.

John Brown was the Minister for Sport and Recreation in the Hawke Government from 1983 to 1988. He was more responsible than any other federal Minister for the development of the Australian sports system. (By permission of the National Library of Australia — see Appendix H for photo credits.)

Prime Minister Fraser had officially opened the Indoor Tennis Hall just before the elections in 1983. The new Minister then opened the Swimming Centre in July of the same year. During the remainder of 1983 the indoor facilities for soccer, weight-lifting, netball and basketball were completed. As well, plans for the Sports Science and Medicine Centre had been drawn up and discussions were in progress regarding the residential complex and the administration centre, which were to be ready in 1985.[5]

Don Talbot resigns

As suggested earlier, John Brown's policy when he took over the sport portfolio was to strike a balance between elite and participation sport. Although the proposed budget was generous given the fiscal stringencies current at that time, Don Talbot, the executive director of the institute, was unhappy with the allocation to the AIS, believing that too much money had been granted to physical recreation and too little to elite sport.

At a meeting with the executive directors of Australia's sports federations before the Federal Budget was brought down, the AIS director declared his dissatisfaction with the new government's policy regarding the funding of elite sport. When the 1983-84 budget was officially announced, Talbot voiced his concern officially and John Daly reported that 'the Prime Minister, Bob Hawke, sought to reassure Talbot on the occasion of his first visit to the AIS'. He expressed pleasure at meeting Australia's young and aspiring sports stars and concluded by saying: 'No-one expects miracles overnight but what we want and expect the institute to do is to lay the basis for a steady improvement in Australia's international performance across a wide spectrum of sporting events.' While the Prime Minister's visit emphasised a definite continuing role for the institute, everyone was also aware of the fact that the AIS would now be more accountable.[6]

In addition to the budget problems, Talbot received a considerable amount of criticism from the House of Representatives Expenditure Review Committee, especially from the Chairman, Leo McLeay. According to Daly,[7] McLeay had pronounced the results of the institute 'not credible' and demanded that funding for sport 'be reviewed'. Moreover, McLeay had insisted to Talbot 'that payment should bring results and that the base of the pyramid of participation should also be funded'. Others such as Dr Jeff Miller, Director of the Cumberland College of Advanced Education, criticised the institute's lack of support for disabled athletes, stating: 'There is no doubt in my mind that the continued expansion and development of the AIS ... in Canberra ... is not in the best interests of the country.'[8] Dr Miller was clearly not aware at that time that the government had already begun gearing up to steadily develop sport for disabled people. Those moves were to lead to Australia's outstanding Paralympic results from 1992 onwards. However, the debate concerning the McLeay review was given wide coverage by the press, and on 10 August 1983 Don Talbot handed in his resignation.

Undoubtedly Don Talbot left a legacy of sports excellence and dedication at the AIS.[9] John Daly stated it well: 'Talbot was critical of the lack of resolve of the government of the day to make a total commitment to elite sport development and was not frightened to say so. Indeed, the value of Talbot had been not only his own unreserved enthusiasm for returning Australian athletes to the victory podium, but also his insistence that all — politicians, public servants, his own coaching staff, the AIS board — should be as committed as he was. This sometimes tested the patience and goodwill of others. Patience was not one of Talbot's strong points and he admitted this himself. But no-one could doubt his resolve. He bullied, cajoled and preached in his quest for an excellent institute for Australia and usually he got his way'.[10]

In many respects it was a pity that Don Talbot left when he did, as the new government had already signalled that the institute's future development was a high priority once the system was brought into balance. Moreover, the Prime Minister and the Minister for Sport were strongly behind it.

However, Talbot's departure from the AIS highlighted the fact that, if Australia's international performances were to be revived, only a total commitment to excellence would suffice. It was unfortunate that he felt obliged to resign in order to make his point.[11]

Paul Brettell takes over

While the search for a new executive director took place, the general manager, Paul Brettell, became acting executive director. Paul, although still a young man, had been at the forefront of sport development in Australia for a decade and had proven to be a competent administrator. During his short period at the helm, a considerable amount of consolidation and steady development took place. By early 1984, the staff had increased to the point where there were 31 coaches and 20 sports science and sports medicine personnel.[12] The team of efficient administrators was led by Bob Hobson, who made an outstanding contribution to the institute over a period of 17 years. One very positive development at this time was the establishment of a marketing and public relations section. John Purnell filled this position and almost overnight the profile of the AIS improved immeasurably.[13]

In addition to the above staff, there were 220 athletes on full scholarship, while 828 athletes had trained at the National Training Centre since its establishment a little over a year before.[14] The popularity of the centre led to the next major initiative, which was the development of the first decentralised unit outside Canberra. Perth became the venue, both because of its high standard of hockey and its international hockey facility already situated at the then Western Australian Institute of Technology (currently known as Curtin University of Technology). Professor Don Watts, the then director, was very supportive of the decentralised concept for the AIS, helping the unit to develop smoothly without teething problems. In fact it was so successful that other decentralised units soon followed, so that today a large number of AIS sports are located outside Canberra.[15]

In mid-May 1984, the second Executive Director of the AIS arrived in Canberra. Dr John Cheffers had spent a decade and a half in the United States, where he had completed his doctorate before rising to the rank of Associate Professor of Education at Boston University. At the time of his departure from the United States, he was the co-ordinator of that university's human movement program. Cheffers was a man of ideas and a lateral thinker whose staff at times had difficulty keeping up with him. He was dedicated to the basic mission of the institute, which was to develop excellence, and possibly because of his early physical education background, he also recognised that the total sports system needed to be in balance. Certainly he understood elite sport, as he had been an Australian (rules) league footballer, a state-level track and field athlete and a respected track and field coach in Victoria and overseas.[16] [17]

John Brown welcomed the new AIS Executive Director, as he felt comfortable with his philosophy relating to the place of the institute within the existing sports system. This had not been the case in the last four months of Don Talbot's term, as Talbot had 'gone public' with his philosophical differences with the government on the role of the institute.[18]

There is no doubt that John Cheffers hit the ground running with his expansive public relations program. He met regularly with his staff to espouse his philosophy, invited people to visit the institute and travelled widely to become more familiar with the Australian sporting fraternity. All this was good, and Cheffers developed a profile as an entertaining speaker and excellent host. Unfortunately his capacity for the latter was to come back to haunt him at a later time during his term in Canberra.[19]

In accordance with the new executive director's specific philosophy for the AIS, he coined the term 'Fortress Bruce', a reference to the locality where the institute was situated in the Canberra suburb of Belconnen. According to Daly, Cheffers stressed the fact that the 'drawbridges of "Fortress Bruce" would be lowered so that the AIS had meaning for the wider Australian community'. In addition, Cheffers stated that the AIS currently practised 'exclusion, elitism [and] favouritism', declaring that in the future it would be more inclusive of other sports in Australia.[20] This caused some consternation among the avowed elitists in the sport fraternity, who had agreed with Don Talbot's straightforward approach. In fact two head coaches, Dennis Pursley and Kelvin Giles, left soon after Cheffers' arrival as a result of alleged differences of opinion and philosophical issues relating to elitism. There was considerable confusion about how inclusive the AIS should be, but some went along with Cheffers' philosophy in the hope that all would become clearer in the future.[21]

A large contingent of AIS athletes and coaches was selected in the Australian team for the Los Angeles Olympic Games, which were held in late July-early August 1984. Australia had a high medal tally of 24, which included four gold, eight silver and 12 bronze. If the Eastern Europeans had competed, the tally probably would have been only 13 or 14 medals, because several of the Australian performances in Los Angeles were inferior to those of Communist Bloc athletes who had competed in the same events that year. Nevertheless, this was a better result for Australia than at either Montreal or Moscow.[22]

The press gave the AIS much of the credit for doing well at the 1984 Games. Daly quoted John Brown as saying: 'Australia's success at the Los Angeles Olympics has underlined the remarkable progress made by the ... Australian Institute of Sport since its beginning in 1980.' This success was reflected in a considerable budget increase in the following year, when the total sport and recreation budget was lifted to $65.5 million. There was also a 60 per cent increase in the AIS budget to finance the inclusion of four new sports, namely squash, diving, rowing and water polo. The first two were decentralised to Brisbane, while the others were established in Canberra and it was planned that cycling would be the next sport to enter the institute.[23]

This was very good news for the executive director and all those associated with the institute, as rapid progress was being made on many fronts. Press coverage was good and John Cheffers was quick to capitalise on it; in addition, John Purnell had been steadily developing an attractive marketing strategy targeting sponsorship. These were heady days for the institute, which seemed to go from strength to strength.[24]

However, the autumn 1985 mini budget brought down by the Labor Government was disappointing. Dr Cheffers challenged the government in a letter to the Secretary of the Department of Finance. John Daly described the letter as 'colourful', reporting some of its content thus: '[Cheffers used] a football analogy and sporting parlance to claim a special exception. He argued that the "final quarter" was about to be played (a reference to the Commonwealth Games of 1986) and that the odds were against Australian sport; and that the Government was aiding and abetting the opposition (especially Canada, Britain and the West Indies) by restricting growth at the AIS.'[25] When the 'special exception request' was not granted, the executive director accused the House of Representatives Expenditure Review Committee of a 'lack of vision' and 'foul play'.[26] This was not a wise public relations move, as several Labor politicians were already of the opinion that the institute was over-funded, and that the money should be used for 'other more needy causes'.[27]

Several observers maintained that following Dr Cheffers' arrival, life was never dull at the institute. Even though the budget had slowed down some developments, future planning and implementation of current programs kept a frenetic buzz alive at Bruce. The executive director continued his enthusiastic promotion of the institute, both to the people he met and the press, with the result that the AIS was no longer just a name, but had become a well-known institution to the Australian sporting public. However, some of the Australian sports fraternity continued to be sceptical about his philosophical approach to sport, as were several members of the press.[28]

Aerial photograph of the Australian Institute of Sport campus, which is located in Canberra, A.C.T. (By courtesy of the Australian Sports Commission.)

At the institute itself, there was a great deal of activity. The Administration Centre had been completed and the Information Centre found a new home there. Nerida Clarke, who had done such a good job in a cramped environment at the Indoor Stadium, was able to operate an even better service as the Co-ordinator of the Sports Information Centre. The Sports Science and Medicine Centre was also opened, as were the Halls of Residence to house over 320 athletes. In the latter

The state-of-the-art Biomechanics
laboratory at the Australian Institute
of Sport has enabled high-level
sports science research to be carried
out over the last decade and a half.
(By courtesy of the Australian Sports
Commission.)

complex, rooms for the scholarship holders, several apartments, accommodation for national training centre athletes and a fine dining room were all constructed. Naturally, the staff to service the above additions were selected and started work, as did the administrative and coaching staff of the four new sports housed in Canberra and Brisbane.[29]

Another important event which took place in October 1985 at Bruce was the athletics World Cup. This proved to be a good opportunity to exchange ideas with various foreign coaches and sports scientists and to show them over the institute. Their reaction was very positive, as was that of the general public, many of whom were taken on conducted tours around the campus. In addition, the August 1985 budget gave the AIS a 23 per cent increase for further expansion, enabling the newly admitted sports to settle in comfortably. Overall, 1985 had been an excellent year for the institute. No-one suspected that a bombshell was about to drop. It landed on 18 November 1985.[30]

The Cheffers affair

The writer had become the chairman of the board of the institute in May 1985. In August and September of that year, information was received from a sectional manager and a head of department which indicated that there were serious problems at the highest level at the institute. This was reported to John Brown, who advised the chairman 'to keep an eye on things'. In mid-September, Bill Mandle, an academic in Canberra who had a weekly sport column in the *Canberra Times* entitled 'Sporting Print', reported: 'The AIS is developing a disturbing tendency to grow fat, to inflate its administrative costs etc'. In hindsight, this statement and similar comments by other critics of the institute were warning signs of what was soon to follow. However, because Mandle and Cheffers had been sparring partners in print for some time, it seemed to many readers to be just another bait dangled before Dr Cheffers.[31]

On 18 November, two journalists from the *Daily Telegraph* in Sydney, Michael Hurst and Ken Anderson, made allegations of serious mismanagement at the institute. For three days the following headlines appeared: 'LEAKED PAPERS EXPOSE SPORTS SPEND-UP';[32] 'THE SPORTING LIFE';[33] 'COACH: WHY I QUIT THE AIS – PROBE ORDERED';[34] 'OFFICIALS WILL PROBE AIS REPORTS'.[35] Some of the allegations made in the above reports included:

- a large increase in the institute's spending on hospitality, from $1581 in 1982-83 to $42 074 in 1984-85;

- the purchase of expensive furniture for the executive director, with a desk costing $8000 and an office chair costing $3000;

- trips costing $2779 to the Victorian Football League Grand Final in Melbourne and the Rugby League Grand Final in Sydney, both on the same week-end, for Dr Cheffers and two senior staff members;

- the misuse of the 'Spot Merit' budget, in sending a senior manager's wife business class to Tokyo to accompany her husband at the World University Games;

- the use of $17 000 of the AIS coaching budget to partially fund the newly-formed Illawarra Sports Institute;

- the employment of the executive director's son and daughter on a part-time basis and of a close friend in a full-time position.

Other allegations concerned the purchase of rowing shells and claims that the documents were altered to favour one of the tenderers. Finally, it was asserted that the executive director had undertaken too much travel, as he had been absent from the institute for 59 out of 110 working days prior to the date of the newspaper's allegations.

The costs mentioned in the reports may not appear excessive today, but when one considers that these allegations were made in 1985, the amounts can be almost doubled in current terms.

The Federal Auditor-General's Department announced that it would investigate the institute with an efficiency audit. In the meantime, John Brown commissioned Price Waterhouse to carry out an internal audit. However, the flak was starting to fly in the direction of the Minister, who had staunchly defended the institute, declaring that everything was in 'apple pie order'.[36] [37]

The Price Waterhouse audit brought several allegations of mismanagement, the most serious being that the institute had overspent its budget by $450 000.[38] The Opposition, using the contents of the Price Waterhouse and auditor general's report, claimed that Brown had attempted to whitewash the affair.[39] A censure motion was then moved in the house by the Opposition, which was lost on party lines, 54 to 74. The affair certainly engendered some heat in the Lower House of the Parliament, with Brown asserting that the Opposition's 'censure motion was as ludicrous as it was laughable'.[40]

To be fair to the Minister, he had played no part in any of the actions leading to the allegations made by the newspapers or the auditors, but he drew a considerable amount of fire as a result of his spirited defence of the institute. Brown advised the Chairman and Deputy Chairman (John Coates) of the AIS board to 'tighten up' the management of the institute, and this was addressed at a meeting of the board in Sydney in mid-December 1985. On that occasion, the 21 allegations made against the executive director were classified into various categories, such as: errors of judgment; actions contrary to board policy; and actions contrary to the chairman's instructions. Dr Cheffers was censured and an executive committee was formed to work closely with him.

John Cheffers resigns

Six months later John Cheffers announced his resignation, declaring that he was unable to work with the executive committee and blaming the board of management for placing too many constraints on him. In his report to president

John Siber and the trustees of Boston University (from which he had been on leave while in Canberra), Cheffers wrote a 425-page discourse entitled 'Raw and Resilient', based on his experience as Executive Director of the Australian Institute of Sport. In this verbose document, he blamed several individuals at the AIS, as well as the Australian Government public service system. Further, he attempted to justify virtually all of his actions over the 27 months he had spent in Australia.[41]

In any assessment of John Cheffers' contribution to the institute, it must be noted that the allegations made about his managerial style and activities concerned either errors of judgment or situations in which he did not carry out the board's or the chairman's instructions. He was never accused of dishonesty, as he was always very direct and prepared to explain the reasons for his actions, even if the board did not always agree with them.

In many ways Cheffers was a man before his time; he was also a man who had been away from Australia for a decade and a half and who had not previously worked in a senior government position. He was therefore somewhat naïve about the constraints of office and the accountability which needed to be maintained at all times. Even though the institute was not yet a statutory body during his term at the AIS, the vast majority of the revenue came from the taxpayer and the government was adamant that it should be spent wisely. There is no doubt that Cheffers finally fell foul of the government of the day and eventually even of the Minister, with whom he had initially had a good relationship.[42] This was partly because censure motions in the Parliament are not experiences which Ministers and their governments enjoy. Having been absent from Australia while the sports system was being professionalised, Cheffers did not fully understand the history of its development, nor was he aware that government support for sport was a relatively new concept in Australia. The Opposition was still only lukewarm about the idea, and apart from a small influential group, which fortunately included the Prime Minister, Bob Hawke, not even all the members of the government were strongly in its favour.[43]

There was never any doubt about John Cheffers' drive, enthusiasm and intrinsic motivation. He may have made a more careful assessment of the situation had he occupied the position at a later time.

The third executive director: Ron Harvey

Several Canberra insiders had tipped that the next man in the executive director's position would, of necessity, be a low-key but highly efficient manager. When Ron Harvey arrived at the institute in December 1986, he fulfilled those expectations. As well as being a former sportsman, coach and sports administrator, he came with a wealth of experience in public administration. Moreover, he had been a high-ranking public servant in the Department of the Prime Minister and Cabinet and a former Principal Private Secretary to Malcolm Fraser during his term as Prime Minister.[44]

A GIANT OF AUSTRALIAN SPORT

Last year Luc Longley, who had been a scholarship holder at the Australian Institute of Sport in 1986-87, returned to the AIS at the time of its 21st birthday. When asked his impression of the place since he was first there, he said: 'It's grown up a lot and I guess I have too ... I came here as a gangly kid and I left as a gangly kid who knew what he wanted.'[45]

From the AIS Longley gained a sports scholarship to the University of New Mexico, graduating in 1991 to enter the United States National Basketball Association (NBA) as a young professional with the Minnesota Timberwolves. They were a struggling team and at first Luc was known as the 'Blunder From Down Under', as he strove to settle into the toughest basketball league in the world. With sheer guts and determination he made the big time as a key player for his next team, the Chicago Bulls, helping them to win the championship in 1996 and backing that up with two more NBA titles. Standing at 218 centimetres and weighing 130 kilograms, Longley was one of the NBA's highly regarded 'big men' until he was forced to retire in 2001 with a chronic ankle injury.[46]

For a decade Luc was a passionate member of the Australian Boomers team and played in the 1992 and 2000 Olympic teams for Australia, having missed the 1996 Atlanta Olympics because of injury. Formerly a Fremantle boy, Luc is a generous supporter of Australian sport, is currently a co-owner of the Perth Wildcats and has been a great inspiration to young Australian basketballers for well over a decade. In late 2002, Luc Longley was chosen as one of the 'Best of the Best' athletes to attend the Australian Institute of Sport during the last 21 years.[47]

When Harvey took over the helm at the institute, AIS scholarship holders had enjoyed an excellent year of competition. The swimmers, rowers, weight-lifters and divers had performed with distinction at the Commonwealth Games in Edinburgh. Basketball and hockey had several young players who were to become top internationals in the future and one of these, Luc Longley, is profiled above. Netball also had ten former or current AIS scholarship holders in Australia's World Cup team. Gymnastics and soccer were on the rise in the institute and cycling had recently been established as a sport in Adelaide. Cricket was to join them in the same city early in the next year. There were now 15 residential sports within the institute, five of which were located outside Canberra.[48] [49]

Future development plans

During 1986 the Australian Institute of Sport Act was passed, and from 1 January 1987 it has operated as a statutory authority. Shortly after this occurred, an unofficial merger between the Australian Institute of Sport and the Australian Sports Commission took place, but it was not until the end of 1988 that the Act was finally passed.[50] [51]

Ron Harvey inherited a budget deficit of $650 000, which made things extremely difficult in his first year in office. With a reduced spending policy over the next two years, some savings from the merger with the sports commission, as well as increased sponsorship money and additional earnings from the various AIS enterprises, the institute steadily returned to a balanced budget. The executive director had done exactly what he was hired to do, which was to run a tight ship, while simultaneously achieving slow but steady growth.[52]

The experience of the previous two years was a stimulus for the AIS board to develop a well-conceived development plan. John Coates, the deputy chairman of the board at that time, chaired a number of meetings in order to define a functional role for the institute within the Australian sports system. In discussions with the new state institutes and many of the national sports organisations, arrangements for future funding were devised. It was at this time that the first Olympic Co-operation Agreement was drawn up, and this was the start of a long and fruitful relationship between the AIS and the Australian Olympic Committee. As previously mentioned, the AIS/ASC merger also enabled sports funding to be better utilised, but more importantly, the programs which accompanied it were also integrated. From the elite perspective, the policies for future developments were laid down at that time.[53]

In 1987 the 'Strategic Plan 1988 and Beyond' was developed. This document was formulated from many sources, the major ones being the AIS review committees for sport, management and sports science. Paul Brettell, the AIS

John Coates played a major role in the development of Australia's sports policy, as well as masterminding the Sydney 2000 Olympics. (By courtesy of the Australian Sports Commission.)

General Manager, was the co-ordinator of the strategic plan project which addressed the development of the AIS, its relationship with other sporting bodies in Australia and the evaluation and assessment of its programs. In addition, it enunciated both its program objectives and its strategic goals, making it a valuable document for future elite sport development.[54] [55]

Because of the almost two-year delay in merging the AIS and ASC, much of this plan was later incorporated directly into the sports commission's strategic objectives.[56] [57]

The first drug episode

With Ron Harvey at the helm, the institute had settled down well as the end of 1987 approached. But suddenly and without warning, it was caught up in a bitter controversy. The ABC *Four Corners* program on Monday, 30 November broadcast a documentary entitled 'The Winning Edge' which examined the use of anabolic steroids in Australia.[58] The program was in fact more concerned with body-building in health clubs around the country, but it cast aspersions on the institute, implying that drugs were readily available there.

The writer chaired the internal committee to investigate the allegations, in which two female AIS field athletes, as well as a head coach, were implicated.[59] These three individuals, all featured on the program, suggested that if an athlete wanted to do well at the elite level it was necessary to use ergogenic aids, and asserted that drug use was widespread internationally.[60] At a later time, three weight-lifters also claimed that an AIS weight-lifting coach had supplied them with drugs between 1982 and 1984.[61] The committee found that the use of drugs at the institute was in fact limited to a handful of individuals, but this did not prevent the Shadow Minister for Sport, John Sharp, calling for an inquiry into drug-taking at Bruce.[62]

The Minister, John Brown, was supportive of the stand taken by the AIS board, who resolved that any scholarship holder caught taking drugs would be immediately dismissed. Sue Howland, a javelin thrower, had already been banned from training at the AIS until her suspension for drug-taking was lifted; and the board imposed a life-time ban on the use of the AIS facilities in the case of the former head coach of track and field, Kelvin Giles. In defence of the institute, there had been a drug policy established as early as 1981 and all scholarship holders had been required to sign the Code of Ethics, which included a clause requiring that they take no drugs while they were scholarship holders at the institute.[63]

THE AUSTRALIAN SPORTS COMMISSION (ASC)

When John Brown had formulated his sports policy before the 1983 elections, one of its central elements was the future establishment of an Australian Sports Commission. Early in Brown's ministry, the Federal Government had provided $274 000 for an interim committee to report on the role, function and structure of the proposed commission.[64] Even the Opposition spokesman, Peter Fisher, had released a press statement in September 1983, endorsing the formation of a sports commission and wishing the interim committee well.[65] Ted Harris chaired this committee, which consisted of Herb Elliott, Libby Darlison, Mike Fitzpatrick and Greg Hartung. Their report had been forwarded to the Minister in March 1984 and in September of the same year, Prime Minister Hawke had announced that the government intended to establish the Australian Sports Commission.[66] The government subsequently announced that the ASC would be a statutory authority and set about preparing the legislation. In the meantime the commission began to function in a preliminary way as an office within the Federal Department of Sport, Recreation and Tourism. This allowed the commission to assume its role immediately as an independent organisation and to report directly to the Minister, while waiting for the relevant legislation to be drawn up. It proceeded through the House of Representatives, was passed by the Senate on 31 May 1985, and was proclaimed on 1 July of the same year.[67]

The Australian Sports Commission's interim report

The report of the interim committee had been wide-ranging, drawing together in a co-ordinated way both the large and small programs which comprise a sports system. It had also recommended that there should be strong inter-governmental links, so that the states and the Commonwealth could share in the various programs. It was a well-conceived document which provided a firm foundation for a professional sports system. The basic objectives of the future commission, as recommended by the interim committee, were:

- to improve Australia's performance in international sport;

- to increase the level of participation in sport in Australia;

- to maximise funding from the private sector to supplement government funds.[68]

The Coalition withdraws support

Despite the fact that Peter Fisher, the Opposition spokesman for sport, had earlier endorsed the Australian Sports Commission Bill, it was an entirely different matter when it came to its passage through the Parliament. In the period between the completion of the interim committee's report and the introduction of the Bill, it was alleged that some members of the Confederation of Australian Sport had been lobbying various shadow cabinet members of the Coalition to oppose it. This was seen as a treacherous act, and the attempt to torpedo one of the most important initiatives ever taken for the development of sport in Australia appeared to occur mainly for political reasons. Fortunately, this move received the scorn it deserved, both within and outside the Parliament, and possibly heralded the beginning of a downward spiral for the confederation.

By a stroke of good fortune, Jack Evans, the Australian Democrat Senator for Western Australia who was about to retire from the Senate, came to the rescue and his last speech in the House saved the ASC Bill. It was not well known in Canberra that Senator Evans had come from a noted sporting family in Western Australia, where he had been a state hockey representative and a prodigious

The administrative centre of the Australian Sports Commission is located on the Australian Institute of Sport campus.

worker and lobbyist for the development of sport. Moreover, he had been a member of several important state government executive committees relating to sport in his state, as well as having been the inaugural chairman of the Western Australian Sports Federation. By lobbying his Australian Democrat colleagues in support of the Australian Sports Commission Bill and delivering a persuasive speech, Evans enabled the most important piece of federal legislation relating to the development of the Australian sports system to be enacted.[69] [70]

Early days of the Australian Sports Commission

As mentioned above, the sports commission began its operations shortly after the interim committee reported to John Brown, even though the Act had not yet been officially proclaimed. Its first business was to plan its core programs, namely: the sports development program; the sport talent encouragement plan; the sport science research program; the drugs in sport program; and the Australian Coaching Council's revamped coaching accreditation scheme.

Since its inception, the Australian Sports Commission has been regarded as an effective statutory body. It was ably led by Ted Harris and his deputy chairman, Herb Elliott, one of Australia's greatest athletes. Greg Hartung, whose profile appears below and who had waged war against the obstinacy of the Fraser Government while still a journalist, became the commission's first and very effective general manager. He had also assisted John Brown to formulate his early Labor sports policy[71] and to prepare his strategic document, 'Sport and Recreation: Australia on the Move.'[72] The above group had the ear of both the Minister and the Prime Minister and this close relationship augured well for the early days of the commission. Undoubtedly the creation of the Australian Sports Commission, allied with the rapid growth of the Australian Institute of Sport, was a very significant step in the establishment of a more sophisticated sports system.

A GREAT CONTRIBUTOR

Greg Hartung has had a long and distinguished career in sport – as a player, journalist and writer, manager and director. A graduate of Queensland and Sydney Universities, Greg first showed both a talent and passion for rugby union, gradually extending his interest from the playing field to the newsroom as a journalist for the News Limited Group.

In 1975 he turned to political journalism in Canberra, but maintained his interest in sport, writing several hard-hitting articles which blamed the government of the day for Australia's poor performances in the Montreal Olympics. He then assisted John Brown, the Shadow Minister for Sport in the Labor Opposition, to develop a policy that was keenly embraced by the Australian sports fraternity. His assistance before the elections led to his appointment by the Federal Labor Government in early 1983 to a committee which reviewed the structure of sport in Australia and made valuable recommendations on future government programs and priorities.

Late in 1983, Greg turned his attention to sports administration, becoming the General Manager of the fledgling Australian Sports Commission, which has become the backbone of Australian sport over the last 28 years. When he stepped down from full-time sports administration in 1988, he turned his attention to business, but shortly afterwards returned to sport as Vice President and then President of the Confederation of Australian Sport. He is currently the President of the Australian Paralympic Committee and the South Pacific Paralympic Committee and an executive board member of the International Paralympic Committee.

Greg Hartung has pursued a varied career in the media, in public administration and in business. For more than 40 years he has been associated with sport and has been one of the great contributors to the development of the Australian sports system.[73]

Greg Hartung has been a great contributor to the development of the Australian sports system for more than 30 years. (By courtesy of the Australian Sports Commission.)

THE AUSTRALIAN SPORTS COMMISSION'S STRATEGIC PLAN

As the commission began operations, a plan was required to provide a framework within which it could function. Its main objectives were:

- to ensure funds were used to develop sport at all levels throughout Australia;

- to provide leadership which would enable both elite and participant sport to further develop;

- to increase funding for sport, especially from the private sector.[74]

So that an evaluation of the plan could be carried out, specific performance measures were outlined in the body of the document. This was so that regular quantifiable measures could be applied when assessing the performance of the commission against its corporate and operational objectives in the future. The results of the 1987, 1994 and 1999 evaluations are discussed in Chapter Four.

This plan was put into effect in June 1986 and was circulated widely throughout the country to all the major sporting bodies, many of whom had been waiting for tangible action from the Hawke Government for some time.[75] Martin Stewart-Weeks, one of the authors of the plan, reported on its reception by the government: 'It was the first one of its type, not only for sporting agencies but one of the early examples of strategic planning, which was introduced widely across the federal public sector as part of new public management in Australia. It received a very favourable response from the Government, particularly from the Federal Department of Finance.'[76]

EARLY FEDERAL - STATE CO-OPERATION

During the Brown era, both the AIS and the ASC had been steadily moving towards creating more links with the states. The Minister and his advisers were very much aware that, without the co-operation of the states, Australia would never reach its full potential as a sporting nation.

As previously stated, from a national development perspective, it was fortunate that Victoria and Western Australia had been steadily building their own sports systems since the early 1970s and they were followed by South Australia only a few years afterward. Within three years of the Hawke Government coming to office in March 1983, these three states were at a point in their development where they could take part in a meaningful dialogue with the Federal Government. At first the discussions centred around ways in which the states and the Federal Government could share various programs and facility costs, but they gradually became more concerned with the integration of their systems, especially at the elite level. This was to prove particularly helpful as Australia entered the 1990s.[77]

Victoria

The rapid development of a state sports system in Victoria during the latter part of the 1970s, under the leadership of Brian Dixon, has already been described in Chapter Two, as have the 1981 Green Papers[78 79] and the 1982 White Paper[80] which followed. The rapid implementation of these reports guaranteed that Victoria was able to take its place in a program and facility-sharing arrangement and, at a later time, in an integrated relationship with the Federal Government.

Western Australia

The Burke Labor Government's election to office in mid-1983 proved to be one of the most significant developments in the history of sport in any Australian state. Strongly supported by the Premier, Brian Burke, Keith Wilson became responsible for several key portfolios in the new government, as well as being the Minister for Sport. A man of great integrity and a former Anglican minister, Wilson would rank with Dixon as one of the two best state Ministers of Sport Australia has produced. His philosophy was similar to that of John Brown, as they both believed that sport was community-based and that a good deal of its policies and management should rest with sport itself. Further, they were convinced that the government's role should be that of a catalyst, in a partnership arrangement with the sports organisations. This type of sport-government co-operation certainly gave good results, as Wilson demonstrated in Western Australia.

His first action was to form the Sport Development Working Party, which was to report to the Minister on a new structure and programs for sport in Western Australia.[81] The writer was appointed as chair of the working party, which consisted of 11 prominent academics, sports administrators, sportsmen and sportswomen. The report recommended that the following initiatives be carried out:

- that the Western Australian Sports Federation's effectiveness in the sports system be increased;

- that a State Sports Council be established;

- that funding for sport be substantially increased;

- that a State Sports Centre be constructed and that additional state/national level facilities be built for eight more sports;

- that a Western Australian Institute of Sport be established.

In addition to the above recommendations, all of which were carried out during the Burke Labor Government's term of office, several important reports were also initiated. These covered the areas of disabled sport,[82] country sport,[83] women in sport,[84] and junior sport.[85] The recommendations from these reports were well received by the members of the relevant state sports associations, as well as by those individuals with an interest in sport in Western Australia. There was also a considerable spin-off to the other states later, particularly for New South Wales, Queensland and Tasmania, whose sports systems were still relatively undeveloped at that time.

South Australia

South Australia had made steady progress following the election of a Coalition Government in 1981. Its first action was to establish a State Institute of Sport, after which it gradually developed a strong sports system. The main initiators of these actions were the Minister for Sport, Michael Wilson, and his chief adviser, Mike Nunan. These early developments had also given South Australia the opportunity to begin some early program integration with the Federal Government during the mid to late-1980s.[86][87]

JOHN BROWN'S LEGACY

In February 1988 John Brown resigned from the sport and tourism portfolio over allegations made by the Opposition relating to an exhibit which had been displayed at the World Trade Fair in Brisbane in 1987. During his term of almost five years, Brown was responsible for the emergence of a highly professional sports system in this country and promoted a constructive dialogue with the states, on which future Labor Government Ministers were able to build. He also oversaw a threefold increase in the sport budget and kept his election promises, a rarity in politics, achieving much more than he had proposed in his original policy for sport.

During his time in office Brown made several well-considered appointments within his portfolio. For example Greg Hartung, who was to become his most valuable adviser, was appointed as the General Manager of the Australian Sports Commission. John Brown had made the establishment of a commission a central plank in his election policy, and by carefully developing it during his tenure, he created a solid foundation for future developments in Australian sport. Apart from his pioneering effort in sports administration, he was well known throughout the country for his achievements in the promotion and development of the Australian tourist industry. Not only did he achieve a great deal in both of the above portfolios, but he did it with panache.

Chapter Four
Consolidation of the
sports system

The Hawke-Keating Labor Governments —
1988-96

Graham Richardson's ministry

Graham Richardson was fortunate to inherit a smoothly running ministry in February 1988. However, some people wondered whether he would follow the policies which had been developed during John Brown's term. At first he did not appear to have the outward enthusiasm which the former Minister had demonstrated, but it soon became clear that he was intrinsically interested in sport; in fact, few people realised that in his youth he had been a talented junior golfer.

There is no doubt that he became very supportive of Australia's athletes during his attendance at the 1988 Olympic Games in Seoul, where Australia won 14 medals. Although the Australian team's performance was marginally better than at the three previous Olympic Games, the opposition, especially from the Eastern Bloc countries, was outstanding. As a result, Richardson felt that more finance was necessary if Australia was to compete on equal terms with the European countries, especially the Eastern Europeans.

Richardson's major strength was his political savvy, as he quickly realised that sport was an item from which he could obtain good political mileage for a relatively modest expenditure. Obviously some funding was needed, but not in the amounts which were essential for the 'big ticket' portfolios, where billions rather than millions of dollars were required. With this in mind, he formulated a strategy which was to pay off handsomely for Australian sport.

MAJOR BUDGET INCREASES FOR SPORT

The contrast in styles between the former Minister and his replacement soon became evident. Even before becoming the Minister, John Brown had produced a political document in the form of an ALP Sport and Recreation Policy in 1982.[1] He offered voters a modern sport and recreation blueprint, while at the same time he was able to score political points against the Opposition for its mishandling of the portfolio. Upon election he quickly produced a comprehensive policy, which he began to implement with considerable political skill.[2]

Graham Richardson used different but very effective tactics to achieve his goals. His approach was to rely on well-researched supporting material to build a case for a more efficient and robust sports system. The first report he commissioned was a joint submission by the Australian Institute of Sport and the Australian Sports Commission (ASC); and the second was a Parliamentary report, which was to become one of the most influential documents in the history of sport development in Australia and which brought with it substantial funding increases.

THE ASC/AIS SUBMISSION

In August 1988 the writer, as Chairman of the AIS, and Ted Harris, as Chairman of the ASC, collaborated to develop a report for the new Minister entitled: 'A Case for Additional Funding to Further Develop Sport in Australia'.[3] Its main thrust was to support the development of sport in its own right and to demonstrate its value from many other perspectives, especially its impact on the nation's health and economy and the role of sport in creating a cohesive society. The report also demonstrated that Australia had been spending only $2 per head of population on sport at the federal level, in comparison to the much larger amounts being spent by its main rivals in Europe and North America. Table 4.1 below illustrates this point.[4]

Table 4.1
Comparisons of federal money spent on sport — 1986

Country	Elite sport budget ($A)	Total sport budget ($A)	Population	$ per head of population
USA*	45m	1800m	242m	7.43
West Germany	44m	420m	62m	6.77
Italy	39m	260m	56m	4.64
France	51m	350m	54m	6.48
Spain	19m	125m	38m	3.29
Canada**	18m	78m	25m	3.12
East Germany	51m	351m	17m	20.64
Czechoslovakia	38m	380m	16m	23.75
Netherlands	18m	68m	14m	4.85
Hungary	17m	105m	11m	9.54
Switzerland	38m	90m	6.5m	13.84
Australia	16m	32m	16m	2.00

* Includes university and college sports budgets and corporate sponsorship
** Does not include university sports budget
SOURCE Bloomfield, J. and Harris, A. (1988) 'A Case for Additional Funding to Further Develop Sport in Australia', Australian Sports Commission and the Australian Institute of Sport, Canberra, August, p.5

THE PARLIAMENTARY REPORT ON FUNDING FOR SPORT

Upon completion of the above report, the Minister requested that the House of Representatives' Standing Committee on Finance and Public Administration commence an inquiry into the administration of and funding for sport in Australia. In early November 1988 a subcommittee was appointed, under the chairmanship of Stephen Martin MP. Submissions were invited and 98 responses were received from sports organisations and private citizens around the country. One hundred witnesses were also called and various facilities were inspected around Australia.

This report, entitled 'Going for Gold',[5] concentrated on elite sport only and was tabled in the Parliament in March 1989. Its major findings were:

- The Commonwealth Government should be basically responsible for the funding of elite sport.

- Funding for elite sport should be substantially increased.

- Because funding in the past had been poorly co-ordinated, a mechanism should be formulated to improve it.

In all, the committee proposed 32 initiatives which required direct funding. It also called for greater accountability from the sports associations, which were the recipients of government funds.

The significance of the report was far-reaching. It had the support of the Parliament, which gave Graham Richardson the authority to 'put the icing on John Brown's cake'. Over the next five months the necessary finance was obtained for what was to be called *'The Next Step'* program, which proved to be a visionary plan for the future funding of sport in Australia.

AUSTRALIAN SPORT – *'THE NEXT STEP'*

The effect of *The Next Step* launch, which took place on 21 August 1989, was electric. It was the largest funding announcement that had ever taken place in the history of Australian sport, and many enthusiasts found it difficult to believe. Graham Richardson's speech at the AIS was simple and convincing. He made a strong case for further elite sports development, drawing attention to the lack of tangible assistance Australia had given to its sportsmen and sportswomen in comparison to similar countries. Richardson stated: 'While as a nation we are proud of our athletes, we certainly cannot be proud of the way we have treated them.' He went on to observe that 'in comparable countries governments and the private sector play a much bigger role in funding and employing [their] athletes'. The Minister declared that the Australian Government 'will provide an unprecedented level of support for our elite athletes as well as encourage much greater participation in sport at all levels in the community'.[6][7]

The increase of $100 million brought the total to be spent on specific sport development by the Commonwealth Government to $230 million over the next four years. The programs to be targeted were elite sport, junior and youth sport, women's sport, sport for disabled people, coaching, sports science and medicine, the development of national sports organisations and an expansion of the Intensive Training Centres, in co-operation with the states [89]

THE SENATE DRUG INQUIRY — THE BLACK COMMITTEE

Allegations concerning the use of drugs at the AIS have already been discussed in Chapter Three. They had been raised in an ABC *Four Corners* program on 30 November 1987 and the AIS had demonstrated that, apart from a few individual offenders, drug-taking was *not* rife at the institute.

When Ben Johnson, the elite Canadian sprinter, tested positive for the ingestion of an anabolic steroid and was infamously stripped of his gold medal at the 1988 Seoul Olympics, the Canadians set up a federal commission under the chairmanship of Mr Justice Dubin, which found that drug-taking in the power events was more widespread than expected. Back in Australia, in response to Graham Richardson's call for a drug inquiry, Queensland Senator John Black was chosen to chair the investigation and Senator Noel Crichton-Browne (WA) was to act as his deputy chairman.

The Minister fast-tracked the inquiry, the object of which was to determine how widespread drug use was in Australia. Submissions were invited and various key people were interviewed. Almost identical allegations of drug use were made against the AIS as had been made one year earlier. Five athletes claimed they had been given drugs by their AIS coaches; the other allegations had little foundation and were greatly exaggerated by the press. The media also failed to report that several of those found guilty of taking performance-enhancing drugs had already been banned from the institute for that very reason, almost a year before the 1988 Olympics. In other words, reportage of the inquiry was little more than a 'beat-up', but the press certainly had a field day in the process.

Ron Harvey, the executive director of the institute, and the writer, who was then the chairman, tried to point out to the Senate Committee that the AIS had a strict doping policy almost identical to that of both the Australian Olympic Federation and the International Olympic Committee. This had been in place since 1981 and random testing had been rigorously administered at the institute since late 1986. In the year prior to the 1988 Seoul Olympics, 160 Australian Institute of Sport athletes had been randomly tested, with *no positive results.*[10][11][12] Despite this record, the Interim Report on Drugs in Sport claimed that drug-taking was widespread in Australian sport; and that the AIS had not done enough to detect drug use.[13]

The committee appeared to take a 'guilty until proven innocent' stance, making it very difficult for the AIS to receive a fair hearing, as some politically ambitious senators on the committee seemed more interested in attracting headlines than in conducting an impartial inquiry. There was also a considerable amount of criticism of Graham Richardson himself over the way in which the inquiry impacted on the good name of the institute. There were allegations that

Richardson had a political motive for calling the inquiry, the implication being that he was more concerned about lifting the profile of one of his political colleagues than about drug abuse in Australian sport. Nevertheless, the AIS agreed that an external body, the Australian Sports Drug Agency, would henceforth accept responsibility for all drug testing in Australia, thus relieving the AIS of the expense of conducting its own 'in-house' testing. It also agreed to the recommendations of the Drugs In Sport Interim Report and those of the Second Report of the Drugs in Sport Committee, as they sought to tighten up the system.[14]

Although several positive recommendations emanated from the above reports, there was a considerable amount of negative fallout at the institute. To some extent, its image had been tarnished and there was both overt and behind the scenes criticism of it, with some coaches reporting that it became more difficult to attract high-level performers to accept scholarships at the AIS. But some who had appraised the situation carefully realised that the media and some of the senators on the inquiry committee had blown the matter out of proportion. John Daly suggested that the outstanding performance of the Australian team at the Commonwealth Games in January 1990 in Auckland 'helped to re-establish confidence and pride in the AIS'.[15] Within a year of the first report, the fallout had dissipated and it was business as usual at Bruce, where some excellent additions to the program were being made as the last decade of the 20th century began.

THE AIS/ASC MERGER

In late 1989 the Australian Institute of Sport officially amalgamated with the Australian Sports Commission. Several coaches and some of those close to the AIS, including its deputy chairman, John Coates, and the writer,[16] had initially been concerned about the move, fearing that the AIS, with its elite sport focus, might be watered down by the commission. However, it went ahead because it was government policy – one which probably rested more on the desire for power and control than any other factor. The main reasons given by the government for the amalgamation were that there was increasing duplication between the sports commission and the AIS and that money would be saved if they were combined. Further, there were several programs which did not fit comfortably with either body.

In fact, when the two organisations were merged, the combined expertise in both groups brought about the creation of several vibrant programs. Notable examples were the National Sports Information Centre, the Sports Science and Medicine Centre, the Sport Talent Encouragement Plan and later the Elite Athlete Assistance Scheme. In hindsight, the amalgamation has proven to be a positive initiative for Australian sport, as it enabled some cutting-edge programs to be established without diminishing the effectiveness of the AIS. By the end of the 1980s, there were 17 residential sports at the institute and the National Training Centre Program, which later became known as the 'National Sports Program', was flourishing.[17]

With the additional government finance, the Australian Sports Commission in 1989 introduced several new programs, the most important one being the selection of seven sports which were targeted to receive $10 million in preparation for the 1992 Barcelona Olympics. These were basketball, canoeing, cycling, hockey, rowing, swimming and track and field. As part of this program, increased assistance was also given to the state institutes and the national sports organisations. This paid off handsomely at the Barcelona Olympics, leading to similar schemes in the 1990s, particularly in preparation for Sydney 2000. As well as the above elite program, sport participation was also being funded by *The Next Step* monies and during the next few years the successful programs of the 1990s were consolidated.[18]

PARTIAL CONSOLIDATION OF THE SPORTS SYSTEM

Since the Labor Government took office in March 1983, there had been substantial developments in the fields of sport and recreation throughout Australia, and John Brown was primarily responsible for those advances.

Life members of the Australian Institute of Sport. Left to right, John Bloomfield, Kevan Gosper, John Brown and Bob Ellicott. (By courtesy of the Australian Sports Commission.)

However, during Graham Richardson's two-year period as Minister for Sport, the partial consolidation of the sports system took place. This was partly as a result of the funding he obtained at a crucial time, and partly because he set up a close relationship with the states and territories, with several elite programs being shared between the federal and state governments.

But just as important was the fact that Richardson established four-year budget programs which were cyclical in nature. As a result, an expectation was created that more funds would flow in the next cycle and those to follow. For the first time in the development of the Australian sports system, forward planning could take place, with the knowledge that money would be available to establish new programs and to fine-tune those already in existence. Certainly the title of his August 1989 initiative, 'The Next Step', summed up Graham Richardson's contribution well.

In April 1990 Richardson left the sport portfolio and Ros Kelly took his place. In addition to the ministerial changeover, Perry Crosswhite, the acting Executive Director of the ASC, and Dr Ross Smith, director of the AIS program, relinquished their positions in mid-1990. The appointments of Jim Ferguson and Robert de Castella to replace them at first went almost unnoticed. Their positive contributions, at a time when there was little dynamic political leadership, will be discussed in the next section.[19]

FINE-TUNING THE SPORTS SYSTEM — 1990-96

Up until the time of Graham Richardson's resignation in April 1990, the major developments had been driven by high-profile Ministers. The leadership of Frank Stewart, Bob Ellicott, John Brown and Richardson himself had been very obvious, but ministerial direction from the early 1990s was not as evident.

The new Executive Director of the Australian Sports Commission, Jim Ferguson, made a quiet start, as the organisation was running reasonably smoothly when he took over and he carefully monitored the current system before starting to fine-tune it. He had been a senior officer in the Department of Sport and Tourism and was familiar with the areas that may have proved to be controversial. Further, the new Minister, Ros Kelly, was not as involved as John Brown and Graham Richardson had been, and seemed happy to let the executive director and the executive of the commission conduct a good deal of the business, despite the fact that her contributions to community sport, women in sport and sport for the disabled were laudable.

At that time both Jim Ferguson and Robert de Castella were aware of the very significant funding increase made available by the Federal Government in the 1989 August budget. The programs which were implemented established several new initiatives, thereby rounding out the system and developing better co-ordination with the states over the next four years. From that point on it would only need fine-tuning.

After Graham Richardson

THE 1990 COMMONWEALTH GAMES

The sports commission had made a grant of $1 million to assist in the preparation of the 1990 Commonwealth Games team. As well, the AIS had been funding the various Commonwealth Games sports for several years, and that combination ensured an excellent preparation for Australia. A total of 162 medals, including 52 gold, were won by Australian athletes in Auckland, with many commentators suggesting that this was their best international performance since 1956. Even the *Canberra Times*, which had been rather critical of the AIS and its athletes for

Robert de Castella was not only a world champion marathon runner, but also the Director of the Australian Institute of Sport in the first half of the 1990s. (By courtesy of the Australian Sports Commission.)

AIS kayak paddlers training on the
Gold Coast. (By courtesy of the
Australian Sports Commission.)

several years, stated that Australian sportsmen and women had regained their
competitiveness at the world level.[20] These accolades were partly true, because
Australia's performances had been steadily improving internationally. However,
it should be remembered that the Commonwealth Games are not as highly rated
as the Olympic Games, the European Championships, and in many respects, the
Pan American Games.

CONSOLIDATION OF THE ASC — 1990-92

Because the 1990 Commonwealth Games were such a triumph for Australia, the
decade started on a high note, with expectations of further international
successes in the near future. The Barcelona Olympics were only two years away,
so the political climate was ripe for further development of the sports system. This
meant that the sports commission and the pertinent national sports organisations
were able to proceed with their elite sport development programs with both
political and community support. Nor did they need to request more money, as
Graham Richardson had ensured that the funding for development had already
been secured and was waiting to be spent.

Even in the early 1990s, Australia was developing a worldwide reputation for its innovative high-performance and participation programs and earning praise for the delicate balance between them.[21] [22]

THE 1992 BARCELONA OLYMPICS AND PARALYMPICS

The Australian team's performance at the Barcelona Games was better than most of the pundits had thought possible. In all, 27 medals were won, seven of them gold, nine silver and 11 bronze. This was Australia's highest medal tally since 1956 in Melbourne and the team also qualified for a record number of finals. The Barcelona performance augured well for the future, as it demonstrated that the depth of the Australian team was steadily improving. A pleasing feature of the results was that Australia had not only performed well in its traditionally strong sports such as swimming and cycling, but also recorded top performances in archery, badminton, canoeing, gymnastics, rowing, soccer, water polo, equestrian and diving. These excellent results were obtained partly because of the ASC's 1989 *'seven sports'* program, and partly through the close association of the AIS with the various state sports institutes or academies and the national sports organisations in the above sports. Of the 240-member team, only three athletes had not received assistance from the AIS or the ASC in their preparation for these Games.[23]

The Ninth Summer Paralympic Games followed the Olympic Games in Barcelona and Australia was represented by 136 athletes, who won 38 gold, 38 silver and 35 bronze medals between them. It was Australia's best-ever position in the medal tally, with the team finishing in sixth place. It now became clear to those involved with disabled sport that Australia had become very competitive at the international level. It was also obvious that, with better coaching and management of disabled sportsmen and women, they could do even better in the future.

OTHER INTERNATIONAL SPORTING TRIUMPHS

During the early 1990s, Australian athletes or teams either won, or were runners-up in, an unprecedented number of international sporting events. In 1991-92 ten world team championships were won, with four teams being runners-up. In individual world championships, 21 were won by Australian athletes, with one athlete placing second.[24] [25] This demonstrated that Australia was performing well not only in the Olympic sports, but also in numerous non-Olympic sports. Details of these results can be found in Appendix B.

When viewed alongside the Olympic and Paralympic results, the above performances were a great start to the last decade of the 20th century. As the sports system became more sophisticated, results were to improve even more as the century drew to a close.[26]

'MAINTAIN THE MOMENTUM' — 1992-96

In order to consolidate the above advancements, the Federal Government announced a further four-year funding program from 1992 to 1996. This grant was $293 million, an increase in real terms of approximately five per cent. This program, which was called '*Maintain the Momentum*', continued to support the existing programs; there was also an enlightened policy change made by the sports commission which greatly benefited the national sporting organisations. This was an increased autonomy and flexibility in both short and long-term planning, which they had been requesting for some time.[27] [28]

SYDNEY WINS THE OLYMPIC BID

After meticulous planning and marketing of the 2000 Olympic bid, the Games were awarded to Sydney on 23 September 1993 by the International Olympic Committee. Just after this announcement, the International Paralympic Committee awarded the 2000 Paralympics to Sydney. Now the various stakeholders had to come to grips with the enormity of their task. The sports commission was faced with the responsibility of co-ordinating the preparation of the Australian athletes. This was done with the assistance of the AIS, the Australian Olympic Committee, the Australian Paralympic Committee, the relevant national sports organisations and the state and territory institutes or academies of sport. Over a period of six months the Olympic Athlete Program was formulated and was ready to begin on 1 July 1994. This gave a lead time of a little over six years to prepare Australia's athletes for the Sydney 2000 Olympics.[29]

THE OLYMPIC ATHLETE PROGRAM (OAP) — 1994-2000

Senator John Faulkner became the Federal Minister for the Environment, Sport and Territories in March 1994 after Ros Kelly's sudden resignation, which followed allegations by the Opposition relating to 'pork-barreling' of sport and recreation funds into Federal Labor electorates. Faulkner was an astute Minister who strongly supported both the staging of the Olympic Games in Sydney and the sports commission's role in it. The initial allocation made to the Olympic Athlete Program was $135 million to be spread over the next six years. A further $5 million was later added. This funding was in addition to the *Maintain the Momentum* athlete development grant, and when added to the Australian Olympic Committee's funding and to grants from the states through their sports institutes and academies, it was sufficient to prepare the athletes well for the 'best Olympics ever'.[30]

But as with anything in the political arena, some behind-the-scenes lobbying at the highest level was required. This was arranged by Peter Montgomery, a former institute board member who had been an outstanding Olympic water polo player and a highly effective sports administrator. He was able to arrange a meeting with the Prime Minister of the day, Paul Keating, and John Coates, the then President of the Australian Olympic Committee, and it was this meeting which clinched the Olympic Athlete Program funding.

The sports commission co-ordinated the above program, which covered funding for international competition, coaching, training camps, intensive training centres and athlete scholarships, as well as research and the provision of sports science and medicine services to athletes. At the beginning of the program the main emphasis was on talent identification in a range of Olympic sports. A Talent Search Advisory Committee was formed and the program was managed through the state institutes or academies of sport. The *'Sport Search Program'*, an interactive computer package for 11 to 15-year-olds, was developed to enable aspiring young athletes to compare their personal physiological and skill attributes in sports which they enjoyed or for which they might have some talent. The program was implemented in many high schools and sporting clubs throughout Australia. While the above strategies were being introduced, the sport participation programs were also being emphasised, so that a balance was kept in the system.[31][32]

The other important feature of the Olympic Athlete Program was the additional funding allocated to the Paralympic athletes. Around this time, the sports commission was also developing the *'Aussie Able'* program, catering specifically for disabled athletes. As well as funds being allocated to fine-tune their athletes, the Australian Paralympic Committee received monies for short-term administrative assistance and to organise the Paralympic Games.[33]

THE 1994 COMMONWEALTH GAMES

These Games were held in Victoria, Canada, in August 1994 and Australia sent its largest ever Commonwealth Games Team of 256 athletes. The team's performance was outstanding, winning 182 medals, including 87 gold, 52 silver and 43 bronze. This record number of medals ensured that Australia easily won the medal tally, Canada placing second with 128 medals and England third with 125. Australian athletes won medals in all of the 12 sports, and gold medals in ten of them. There were significant improvements since the 1990 Auckland Games in track and field, swimming, shooting, boxing, weight-lifting and cycling. It was evident that the *Maintain the Momentum* program was working well, as 60 per cent of the team were current or past AIS scholarship holders and the vast majority of the other athletes were in programs supported by the sports commission.[34] Jim Ferguson stated that 'the programs which had been in place for three years were starting to mature. The Intensive Training Programs were paying off, the national coaches were becoming more effective and the sports scientists were working more closely with the coaches'.[35]

EVALUATION OF THE ASC PROGRAMS

The Australian Sports Commission (ASC) had prepared a Strategic Plan in 1986, in which it had outlined the procedures for the evaluation of its policies and programs. This was to happen at regular intervals and the outcomes were to be compared with the commission's corporate objectives and performance indicators. This process of self-regulation was developed so that equal emphasis could be given to both participation and the development of talented athletes. It was also important to create a positive environment in which both the physical and mental health of Australians could be improved through sport and physical recreation. The corporate objectives and sports development policies of the commission which form the basis of comparison for the above-mentioned evaluations can be seen in the ASC's 1986 Strategic Plan.[36]

The first evaluation undertaken by the commission, known as 'Outcomes – 1986 to 1987', was done under the above guidelines, and because the system had only been running for about two years, it lacked detail. In fact, the ASC stated in the introduction: 'The report is primarily an information document. It does not set out to present a detailed analysis of that information, nor does it pretend to be, in itself, a full evaluation of the commission's performance.' Nevertheless, the report did provide a brief outcome statement of the major ASC programs, giving enough information to later implement a 'management information system'. This was to be used in the transition to 'program budgeting' in the future, which would enable the commission to determine whether it had been successful in meeting its objectives.[37]

The 1994 'Evaluation of the Australian Sports Commission's Impact on Sport Performance and Participation' was carried out by a joint working party of the Department of Finance and the Sports Commission. They selected 44 national sports organisations and investigated their outcomes in depth, as well as analysing the impacts of the Aussie Sport and Australian Coaching Council programs. Results indicated that significant improvements in both high-level performance and participation had been made, probably due to the influence of *The Next Step* (1989-1992) and *Maintain the Momentum* (1992-94) programs. In addition there had been significant increases in junior sport participation and in the number of qualified coaches currently active in Australia.[38] [39]

Some years later, in 1999, a task force under the chairmanship of Ross Oakley was set up by the Minister for Sport and Tourism, Jackie Kelly, in order to examine the 'effectiveness of strategies, roles and relationships of the key agencies responsible for ... sport in Australia'. The findings of this report were positive, demonstrating that the current stakeholders in Australian sport were operating efficiently, and this document will assist in policy development for at least the next half decade. Because Chapter Eight deals mainly with the initiatives required if Australia is to continue as a world power in sport, general discussion of this paper and its ramifications for the future will be carried out later in the book.[40]

COMMENTS ON THE ASC EVALUATIONS

The 1994 evaluation of the ASC was more detailed than the 'Outcomes 1986-1987' report, demonstrating that the commission, assisted by the Department of Finance, was not afraid to scrutinise its own policies and programs. The 1999-2000 Report to the Federal Government, entitled 'Shaping Up – A Review of Commonwealth Involvement in Sport and Recreation in Australia', which had been carried out by several high-profile individuals not connected to the Australian Sports Commission, was another useful exercise. Both the 1994 and

2000 evaluations, for which external assessment was carried out, were valuable examinations for the sports commission in particular and the sports system in general. Government and, to a lesser extent, non-government sports bodies need to have their outcomes compared with their strategic objectives and the commission's willingness to submit to this process augurs well for the future of sport in Australia.

EVALUATING THE SPORTS SYSTEM

The evaluations of the sports commission's programs were very positive. However, a more global assessment of the entire sports system is also necessary. Both in Australia and overseas, the accepted criterion for judging the success of a sports system has been to assess the medal tallies in various international competitions. More recently, the success rate in the top eight places, or the equivalent of finals, has also been used. For example, the Australian Olympic team members gained 57 top eight places in Seoul, 66 in Barcelona, 94 in Atlanta and 120 in Sydney. This analysis gives a better indication of depth in the team and, when added to the medal count, is a reasonably good indicator of elite performances.

In addition, sport participation statistics have become more accurate in the last few years, as national sports organisations are keeping better registration figures and non-sports organisation participants, who play sport on a less competitive basis, can be recorded in the census. In order to reach a more objective evaluation of overall effectiveness than can be assessed by elite performance and participation levels alone, physical fitness and sociological variables could also be added to the formula.

AUSTRALIAN SPORTS COMMISSION PUBLICATIONS

In 1986, the sports commission's Strategic Plan had enunciated a policy relating to the publication of various instructional and educational brochures, booklets and books on many aspects of sport. From 1987, these educational materials were produced mainly to inform the volunteers in the sport as to how they could perform their various duties more efficiently. In all, several hundred thousand copies of these publications were distributed free around Australia, while the more sophisticated instructional manuals were available for sale at a price close to the cost of production. These materials have been readily available through national and state sporting organisations, state ministries of sport and recreation and sporting clubs *(see Appendix G for further information)*.

THE 1996 ATLANTA OLYMPICS AND PARALYMPICS

Australia's international performances for the two years leading up to the Atlanta Olympic Games were extremely good. A medal tally of approximately 35 had been forecast, but with 41 medals being won, it was the best performance in any Games by any Australian team — including Melbourne, where Australia had won

Figure 4.1
The Australian
Olympic medal
totals from
1956 to 2000.

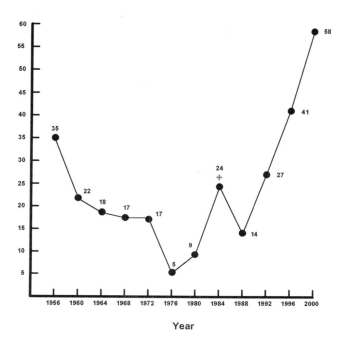

+ Australia's medal count would have been considerably lower if the Communist
  Block had competed. (See text for more detail)

Sources: Sarsfield, R. (1999) The Olympic Games, Dorling Kindersly, Sydney.
Weston, J. (2000) Sydney 2000, News Custom Publishing, Melbourne.

Figure 4.2
Federal
government
expenditure on
the Australian
sports system.

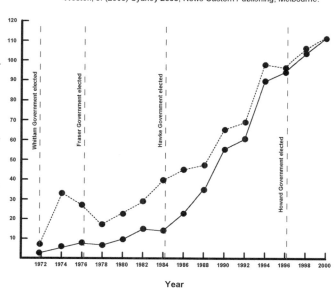

--------------- Shown in 2000 dollar values

——————— Actual dollars

Source: Australian Sports Commission Annual Reports

35 medals. At Atlanta, nine gold, nine silver and 23 bronze medals were won in 14 sports, compared to the total of 27 medals in only nine different sports in Barcelona. The Australian team, consisting of 424 members, also finished seventh at Atlanta in the overall medal tally, in comparison to their tenth position in Barcelona. As well, 94 Australian athletes rated among the top eight places, compared to 66 in Barcelona and 57 in Seoul.[42]

One of the main reasons for the outstanding performance was that the team was better funded than any previous Australian Olympic team in history. There was also a high level of co-operation with the federal, state and territory governments, the various national sports organisations and the Australian Olympic Committee. The additional funding enabled high-level competition, intensive training and sports science and medicine support to be available to the athletes for two years before the Games, and much of this was offered at the local level in the various state capitals. It is clear that the assistance given to Australian athletes by the AIS and the state institutes or academies of sport through the Australian Sports Commission was a crucial factor in the outstanding performances of the Australian team.[43]

As had been the case for several Olympics, the Tenth Summer Paralympic Games followed the 1996 Olympics in Atlanta. The Australian Paralympic team of 166 athletes was relatively small in comparison to the American, German, British and Spanish teams. Nevertheless, Australia led the medal tally until the last day, finally taking second place with 106 medals, including 42 gold, 37 silver and 27 bronze. This was five fewer medals than in 1992, but the competition was considerably stronger, as numerous records were broken in Atlanta and more countries competed than previously. It was obvious that the Olympic Athlete Program had greatly assisted the Australian Paralympic team and on its return, it was hailed as the most successful sporting team of the year in Australia.[44]

BILL BRYSON'S COMMENTS RE AUSTRALIAN SPORT

Bill Bryson, the celebrated journalist and author of various travel books, had some amusing and informative comments to make in his recent book about Australia, entitled *Down Under*. After describing Test cricket and commenting that Australia gave England a 'good thumping', he goes on to say: 'In fact, Australia pretty generally beats most people at most things. Truly never has there been a more sporting nation. At the 1996 Olympics in Atlanta, to take just one random but illustrative example, Australia, the fifty-second-largest nation in the world, brought home more medals than all but four [sic 'six'] other countries, all of them much larger ... Measured by population, its performance was streets ahead of anyone else. Australians won 3.78 medals per million of population, a rate more than two and a half times better than the next best performer, Germany, and almost five times the rate of the United States. Moreover, Australia's medal-winning tally was distributed across a range of sports, fourteen, matched by only one other nation, the United States. Hardly a sport exists at which the Australians do not excel. Do you know, there are even forty Australians playing baseball at the professional level in the United States, including five in the Major Leagues – and Australians don't even *play* baseball, at least in any devoted manner. They do all this on the world stage *and* play their own games as well, notably a very popular form of loosely contained mayhem called Australian Rules Football ... '[45]

THE HAWKE-KEATING GOVERNMENTS' CONTRIBUTION

In reviewing the contribution of the Hawke-Keating Governments, it is clear that there were two major factors responsible for the evolution from an amateur to a modern professional sports system.

The first was the additional funding provided by the Federal Government. Table 4.1 demonstrates that in 1986 Australia was spending much less on sport development per head of population than its major rivals, and that in order to seriously compete with them, similar amounts would be needed. The Hawke-Keating Governments steadily increased the funding for sport and Australia's results improved to the point where they correlated highly with the amount of money allocated. Figures 4.1 and 4.2 demonstrate the closeness of this relationship.

The second crucial factor was the expertise of the personnel who guided the program as it developed. This process was begun by the Whitlam Government in 1973 with Frank Stewart as its first Minister for Sport, and John Brown was a key player in the next stage of development. Brown was ably supported by Greg Hartung, who had helped him to formulate the Labor sport and recreation policy and who oversaw its implementation until the end of the 1980s. Graham Richardson, John Faulkner and Warwick Smith were effective Ministers who continued the Brown tradition; and Jim Ferguson, the longest-serving Executive Director of the Australian Sports Commission, was very instrumental in fine-tuning the system; his impressive profile appears below. A vital role was also played by John Coates, President of the Australian Olympic Committee, who masterminded the Olympic bid and played a key role in the formulation of the Olympic Athlete Program.

The above developments and the success of the Australian teams in the 1996 Atlanta Olympics and Paralympics demonstrated that a modern professional sports system had evolved in this country. From that point on only minor adjustments were needed, as Australia progressed towards the biggest sporting challenge it had ever faced, namely the Sydney 2000 Olympic and Paralympic Games.

THE PUBLIC SERVANT-SPORTS MANAGER

Jim Ferguson was a keen sportsman in his youth and had a wide variety of work experiences as a jackaroo, a taxi driver and a publisher's editor while completing his university studies. He then led an impressive career as a high-level Commonwealth public servant before entering the sports administration area.

As a career diplomat with the Department of Foreign Affairs from 1966 to 1986, during which time he undertook several overseas postings, Jim rose to the level of Ambassador to Peru in 1980. In 1986 he joined the Department of Tourism and Sport in Canberra under John Brown, the then Minister. Together they helped to place Australian tourism on the international map.

Jim Ferguson's reputation in Canberra was such that in 1990 he was invited to become the Executive Director of the Australian Sports Commission, a position he held until after the Sydney Olympics in 2000. As executive director his contribution was enormous, as he was able to develop both elite and participant sport, establishing a better balance between the two. When the Sydney Olympic bid became a reality in 1994, Jim's diplomatic and communication skills were invaluable, as he co-ordinated the preparation of Australia's athletes in both the federal and state sports systems.

Jim Ferguson has held many important positions in both tourism and sport, such as board membership of the Australian Tourist Commission, the Great Barrier Reef Marine Park Committee, and organising committees for the World Youth Soccer Cup and World Masters Games. He is currently a member of the Migration Review Tribunal and President of the China Australia Sports Association. Jim is also the President of the Australian Capital Territory Rugby Union and in this role acts as chairman of the prestigious ACT Brumbies.

However, Jim Ferguson will be best remembered for his important role in guiding Australian sport through its most successful decade and for his smooth management of the sports system, culminating in such a resounding success at the Sydney 2000 Olympic Games.[46]

Jim Ferguson guided Australian sport through its most successful decade up until the Sydney 2000 Olympics.

Chapter Five
How governments
assist sport

The role of various government agencies

The previous chapters have chronicled Australia's sports performances up to the Atlanta Olympic and Paralympic Games. During this period, a more sophisticated sports system developed steadily as more funds were made available by the Hawke-Keating Labor Governments. Much of this funding was utilised to develop various government services, which have played a significant role in Australian sport during the last two decades.

Government sports services are very basic to Australian sport, because they supply crucial support for the national sports organisations, the state sports organisations and the tens of thousands of sports clubs throughout this country. The services discussed in this chapter are mainly supported by the Federal Government, but state and local governments also give assistance to some programs.

Specific sports services

AUSTRALIAN COACHING COUNCIL (ACC)

In the section in Chapter Two entitled 'The Early Period – 1975-78', the establishment of the Australian Coaching Council was briefly discussed. The National Coaching Accreditation Scheme, which the coaching council previously oversaw, is one of the most effective programs ever to have been set up in the Australian sports system.

As previously mentioned, an embryonic coaching accreditation scheme had commenced in Western Australia in mid-1969. The first course was a 30-hour unit on the general theory and principles of coaching, with specific sport courses being added five years later.[1] The former Western Australian program was upgraded in 1978 after it became the responsibility of the Commonwealth and three levels of accreditation were established nationwide. The Level 1 course consisted of the general principles of coaching; the Level 2 course comprised specific theory and practical work and an introduction to the field of sports science; and the Level 3 course contained advanced sport-specific material and advanced sports science. There were regular curriculum revisions during the first seven years, by which time 44 000 coaches had been accredited in 70 sports.[2] Several high-quality coaching manuals were published by the council in the 1980s and 1990s and newer editions are currently available from the Australian Sports Commission. In addition, the above courses were steadily upgraded during the late 1980s and early 1990s and by 1994, 132 726 coaches had been accredited in Australia.

Since 1994, with special funding from the *Maintain the Momentum* program, there has been further expansion in the coaching field. It is estimated that there are currently more than 600 000 coaches in Australia and of that number, 289 000 coaching qualifications have been gained in 96 different sports since 1978.[3] The Australian Sports Commission, which has become directly responsible for this program, now realises that more coaches are needed at the elite level, because Australia has been partially relying on some highly qualified overseas coaches for various national teams. Since the Sydney Olympics, several top coaches have left Australia to coach overseas, mainly in Britain, as the Howard Government was too slow to commit funds for international-level sport immediately after the Sydney 2000 Olympic Games. Funding was later restored, but during the nine months in which it lapsed, considerable momentum was lost. Other coaches in non-Olympic sports have also been attracted overseas, because there is now a lucrative global market in coaching, especially in Europe. With recently established sports commission programs like the Sports Assistance Scheme, the National Coaching Scholarship Program and the Graduate Diploma of Elite Sports Coaching, a coaching career pathway has now been created which will enable Australia's coaches to move to the highest level of coaching in this country.

If one looks back beyond the last three decades, when almost all coaches were trained in an informal apprentice system and Australian coaching standards were low, it is clear that significant progress in this field has been made and these developments correlate highly with the modernisation of the Australian sports system. With a carefully planned career path and excellent human movement and sports science courses around the country underpinning coaching, Australia is well placed to be one of the international leaders in the coaching field from this point on.

Although many people have assisted in the development of the coaching accreditation scheme, Laurie Woodman stands out as the architect and founding director of this very successful program. It is fitting that he is acknowledged for his foresight and dogged persistence in the accompanying profile.

THE NATIONAL SPORTS RESEARCH PROGRAM (NSRP)

It was not until 1983 that the Federal Government displayed any interest in sports research in Australia. When John Brown became the Minister for Sport

THE COACH OF THE COACHES

Australia's coaching standards are highly respected by our overseas opponents and for proof of this, one only has to look at the number of elite-level coaches who have been lured to lucrative positions abroad. Australia's real strength in coaching comes from the thorough education coaches receive as they progress through the various coaching accreditation levels.

The man responsible for the development of this program during its first 13 years in Australia was Laurie Woodman. Laurie first trained as a physical education teacher, then completed a Master's Degree at the University of Western Australia. After a short period lecturing at the Royal Melbourne Institute of Technology and holding various part-time coaching appointments, Laurie became the Development Officer and later the Director of the Australian Coaching Council. As well as 'coaching the coaches', he also wrote, edited or published numerous very useful publications on coaching.

Laurie Woodman has always been the epitome of the dedicated educator. The courses and units offered within the coaching curriculum were carefully structured, each level steadily progressing from the previous one; and the manuals developed during his term of office presented the curriculum in a simple and well-illustrated form.

As talent identification and development became a more important part of the AIS program, Laurie moved from coaching accreditation to become the AIS Elite Sport Performance Co-ordinator in 1996. For a time he was instrumental in establishing a formalised talent development program which is currently expanding rapidly both at the AIS and throughout the state and territory institutes and academies of sport. Recently Laurie became the National Training Manager for the Australian Football League, where he continues to apply his considerable expertise to our national football game.[4]

and Recreation in March of that year, he was the first federal Minister to actually formulate a sports science and medicine research policy. The National Sports Research Program was established during his term in office. The aim of the program was to bridge the gap between science and sport.[5] This was a daunting task, as sports science was still almost unknown in Australian sport, except in Western Australia. The interim committee for the Australian Sports Commission had strongly recommended to John Brown in 1984 that the new commission should play a 'central role in both overseeing and [in] the co-ordination of ... research ... in all areas of sport'.[6]

The National Sports Research program was set up in 1983, with policies similar to those of Sport Canada. When funding became available in the 1983-84 financial year, grants were made to various tertiary institutions and national sports organisations. The research was expected to be of an applied nature and by 1990 almost $1 million had been allocated for this purpose. The program functioned until 1990, when it came directly under the auspices of the Australian Sports Commission. It became known as the Applied Sports Research Program and now operates under the aegis of the National Sports Research Centre in Canberra.[7]

This centre has carried out some very valuable applied research, as well as establishing the Laboratory Standards Assistance Scheme, which supervises national standards for sports science laboratories throughout the country.[8] Another welcome development which has emanated from the National Sports Research Centre and the National Sports Information Centre is a Sportscan database, which has been developed in conjunction with various national sporting organisations.[9] This database is used to identify articles and reviews which will be of interest to coaches, sports scientists and sports medicine specialists. It currently ranks among the best available in the world and is a credit to the sports commission.

SPORTS SCIENCE AND SPORTS MEDICINE RESEARCH IN AUSTRALIA

A critical analysis of sport in Australia would rate almost all the services within the sports system highly, except for basic research in sports science and sports medicine. There is no doubt that Australia's scientists have skillfully applied research findings emanating mainly from Europe and North America in both of the above fields, as there are many well-trained professionals in these fields in this country. However, as sport becomes more competitive and scientific, Australia will need to build up its own basic body of knowledge in these areas. Research in sports science and sports medicine reflects the general decline in research in Australia and this nation must soon face the challenge of developing its own intellectual property. Unfortunately for Australia, sport is just one of the many fields in which this must be done.

However, it is important to emphasise that this neglect of basic research in sport is not the fault of the Australian sports scientists and sports medicine doctors. They are dedicated professionals who have done an excellent job with very meagre funding and little support. The Sport 2000 Task Force, in its review of the Commonwealth's involvement in sport, also pointed out that Australia's research in sports science and sports medicine will need to be upgraded if Australian athletes are to have continued success at the international level. Additional points concerning the need for more research in sports science and sports medicine are presented in Chapter Six.[10]

THE JUNIOR SPORT PROGRAM (ORIGINALLY 'AUSSIE SPORT')

Of all the programs conceived and developed for the Australian sports system, 'Aussie Sport' has been the most innovative and successful. Sport for young Australians over the age of 12 had become reasonably popular in Australia by the late 1960s and early 1970s, and was similar to the US Age Group sport program which had been in operation from the early 1960s. However, some coaches and educators in Australia felt that in many games the rules were too complicated, the courts and fields too large and the equipment too heavy or awkward for younger children. With several rule modifications, various games were simplified. The sport development officers and coaches, who initiated these changes in the early 1980s, realised that more complex rules could be introduced as the children became familiar with the games and as their skill levels improved.[11]

One of the first initiatives of the new sports commission in 1984 was to investigate how junior sport within Australia could be fostered. In 1985 a grant of almost $1 million was allocated to develop modified rules to suit young children. These were tested by a group of sports development officers from various associations and the commission, and together they developed the instructional material required for the various sports.

In April 1986 the Aussie Sport program was launched by the Acting Prime Minister, Lionel Bowen. The commission's Aussie Sport committee was chaired by Roy Masters, who had a deep interest in junior sport and good connections with the media; a profile outlining his contribution appears at the end of this section. With the able assistance of Jenny Oldenhove, 8000 primary schools were contacted in the first year and Aussie Sport Resource Kits, which included an accompanying activities manual for 30 modified sports and a 60-minute video tape, were placed on sale. In addition to the resource materials, codes of behaviour for conducting the various games were set up and an extensive media campaign was introduced. Coaching courses and an awards system were established by the commission for the various sports and co-ordinators were appointed to all the states and territories.[12]

Since 1986, modified junior sport has grown to the point where it is now a very large national program. By 1995, the number of children annually competing in Aussie Sport had reached two and a half million and the program was in operation in 100 percent of the primary schools in Australia by 1991.[13] [14] It currently covers four areas: early childhood sports skills, modified sport, youth leadership and sports counselling.[15]

Australia has become the world leader in adapting junior sport to suit young people and programs which are modelled on the Aussie Sport system are now in operation in 16 overseas countries, with five more intending to implement the program in the near future.[16] [17]

The Matthews Netball Centre
in Perth on a typical Saturday
morning, when at least 5000
girls from six years of age
upwards use the facility.

DRUGS IN SPORT AND THE AUSTRALIAN SPORTS DRUG AGENCY (ASDA)

The first sports agency in Australia to establish a drugs policy was the Australian Institute of Sport, yet just seven years later it became the first institution to be accused of supporting performance-enhancing drugs.

The first policy in Australia on the illegal use of drugs had been introduced at the AIS as early as 1981 and was an important part of the Athlete's Code of Ethics which every scholarship holder had to sign. After the Black Committee inquiry, a National Drugs in Sport Co-ordinator was appointed and since that time various upgrades of the program have been carried out. In the lead-up to Sydney 2000, Australia refined its anti-doping policies and developed a program of drug education. The Australian Sports Drug Agency has established itself as a reliable unit for the testing of athletes. With the co-operation of the various national sports organisations, an efficient system is now in operation.

The Sport 2000 Task Force became aware during the data-gathering phase for its final report that some national sporting organisations would prefer to have more extensive drug testing, but found it far too costly for their existing budgets. They also noted that there are 'limitations of the current analytical detection methods and the legal robustness of the system'.[18] These concerns are currently being addressed by the related agencies.[19] However, in early June 2001 a senate committee was told that women's and men's basketball, soccer, athletics and cycling had reduced their drug testing because of the increased cost of the tests. Furthermore, Senator John Faulkner recently forecast a fall in ASDA funding over the next two years, which is the lead-up period to the 2004 Athens Olympics.[20] If this is correct, it is disturbing news and the national sporting organisations involved and the Australian Sports Commission should urgently address any shortfall.

THE FOUNDER OF *AUSSIE SPORT*

Roy Masters was both a school teacher and a very successful first-grade rugby league coach — two professions which equipped him well to conceive and head up the Australian Sports Commission's *Aussie Sport* (or modified sport) program.

As coach of the Western Suburbs Magpies (1978-81) and the St George Dragons (1982-87), he was a member of the NSW Rugby League coaching panel which developed the first modified football game in Australia. When John Brown appointed Masters to the inaugural board of the Australian Sports Commission in 1984, he asked him to introduce primary school children to as many competitive sports as possible. Minister Brown was concerned with child obesity levels and felt that more participation in sport may alleviate this serious health problem. Roy Masters developed the concept of *Aussie Sport*, encouraging Australian sports federations to modify their rules so that primary school children could compete in games with simple rules. He also modified courts, fields and equipment, as well as encouraging girls and boys to play in mixed teams for the first time in Australian junior sport. There was some opposition to the project from a few quarters; nevertheless, by 1988 *Aussie Sport* had been taken up by approximately 80 percent of schools in Australia.

Aussie Sport has now been exported successfully to many countries around the world, but the significant point as far as Australia is concerned is that two and a half million young Australians currently compete each year in modified sport in this country.

Roy Masters is well known in New South Wales, where he is a senior writer for the *Sydney Morning Herald* and a regular commentator on Channel Seven.[21]

WOMEN AND SPORT

While women's participation in sport has historically been discouraged in many countries, Australia has proved to be one of the more enlightened Western democracies in generally promoting it. Female swimmers such as Fanny Durack, Mina Wylie and later Claire Dennis placed this nation on the international swimming map at the beginning of the 20th century. However, there was a body of opinion at that time suggesting that vigorous activity might be harmful to a female's health and that intense competition was not suited to a woman's feminine personality. Partly as a result of women's participation in the Second World War effort, however, these attitudes had largely been discounted by the second half of the last century and Australia subsequently developed many outstanding international sportswomen. The most famous of these were Shirley de la Hunty-Strickland, Marjorie Jackson, Betty Cuthbert, Marlene Matthews, Dawn Fraser, Lorraine Crapp, Ilsa Konrads, Shane Gould, Margaret Court, Evonne Goolagong, Raelene Boyle, Heather McKay and more recently Karrie Webb, Belinda Clark and Michelle Martin. Two other outstanding sportswomen whose profiles appear later in this section are Rechelle Hawkes and Sarah Fitz-Gerald.

Belinda Clark, the Australian women's cricket captain and top batter, guides a ball through mid-wicket. (By courtesy of the Australian Cricket Board.)

THE HEART OF THE HOCKEYROOS

Rechelle Hawkes started playing junior hockey in Northam, a country town approximately 100 kilometres north-east of Perth. Identified through state junior development squads, she was awarded a scholarship by the Western Australian Institute of Sport in 1984. In 1987 she became a dual scholarship holder when she also won an award from the AIS, retaining both scholarships until her retirement in 2000.

Rechelle was first selected in the Australian team in 1985 for a five-Test series against England in Australia. Despite several injuries in her earlier career, she went on to represent Australia with great distinction for the next 15 years, the last eight as captain. A senior member of the Hockeyroos, Rechelle was highly respected as one of Australia's most consistently outstanding players. With her great acceleration, elimination skills and excellent vision, there were few players in the world who could set up plays as well as she did.

Rechelle scored 49 goals in the 279 matches she played for Australia. When she retired after competing in her fourth Olympic Games at the Sydney 2000 Olympics, she was recognised as the most successful female hockey player in the world and is regarded as one of Australia's greatest captains.

Rechelle Hawkes is one of only two Australian females to win Olympic gold medals at three separate Games. This feat was achieved in 1988 in Seoul, 1996 at Atlanta and 2000 at the Sydney Olympics. She received many awards for leadership and was an inspiration to younger players, but her highest accolade came when she was awarded an Order of Australia Medal for service to the sport of hockey.[22]

In his 1983 policy document, 'Sport and Recreation: Australia on the Move',[23] John Brown drew attention to the lack of financial support for women's sport in Australia. In June 1984 he announced the establishment of a Working Group on Women in Sport which was chaired by Senator Rosemary Crowley from South Australia. This report was tabled in the Parliament in May 1985 and launched shortly afterwards by the Prime Minister as the future policy for women's sport.[24] By 1986, women's sport had became one of the major programs in the Australian Sports Commission's Strategic Plan,[25] and a Task Force for Women's Sport was established in early November 1986 by the commission. Their report was approved in December 1987 and the Women's Sport Promotion Unit (WSPU) was formed.[26]

Margaret Pewtress, who had been very active in women's sport and who was the President of the Australian Netball Association at the time, was appointed chairperson of the task force and later of the Women's Sport Promotion Unit.

Her positive influence was felt well into the early 1990s, as was that of Libby Darlison, who had been a member of the Interim Committee for the Australian Sports Commission before becoming an inaugural member of the WSPU. She was also a valued member of the AIS board, with a special responsibility for athlete welfare.

The commission increased its support for women's sport in early 1991 by establishing the Women and Sport Unit, which had a wider focus and increased influence in the Australian sporting community.[27] The above unit has recently been disbanded and the government has replaced it with a program entitled *Active Women: National Policy on Women and Girls in Sport, Recreation and Physical Activity 1999-2000*. This change brought considerable criticism from several sports organisations and the Sport 2000 Task Force reported that 'discussion with sporting organisations revealed a perception that the Australian Sports Commission's commitment to women's issues had decreased'.[28] However, the task force felt that this was not the case and was confident that the commission would continue its strong support of women's sport at the grass roots level.[29] If this does not occur, women's sport is in danger of losing the positive momentum it has built up over the last two decades.

SPORT FOR PEOPLE WITH DISABILITIES

Interest and support for people with disabilities was one of the most neglected areas of Australian sport until 1984. Seven Australian disabled sports associations were formed between 1954 and 1984, catering for amputees or people with blindness, cerebral palsy, deafness, intellectual disabilities, transplants, paraplegia and quadriplegia.[30] However, these associations had almost no funding and were obliged to rely on volunteers for assistance.

The first government interest was shown soon after John Brown came to office and in his December 1983 statement, entitled 'Sport and Recreation: Australia on the Move',[31] he announced his policy for 'Sport and Recreation for the Disabled', enunciating both his future program and funding policies. The government decided to increase annual funding to $400 000; to hire a consultant to advise the Federal Department of Sport, Recreation and Tourism; and to consult with the AIS about the admission of talented disabled athletes to the National Training Centre Program. Following the Minister's initiatives, the Australian Sports Commission was asked to examine the field more closely and to propose a better system than the existing one.

The only substantial document available at the time was the 1983 report of a Western Australian State Government committee on 'Sport and Recreation for Disabled People'.[32] This committee had been chaired by Dr Richard Lockwood, then a lecturer in human movement at The University of Western Australia. However, it was not until November 1987 that the commission accepted responsibility for disabled sport and launched a program known as the Disabled Sports Program in early 1988. Its objectives were designed to co-ordinate all the bodies then operating around Australia which had assisted with the various facets of disabled sport. Substantial funding was made available for programs designed to boost participation and improve elite performance.[33] Louise Sauvage is an example of an outstanding disabled athlete who was first supported by the Western Australian Institute of Sport and later by the NSW Institute of Sport. She is profiled at the end of this section.

In February 1991, the name was changed to 'Aussie Able', as the sports commission felt that the new title gave a more positive identification to disabled sport. Not everyone agreed with this decision, but the name was not as important as the changes which soon occurred, the main one being a budget increase to $1.6 million per year. There were several other significant policy changes, such as:

- employment of specialised personnel in the area;

- funding of travel costs to international competitions;

- provision of travel costs for officials to overseas meetings and conferences;

- availability of additional funding for coaching development and research;

- offering several scholarships to elite disabled athletes to attend the AIS.

A CHAMPION TO RIVAL THE GREAT MACKAY

Sarah Fitz-Gerald began playing squash at the age of six, and as a 14-year-old she was already representing Australia. After gaining a scholarship at the Australian Institute of Sport, which she held until 1990, Sarah won the world junior championship in 1987, setting her on the path to international sporting fame.

Sarah has represented Australia 68 times in her long and illustrious career, winning 60 Women's International Squash Players Association (WISPA) and world tour titles, including five World Open championships. After extensive knee surgery in 1998-99, she regained her position as the world's number one player in 2001, but one of the most prestigious jewels in her crown is the gold medal she won at the 2002 Commonwealth Games.

Since 1991 Sarah has held a scholarship from the Victorian Institute of Sport and is very supportive of junior players in her home state and throughout Australia. She is also very active in her role as President of the Women's International Squash Players Association.

Named the Dawn Fraser Australian Athlete of the Year as well as the Australian Female Athlete of the Year in 2002, Sarah looks set to continue her winning streak, along with her role as a mentor in support of younger players, for some time into the future.[34 35 36]

In addition, the commission funded several programs with the aim of integrating them into the existing national sports organisations.[37]

After a decade of operation, and not without some acrimony between the ASC and the various groups involved in the Disabled Sport Program, it has proven to be very successful — both for high performance sport, where the results have spoken for themselves in several Paralympics, as well as in its high-quality education program. Known as the Disability Education Program, it has focussed on the four key areas of: resource development, training and education, systems development and elite sport support.[38]

The most important goal to strive for in the future is the integration of programs for disabled athletes with mainstream sport. The Sport 2000 Task Force Report states that 'the success or otherwise of this policy is still under scrutiny by disabled groups. It has been successful in some sports, but this is so only when the particular sport is supportive of the programs. However, there is growing support for additional assistance for sports to achieve integration goals'.[39] If this can be accomplished by the national sports organisations over the next decade, Australia will retain its reputation as a leader in the field of sport for disabled people.

A wheelchair rugby game with the Australian Steelers in action at the Sydney 2000 Paralympics. (By courtesy of Sport the Library.)

Louise Sauvage, the greatest disabled athlete ever to represent Australia, in training at the Australian Institute of Sport. In 2000 she was recognised as the World Sportsperson of the Year with a Disability. (By courtesy of the Australian Sports Commission.)

WHEELING TO VICTORY

Louise Sauvage first hit the headlines when she won the 100 metre event in world record time at the International Paralympic Committee's World Championship in 1990. She cemented her place as the new star on the Paralympic world stage at the 1992 Paralympic Games in Barcelona, where she triumphed with three gold medals and one silver. Over the next decade, Louise travelled to various overseas locations for six to seven months of each year, winning not only track racing events but also many road races, from five kilometres to marathons.

Born with a spinal condition called myleodisplasia, Louse was first taught to swim to develop her upper body, but a spinal operation at the age of 14 ruled out competitive swimming. Her strong desire to compete was channelled into wheelchair track racing, where she has consistently defied the odds and inspired athletes with her inner strength and determination.

Louise spent a decade at the Australian Institute of Sport before taking up a scholarship with the NSW Institute of Sport. She has won many awards, including the Abigroup Young Australian of the Year and the Australian Paralympian of the Year four times out of five. She has twice been named the International Female Wheelchair Athlete of the Year and was recognised as World Sportsperson of the Year with a Disability by the inaugural Laureus Sports Awards in 2000.

As Louise winds down her international sporting career, she is devoting more of her energy to promoting sport for people with disabilities. She looks forward to coaching other Paralympic athletes to international level, to give them 'the chance to fulfil their aspirations just like I have'.[40]

DEVELOPING AUSTRALIA'S TALENT

It was previously claimed that the Junior Sport Program (originally *Aussie Sport*) was the most successful government initiative since the rapid growth of the Australian sports system took place after 1983. Undoubtedly, however, the National Talent Search Program runs it a very close second.

IDENTIFYING THE TALENT

Research into talent identification began in the early 1970s in Eastern Europe.[41] In 1973 Bloomfield and Blanksby were the first Australian research team to profile elite rowers, before later working with swimmers in the early 1980s.[42][43] Allan Hahn began his research in this field in 1987, working with elite female rowers at the AIS in Canberra, and by 1994 a strong talent identification and development program had emerged at the AIS under his leadership.[44] Just as the 2000 Olympic Games were allocated to Sydney and the Olympic Athlete Program (OAP) was being formulated, the Sport Search Program became a very important element in the preparation for Sydney 2000.

As the OAP progressed, a vigorous talent search took place throughout Australia. At first it relied heavily on identifying raw sporting talent in the schools and was very effective. However, those closely connected with the program were convinced that many potential athletes were being missed and that other methods should be used to identify and then recruit them into the sports system.

In an article in *Sports Coach*, Dr Jason Gulbin, the National Talent Search Co-ordinator from the Australian Institute of Sport, outlined several additional methods which are now being used to identify talent.[45] Several of these, although only recently initiated, appear promising and have already borne fruit. Table 5.1 below will substantiate this statement.

- *Media call-ups* — Talent scouts have found that an effective way to recruit novice talent is to advertise over the radio or in the press, and the AIS is currently developing such a program. It recently tested 250 young women who were interested in cycling, selecting 26 of them to do an eight-week training program. Seven members of this group performed well at the national level, with Jessica Ridder winning a silver medal in the team sprint at the 2002 national championships.

- *Older athletes* — The conventional talent search program traditionally catered for high school and upper primary students. This program currently targets university-aged young people for events in which they are expected to reach their peak performance at a later age, such as the field events, rowing, kayaking or long-distance running. Some examples are Clint Robertson, a promising surf ski paddler who changed to sprint kayaking and won an Olympic gold medal in Barcelona; and Nova Peris, who moved from hockey to track sprinting in the late 1990s, with good results.

- *Talent recycling* – Gulbin points out that 'a number of multi-talented athletes with an extensive training and competition background in one sport may have common attributes that can be applied to another sport'.[46] At present, this is one of the most productive sources from which potential elite athletes are being identified. Examples are Alisa Camplin, who was first a little athlete and then a gymnast, before becoming a gold medallist at the 2002 Winter Olympics in aerial skiing; and Jane Saville, who became an internationally reputed race walker after being an elite ironwoman in surf lifesaving and a national-level junior swimmer in the butterfly and individual medley events.

- *Sibling profiling* – This relatively new program tests the siblings of successful athletes, assuming that if there is already a talented member in a family, there could be others with a similar genetic make-up. This means of identifying talent is only in its infancy, but it is expected to become a mainstream method of identifying potential athletes in the future.

- *Foreign athletes* – Several athletes from other countries, primarily Eastern Europeans, have moved to Australia to continue their sporting careers and have been welcomed into this country's sports system – firstly because they usually perform well for their adopted country in events where Australia has not been particularly strong, and secondly they are a stimulus to our athletes, who benefit from the competition they create. One example is Katrin Borchedt, who defected from East Germany in 1989 after winning the World Junior Kayak Championship, then came to Australia in 1993 via West Germany. Since her arrival, she has won several international events, two world championships and an Olympic bronze medal at the Sydney 2000 Olympics. Another example is Kostya Tszyu, a former Russian amateur boxer who came to Australia after the communist government lost power. He has been a very successful professional boxer, winning the IBF, WBC and WBF super-lightweight world titles since becoming an Australian citizen. Yet another example is Tatiana Grigorieva, whose profile appears below.

DEVELOPING THE TALENT

The talent development stage is the most difficult part of this program, because it often entails many years of careful planning and guidance by those advising the athlete. Obviously it is important to choose a good coach and to find a positive training environment. Each state in Australia has State Talent Search Co-ordinators (STSCs) who are a part of the national program. Recently Talent Search set up a national development blueprint, which Gulbin describes as being 'designed to optimise the transition from novice to elite athlete. It supplements an existing quality ... program with a ... set of worthwhile experiences delivered at critical developmental time periods.'[47] By using this procedure, the STSCs can deliver a quality talent development program for every young elite athlete in this country.

A MODEL ATHLETE

Tatiana Grigorieva is an example of a foreign-born athlete who successfully changed events after coming to Australia at 22 years of age. Ranked sixth in the 400 metre hurdles when she left Russia, she managed to win a bronze medal at the world championships in the pole vault just two and a half years after her arrival in Australia.

Tatiana came to Australia to join her husband Viktor Christiakov, who was being coached in Adelaide by his former Russian pole-vault coach, Alexander Parnov. Viktor encouraged his wife to try the pole vault, so between modelling assignments, she began to coach herself in this challenging new event. Within 12 months she was rated sixth in the world and was able to win a South Australian Institute of Sport scholarship.

At the Sydney 2000 Olympics, Tatiana struck a real chord with the Australian public, as she was engaged in an absorbing head-to-head battle with her American opponent, Stacy Dragila, in the pole vault final before having to settle for a silver medal. Since that time she has continued to soar, winning the women's pole vault at the 2002 Manchester Commonwealth Games.

Since coming to Australia Tatiana has been in demand as a model, particularly following the Sydney Olympics. She has also embraced the relaxed Australian way of life and is now an enthusiastic fan of Australian (rules) football. She hopes to continue pole vaulting until 2004 or 2006 before resuming her studies in sports psychology, which she was studying when she left Russia. [48 49 50]

Table 5.1
Talent Search Under-23 — achievements from 1994 to 2002

Achievement	Total
World Age Championships — medals	35
World Age Championships — representation	128
National Age Championships — medals	1297
Age Championships — top ten placing	2538

SOURCES Adapted from Gulbin, J. (2001) 'From Novice to National Champion', *Sports Coach*, Vol. 24, no.1. pp. 24-26. Gulbin, J. (2002) Updated data for Talent Search Program — personal communication with the author.

ATHLETE DEVELOPMENT PATHWAYS

During the last decade, the AIS, the state institutes or academies of sport and the national sports organisations have been streamlining the way in which athletes proceed towards the elite level. As a result, they now have a variety of developmental pathways along which they can progress. These are flexible and allow for the athlete's age, level of skill, educational level, future work aspirations and geographical location, as well as coaching, facilities and equipment preferences, which are all taken into account when setting up their program. The State Talent Search Co-ordinators can offer a wide range of choices which create a flexible development program for young elite athletes.

In order to illustrate how the system works, four different types of athletes will be used as examples. The first is a female rower from the northern beaches in Sydney, who was selected in a rowing talent identification program in 1993. Kristina Larsen had already excelled in surf life saving, netball and athletics and was regarded at that time as a promising all-round athlete. Her early rowing training was undertaken at Narrabeen Lakes, where she rapidly developed her skills before receiving support from the AIS and then the NSW Institute of Sport. In 1997 and 1998, she won two world under-23 sculling championships and was a member of the Australian women's eight which gained fifth place at the Sydney 2000 Olympics. Then in 2001, her team won a gold medal at the world women's senior eights in Switzerland and were runners-up in Spain in 2002. If everything turns out as Kristina plans, she will be competing with distinction in the 2004 Olympic Games in Athens.[51]

Kristina Larsen progressed through a typical 'athlete development pathway' to the international level in women's rowing. (By courtesy of James Rankin JRP.)

Ryan Bayley is an example of a young international-level cyclist whose development has mainly taken place in his home state of Western Australia. (By courtesy of the Western Australian Institute of Sport.)

The second example is a 20-year-old male cyclist from Perth, Ryan Bayley. Ryan first raced in junior motocross and then went to BMX competition. He began track cycling at 15 and was selected for the Western Australian Institute of Sport (WAIS) development squad one year later, in 1998. In 2000 Ryan won the world junior track sprint title at 18 years of age and in 2001 the world keirin title. At the Manchester Commonwealth Games he won gold medals in both the sprint and team sprint events. After his wins in Manchester, this fine young cyclist praised the assistance he had been given by both his WAIS cycling coach, Daryl Benson and former WAIS coach, Martin Barras, who is now head coach of the Australian cycling team.[52]

The third example is Adam Miller, a young male sprinter who lives in Port Macquarie in New South Wales and who has already represented that state in junior baseball. He is the hottest male prospect seen in track and field for many years in Australia and was discovered by the NSW Institute of Sport sprint coach, Michael Khmel, at the NSW Combined High Schools Track and Field Championships in 2001. He has already run 10.4 seconds for 100 metres as a 17-year-old and has been granted a NSW Institute of Sport scholarship. Last year Adam trained at home while completing his last year of high school, but spent as much time as he could with Khmel at the Sydney Academy of Sport at Narrabeen. If Adam Miller is able to perfect his technique in the next few years, he has the potential to be a great Australian sprinter in the future.[53]

Finally, Kym Howe is a good example of an athlete who has successfully adapted to a different sport. Kym was an outstanding young gymnast till the age of 16, when she was advised that she had become too tall for the sport. Based on testing by the West Australian Talent Identification Program, which carries out scientific and functional assessment of adolescent physical attributes, she was strongly recommended to try pole vaulting. By 1999 she had become the Australian junior pole vault champion, holding both the National and Commonwealth under 20 records, followed by the Western Australian state record in 2000. Initially selected and coached by WAIS pole vault coach Steve Rippon, she is currently under the direction of Alex Parnov, also at the WAIS. Kym was a silver medallist at the Manchester Commonwealth Games and shows great promise.[54]

The young athletes discussed above have all been identified within their own state sports systems. Apart from Kristina Larsen, who has reached international level in the highly sophisticated team sport of rowing, they will be able to develop their skills at the state level. From time to time they may take part in the national development program and probably have some association with the AIS, but by and large they are likely to remain state-based athletes for the majority of the time. The fact that they are able to train in a first-class institute or academy in their home state indicates that Australia now has a high-quality, uniform system throughout the country. A more comprehensive discussion of the elite program appears at the end of this chapter.

'ACTIVE AUSTRALIA'

Traditionally Australia has had high levels of sports participation. This is largely because of this country's early social history, the way in which the sports club system developed, the temperate climate in which most Australians live and the relatively high standard of living available to a large number of people in this country. In 1999–2000, 7 500 000 Australians from a population of approximately 19 million participated in sport, either within the organised club system or outside it. This is one of the highest participation rates of any country in the world.[55]

Adam Miller is Australia's hottest male sprint prospect for many years, having covered 100 metres in 10.4 seconds as a 17-year-old. He is currently a scholarship holder at the NSW Institute of Sport. (By courtesy of Sport the Library.)

Kim Howe, a rising star in
the women's pole vault after
converting from gymnastics,
soars above four metres as
she prepares for the Athens
Olympics. (By courtesy of Kim
Howe and the Western Australian
Institute of Sport.)

As previously mentioned, there have been various initiatives, such as the *Fitness Australia* campaign in 1969 and the short-lived *Life Be In It* campaign of the late 1970s, aimed at stimulating higher levels of physical fitness. However, Australia has never had a long-term national 'sport for all' program, like those which were popular in Europe in the 1970s and 1980s, or the *Participaction* program, which was mounted at a similar time in Canada. Because the programs of the 60s and 70s ceased in Australia, no vehicle existed which could stimulate participation and fitness 'across the board'.

The *'Active Australia'* program was established by the sports commission in 1996 to stimulate participation and physical fitness. It was not exactly a program as such, but more of an alliance of many programs. Some of these, such as junior sport, women and sport, disabled sport, indigenous sport etc, were sponsored by the sports commission, while others were already in existence in the local communities. The mission of *Active Australia* was to encourage more Australians 'to become active in sport, community recreation, fitness, outdoor recreation and other physical activities.' In addition, the sports commission stated that 'the program contributed to health, welfare and productivity of the nation'. With relation to its mode of operation, the commission has pointed out that the program has a nationally integrated approach, bringing together elements of federal, state, territory and local governments, as well as commercial providers.

There are currently three *Active Australia* Provider Networks which help to improve the delivery of sport and physical activity to the Australian community. These are:

- clubs and similar organisations within the community;

- local councils, which provide programs, facilities and services in their regions;

- schools, which provide many opportunities for the development of positive attitudes and behaviour through their health, physical education and sport programs.[56]

The evaluation of the Australian sport and recreation system, which was carried out by the Sport 2000 Task Force, indicated that *Active Australia* is achieving its objectives and that it should be expanded through sporting organisations and other government agencies. The task force suggested that it is now in a position 'to create partnerships, set goals and provide the impetus for an improved system to increase participation and physical activity. In particular, health outcomes can be delivered through *Active Australia*.'[57]

Finally, the last observation of the task force report was that 'the emphasis on elite sport has overshadowed the importance of delivering increased participation in sport and recreation, and that the current funding level is inadequate'.[58] This recommendation should not be interpreted to mean that the elite sport program should be cut and the savings transferred to fund a more vibrant *Active Australia* program. The best outcome for Australians would be for the existing budget, currently $12.9 million, to be substantially increased. Several countries in the past have funded similar programs in Europe and North America at around $A2 per head of population, which would mean a figure of approximately $38 million for Australia. Such a funding allocation would allow this program to have real impact around Australia. As this book goes to publication, it would appear that *Active Australia* might, in the future, be placed under the health banner and that a Target Sports Program, in conjunction with the national sports organisations, will take its place in partnership with the sports commission.

INDIGENOUS AUSTRALIANS IN SPORT

Mike Jenkinson, in an article on the social impact of sport in Australia, suggests that Indigenous Australians have used 'European-style sport to improve their position in society, although their progress was seldom easy or free from cultural conflict'.[59] Certainly many Indigenous athletes have been very successful in the limited number of sports which they have played in this country, and Darlison makes some valid points when discussing several aspects of Aborigines and sport, in an article on equality. First she suggests that 'the treatment of Aboriginal Australians by white Australians is generally little different to the treatment of the colonised by the colonisers anywhere in the world. Within sport, however, the picture is often held to be different, with sport being seen as providing a unique vehicle for upward social mobility for Aboriginal people. Once again sport is advanced as the great social leveller, transcending barriers of race and providing opportunities for success for all those who are prepared to make an effort'.[60]

In a section of the above article, Darlison also draws attention to the sports in which Indigenous athletes have traditionally excelled. She suggests that Australians 'take comfort and display pride in the fact that "they" have produced many first-rate Aboriginal athletes and see such a phenomenon as a living example of treatment of minority groups in sport as different from the treatment they receive in society generally'. She also raises the point that few white Australians query why the success of Aborigines up until the mid-1980s had been restricted almost entirely to boxing and the various football codes.[61] There are many prominent examples, such as Dave Sands, Ron Richards, Lionel Rose and Tony Mundine in boxing; Arthur Beetson and Ricky Walford in rugby league; Sir Douglas Nicholls and Graham 'Polly' Farmer in Australian football; and the Ella brothers in rugby union.

More recently the sports commission has stated that 'sport is especially important in increasing the opportunities available to Indigenous people and has devoted extensive resources to ... sport development'. Further, the Federal Government aims to increase the opportunities and pathways available to the indigenous population through sport. The sports commission and the Aboriginal and Torres Strait Islander Commission (ATSIC) currently have a program with two components: community development and athlete development, which are described below.[62]

The Community Sport Development Program has a national network of development officers who work at the regional level in co-ordinating sport and recreation programs. These programs complement existing services in health, education and the justice system, and are located in the 35 regional Aboriginal and Torres Strait Islander Councils throughout Australia.[63]

The Athlete Development and Elite Sport Program is integrated with existing sport structures and assists athletes, coaches, officials and administrators. Scholarships are offered to Indigenous athletes to participate in mainstream sport at the elite level and so far, more than 600 athletes have benefited from the program, from the junior to the Olympic level.[64] It is heartening to see some very fine young Indigenous athletes in recent years emerging from this program in a much wider range of sports. Eleven were members of the Australian Olympic team at the Sydney Olympics, led by Cathy Freeman, whose profile appears below. In addition, a great many footballers are now playing at the top level in Australian football and the two rugby codes. Currently several young Indigenous athletes in track and field, netball, hockey, tennis and golf are performing very well at the junior level; and an Indigenous Australian cricket team completed a successful tour of the United Kingdom in the latter part of 2001.

ADDITIONAL PROGRAMS SUPPORTED
BY THE FEDERAL GOVERNMENT

The programs discussed to this point are all major Australian Sports Commission initiatives and many of them have steadily developed since the commission's early days. In addition to those discussed above, some programs have been smaller in their scope, but nevertheless are very important to a well-integrated sports system. These are briefly discussed below.

THE ATHLETE CAREER AND EDUCATION PROGRAM (ACE)

This program is delivered through the state and territory institutes or academies of sport. There are approximately 3000 young elite athletes who have access to the program, which provides educational guidance, personal development, career planning, job skilling assistance and post-sport transition planning. The licence for the ACE program has already been purchased by a number of sporting bodies in Australia, as well as the United Kingdom Sports Institute and the New Zealand Sports Foundation. Other countries interested in adopting this program are the United States, Canada, South Africa, Italy and France.[65]

INTERNATIONAL ASSISTANCE

In 1996, the International Section of the sports commission was established. This created an additional dimension to sport in this country, enabling Australia to export sport both as a business and also as foreign aid. Specific programs are now being managed by the commission, in co-operation with the Australian Agency for International Development and the Department of Foreign Affairs and Trade in Africa, Asia, Oceania and the Caribbean, in a total of 29 countries.[66]

Australia has some fine Indigenous athletes but sprinter Patrick Johnson (left lane) is among the best of them, consistently challenging Matt Shirvington for the title of Australia's fastest man. (By courtesy of the Australian Sports Commission.)

International assistance is also being given in the form of sports training for foreign athletes at the Australian Institute of Sport. During the last decade, since the programs were finalised with Oceania and the African countries, overseas athletes training in Australia currently number more than 70 per year.[67]

SPORTS EDUCATION

No sports system can operate efficiently without a repository of up-to-date information and a sports education program. The National Sports Information Centre is Australia's premier sports information resource and is housed on the AIS campus in Canberra. It oversees the activities of the network of Australian Sport Information Providers. This group co-operates with the state departments

A NATIONAL INSPIRATION

Cathy Freeman burst on to the world athletics scene at the 1990 Auckland Commonwealth Games, where she won a gold medal as a member of Australia's 4 x 100 metre relay team. Four years later, in Canada, she produced stunning Commonwealth Games victories in both the 200 metres and 400 metres.

Apart from her fine athletic perfomances over the years, her charming personality radiates to her supporters as she strives to repeat her many Olympic and Commonwealth Games successes, weighed down by the nation's expectations and her husband's recent illness.

Cathy came from a large family in Mackay, Queensland, and for more than a decade has been an inspiring example for other indigenous athletes and for the nation as a whole. She was named Young Australian of the Year in 1991 and several years later also became Australian of the Year. In 1997 Cathy was ranked as one of Australia's best sports people of all time, among traditional greats such as Sir Donald Bradman, Dawn Fraser, Greg Norman and Kieren Perkins. She has won many other awards, including Telstra's Female Athlete of the Year, the Aboriginal and Torres Strait Island Sportswoman of the Year, *The Age* newspaper's Sportsperson of the Year, the *Australian Runner And Athlete* magazine's Athlete of the Year, and has twice been named in the achievement roll of the Australian Sporting Hall of Fame.

However, perhaps Cathy's most memorable moment was the lighting of the Olympic flame at the Sydney 2000 Olympic Games. The whole world witnessed her grace and poise as she performed this traditional honour before winning gold just a few days later in spectacular fashion in the 400 metre event.[68]

Cathy Freeman, the icon of Indigenous athletes, and Nova Peris, an Olympic hockey gold medallist who later became a world-class sprinter. (By courtesy of the Australian Sports Commission.)

of sport and recreation and the state institutes or academies of sport, as well as providing educational assistance and advice to various sports organisations. Not only do they act as sophisticated libraries, but they also have several other ways in which information can be disseminated around Australia. There is no doubt that this centre has played a major role in Australia's recent sporting successes.[69]

The sports education programs which are offered by the commission cover several areas. Management is a major one, while the education of officials at all levels is seen as very important also. Because Australia has a large number of volunteers, who are basic to the operation of the sports system, courses to upgrade their understanding of their sport and the way it functions are offered regularly.[70]

THE FEDERAL DEPARTMENT OF SPORT AND RECREATION

During the period from 1973 to 1986, the Department of Sport and Recreation played an important planning and policy development role in the evaluation of the Australian sports system. Lloyd Bott, the first secretary under the Whitlam Government, Graham Dempster, head of the sport and recreation divisions under both the Whitlam and Fraser Governments, and Bruce McDonald, secretary under the Hawke Government, all played significant roles in the establishment of a more sophisticated sports system. The department gradually passed over its programs to the Australian Sports Commission, so that by the end of the 1980s it was responsible only for monitoring policy implementation. In more recent times it has carried out executive functions to assist whichever Minister was in office. There have been occasional suggestions of interference by the department from some members and executive officers of the sports commission, with the main complaints relating to departmental meddling in commission policy development. With the strong Ministers of the 70s, 80s and early 90s, the system was kept in balance. However, some of the more recent 'lightweight' Ministers may have allowed imbalances to develop within the system, affecting the harmony between the groups.[71]

NATIONAL ELITE SPORTS COUNCIL (NESC)

The National Elite Sports Council, which was conceived by Dr Frank Pyke, Director of the Victorian Institute of Sport, is a unique sport body which was formed in 1993 and consists of the directors of the national, state and territory academies and institutes of sport. The current membership of the council includes the Australian Institute of Sport, the Victorian Institute of Sport, the NSW Institute of Sport, the Western Australian Institute of Sport, the Queensland Academy of Sport, the Tasmanian Institute of Sport, the South Australian Sports Institute, the Northern Territory Institute of Sport and the Australian Capital Territory Academy of Sport. The Australian Olympic Committee and the Australian Commonwealth Games Association attend the council meetings as observers.

The council's mission is to be 'an effective agent for the enhancement of high performance sport in Australia' and its main objective is to ensure that 'sport institutes and academies are recognised as significant contributors to Australia's international sporting success, through the effective co-ordination and successful delivery of quality programs'.[72] Because the directors of the above bodies realise that the state and the national systems will be stronger if they work closely together, they have become a very cohesive group in recent years.

STATE GOVERNMENT SPORTS SERVICES

All the Australian states and territories now have well-developed *Departments of Sport and Recreation,* or their equivalent. The sports systems in the states of New South Wales, Queensland and Tasmania evolved later than in Victoria, Western Australia and South Australia, but in the last decade the gap has been closed. All these state bodies currently formulate their own policy with relation to sport and recreation and play the major role in its implementation. The exception is for elite sport, which is delivered by state or territory institutes or academies of sport. Currently the states and territories of Australia contribute approximately $350 million directly to the Australian sport and recreation budget, which at the present time is approximately $6.0 billion.[73] See Table 8.1 in Chapter Eight for further information on the funding of the sports system.

The state or territory institutes or academies of sport have become very sophisticated since 1994. The emphasis on federal-state co-operation began under John Brown in the late 1980s and was carried on by Graham Richardson. When Sydney won the 2000 Olympic bid in 1993 and the Olympic Athlete Program commenced in early 1994, the federal-state elite sports model changed from one in which there was a degree of competition between the states and the AIS to one in which there was a high level of co-operation. This has led to the development of a national network of sophisticated training centres which have several programs partially funded by the Australian Sports Commission. It is this co-operative system which has enabled the athlete development pathways to flourish, catering for a large number of young elite athletes throughout Australia.

In addition to the state bodies mentioned above, the larger states have established, or are currently investigating, the setting up of district-level institutes. For example, the NSW Institute of Sport, which in the last seven years has become one of the most highly developed state institutes, now has eight country regional 'satellites', or mini-institutes known as academies. These cater for elite-level juniors and some senior athletes who cannot reside permanently in Sydney, where the state institute is located. An example of a state institute which initiated some very good programs quite early is the Victorian Institute of Sport (VIS). This is directed by Dr Frank Pyke, who is profiled below.

ACHIEVING THE RIGHT BALANCE

The motto of the Victorian Institute of Sport (VIS) is 'Success in Sport and Life'. This encourages athletes to adopt a balanced approach to sporting excellence while also pursuing a future career path; it is an approach which prepares them for life after sport by teaching them various skills while keeping their sporting performances in perspective.

Balancing sport and education has always been the philosophy of Dr Frank Pyke, who has directed the operations of the VIS since its inception in 1990. He was an outstanding Australian (rules) footballer in Western Australia before completing his PhD in exercise physiology.

Frank Pyke has been at the forefront of sports science, coach education and elite athlete development in Australia for many years. Between 1970 and 1990 he lectured and carried out research in exercise physiology at several universities in North America and Australia. Before taking up his present post, he was Professor of Human Movement Studies at the University of Queensland.

During his academic career, Dr Pyke always endeavoured to apply scientific knowledge to sport, particularly through the education of coaches. Among his several books are three editions of the internationally recognised *Better Coaching* manual, which has been used in the National Coaching Accreditation Scheme since 1980.

The VIS has become an integral part of Australia's sporting success and during the past 13 years its athletes have competed successfully in various Commonwealth, Olympic and Paralympic Games and many world championships. The contribution made by VIS athletes to Australia's international medal tally has been more than might be expected from a state with only one-quarter of the nation's population.

Finally, the VIS and its director, Frank Pyke, are to be congratulated on the healthy balance they have achieved for their athletes. Their positive initiatives have been adopted by other states and territories and have assisted in the evolution of the National Athlete Career and Education program developed by the Australian Sports Commission.[74]

In addition to the above, various state and territory education departments around Australia support sport to a greater or lesser degree. They all have *School Sport* branches for organisational purposes which are co-ordinated by the peak body, entitled *School Sport Australia*. The larger eastern states have traditionally supported regular high-level competitions, such as those organised for the Combined High Schools of New South Wales; however, some of the smaller states have never developed such a competition. These programs are generally well organised and coaching and performance levels are reasonably high, largely because of the many millions of hours which state school teachers have spent with students on a voluntary basis for more than 50 years. Unfortunately, however, sport in some schools is now becoming less structured and with ever-increasing pressures being placed upon teachers, many of them are no longer willing or able to carry out voluntary extra-curricular roles as coaches and sport co-ordinators.

A more recent innovation at the secondary school level is the establishment of specialist *sports high schools* in the majority of the Australian states, where the coaching is generally above average. These have been developing steadily for the last 15 years, and there are now enough of them around Australia for the impact to be felt in the national sports system. Experience over the last decade indicates that dedicated sports high schools seem to flourish more in lower-middle-class areas, whereas schools where only two or three high-level optional sports are offered are more popular in middle-class suburbs. It is also important for teachers with high levels of coaching expertise to staff these schools, as this was not always the case in the first half-decade of their evolution. As with academic subjects, it is also of value if these schools can be associated with a local university or a state or district institute or academy of sport.[75][76] With more funding to improve facilities and well-trained coaching personnel, they will have an even greater impact on elite sport in Australia in the future.

LOCAL GOVERNMENT SPORTS SERVICES

Australian local governments contribute by far the largest amount of money to sport and recreation of any government sector in Australia. Their contribution currently is approximately $1.13 billion per year, or almost 19 per cent of the entire Australian sport budget. This funding supplies the majority of the 'grass roots' facilities such as sport and leisure centres, pools, courts, ovals, fields, golf courses and many other specialised venues, as well as the employment of recreation officers, who are mainly responsible for the co-ordination of sport and recreation within their municipalities. See Table 8.1 for further details relating to funding of sport and recreation at the local government level.[77]

UNIVERSITY SPORTS SERVICES

Input into the Australian sports system from universities is indirect. Nevertheless, they play a vital role in the training of professionals for several fields relating to sport in this country. In previous sections of this book, several university departments have been singled out for various reasons, especially where they played a crucial part in the early development of the sports system. During the last three decades, 12 very reputable schools of study around the country have matured and now offer high-quality undergraduate education, as well as postgraduate studies. Their major thrusts involve human movement, sports science, sports studies and physical education, and many of their graduates enter the sports system in one capacity or another. There are 11 other smaller courses around Australia which are at various stages of development and one would expect that within a decade, several of these will be in a position to offer in-depth courses and post-graduate training for their students.[78]

A new trend has recently developed in which universities have been assisting national or state sporting organisations and state sports institutes or academies with sports science services. This occurs in Victoria in co-operation with the Victorian Institute of Sport and is now well established in that state; and the Centre for Rugby Studies, which operates from the Queensland University of Technology, also caters for young rugby union elite performers. Anecdotal evidence currently points to similar programs still on the drawing board as other tertiary institutions become more involved in high-level sport.

The newest development within some universities is the offering of sports scholarships to elite-level athletes. Who could have imagined two decades ago that the oldest and one of the most conservative Australian universities, Sydney, would be the first to take such a daring step? (The writer has been told on many occasions over the last three decades that 'sport has no place in Australian universities' and that it was appropriate 'only for the second-rate universities in the United States'!) This is certainly an interesting initiative and it is encouraging to know that several Australian universities are finally entering the real world as far as sport is concerned. The University of Sydney now grants scholarships in swimming, rugby, cricket, rowing and water polo. John Boultbee, a former Director of the Australian Institute of Sport, strongly supports the move. He also suggests that the university sector should be encouraged to play a more active role in the Australian sports system and maintains that a more direct liaison between state institutes and academies of sport and various universities around Australia could be of great value.[79]

CO-ORDINATING GOVERNMENT SERVICES FOR ELITE SPORT

As already outlined in this chapter, the national and state governments assist sport in this country by establishing various athlete development programs, particularly for elite sport. Not only are the programs of a high quality, but they are also uniform as far as standards are concerned. In addition, they are highly co-ordinated and utilise regular interaction with each other, as demonstrated in the following sections.

THE SPORTS INSTITUTE/ACADEMY NETWORK

When the AIS was established in Canberra in 1981, there were no state institutes or academies in place. Its role was that of a centralised residential training institution which selected its scholarship holders from around Australia. Within the next few years, the most distant and least populous states of South Australia, Western Australia and Tasmania developed their own institutes or academies but they were not linked with the AIS, operating in isolation and often in competition with one another.

Gradually it became obvious that many young elite athletes were not able, or did not want, to leave their home states and re-locate to Canberra. This led to more growth in the already existing state institutes/academies and the establish-ment of others in the more populous eastern states.

By the early 1990s it was clear that more co-ordination was needed between the Commonwealth and the states if the sports system was to reach its full potential, and the Australian Sports Commission began to forge close financial links with the states. By 1996 there were eight state or territory institutes or academies of sport as well as the AIS, providing programs for this country's elite athletes wherever they wanted to reside. This close linkage has allowed flexible development pathways to be established, enabling individual athletes to choose whichever location suits them best. The other important point is that the institutes/academies around the country are now reasonably uniform as far as coaching standards are concerned. The National Elite Sports Council (NESC) currently co-ordinates this program and the national sports organisations play a vital role in its delivery.

The Western Australian Sports Centre (Challenge Stadium) is shown hosting the 1998 World Swimming Championships. This centre currently houses the Western Australian Institute of Sport. (By courtesy of the Western Australian Sports Centre Trust.)

THE TARGETED SUPPORT PROGRAM

In 1989, the ASC decided that it would target sports in which Australia could do well internationally and *seven sports* were chosen. The budget for the program was $10 million, to be divided between basketball, canoeing, cycling, hockey, rowing, swimming and track and field. The additional funding was available to hire an international-level head coach for each sport, to establish a state-based Intensive Training Centre (ITC) and to make international competition more available for athletes in the above sports.

By the early 1990s, targeted support was beginning to work well and was given greater impetus in 1994, when the Olympic Athlete Program commenced. The combination of the establishment of more state or territory institutes/academies of sport, the increasing development and decentralisation of the AIS and the co-operation of the national sports organisations has contributed to an effective and efficient national elite sports program in this country. As well, the former ITCs (now the National Training Centres) have become well established and their results speak for themselves. For example, the medal tally from the targeted sports increased from 12 in Seoul in 1988 to 22 in Barcelona in 1992 to 31 in Atlanta in 1996, reaching a total of 37 in Sydney in 2000. Pyke and Norris suggest that 'the contribution of state-based athletes to the medal tally has increased progressively during this time'.[80] Table 5.2 gives more details of the targeted support program up to the Sydney 2000 Olympics.

Table 5.2
Olympic medal tallies in targeted sports

Sports	Seoul 1988	Barcelona 1992	Atlanta 1996	Sydney 2000
Track and field	2	2	2	3
Basketball	0	0	1	1
Canoeing	2	3	3	2
Cycling	4	5	5	6
Hockey	1	1	2	2
Rowing	0	2	6	5
Swimming	3	9	12	18
Totals	12	22	31	37

SOURCE Adapted from Pyke, F. and Norris, K. (2001) 'Australia from Montreal to Sydney: The Evolution of a Model', Presented at the Second International Forum on Elite Sport, Barcelona, Spain, 21 September, p.6.

In summary, there is no doubt that the National Training Centre programs in the currently targeted sports enable this country to fully co-ordinate all the resources which are available to elite athletes. The co-ordination of the European sports systems is not yet as efficient as Australia's. However, several of them have observed the way in which the Australian programs operate and are currently streamlining their systems in an effort to obtain better results.

THE VITAL ROLE OF GOVERNMENTS IN AUSTRALIAN SPORT

If the various governments do not continue to support sport, Australia's current system will partially collapse and return to the 'horse and buggy' days of the 1960s. Federal governments from Whitlam to Howard have viewed these agencies as central to Australian sport and, by and large, have funded them adequately. The majority of them now only require fine-tuning from time to time in order to be effective agents in the sports system. However, the *Active Australia* program needs half a decade of affirmative action in order for it to become a viable health-oriented program.

Chapter Six
Community support for sport

The role of non-government agencies

The bodies which make up the non-government sports services sector are essential ingredients in the Australian sports system. To be effective, several of them require some government funding to function efficiently, while others are regulatory or service bodies which are partially or fully self-funded. Without them sport could not exist in its present form, as they are the fundamental service components of Australian sport.

The voluntary services which are currently extended to the Australian sporting public have been developed over a long period. Before the sports system became professionalised, these bodies were formed by highly-trained volunteers who generously donated their expertise to develop the various non-government service agencies in this country. Without these dedicated individuals, none of Australia's high-profile sports service agencies would have developed to the point where they could support this country's rapidly growing sports system in the 1990s. Several of the high-profile pioneers responsible for these developments are mentioned in this chapter.

Specific sports services

THE CONTRIBUTION OF SPORTS SCIENCE

During the last 25 years there has been an extraordinary improvement in international sport performances. This is partly due to the increased participation in sport, especially among athletes of other races, who sometimes have an advantage in certain sports and events because of their particular body build and/or body biochemistry.[1] Other factors, such as higher living standards and better facilities, equipment and coaching methods, have also been responsible for these improvements. However, the biggest single factor is the rapid development of sports science and its recent application to training and sports techniques.

Sports science was originally a very small sub-discipline of sports medicine, which was practised in a rudimentary form for more than 200 years in northern and central Europe. Sports medicine came from the Continent to the United States in the latter part of the 19th century and there developed almost in parallel with European advances. In the late 1920s and early 1930s, sports science slowly moved away from sports medicine, setting up a basic discipline of its own. It was traditionally stronger in the United States at that time because it became the scientific basis of physical education in many American universities, whereas Europe had no such systematic development in the field of physical education until after World War II.[2]

The father of sports science in Australia was Professor Frank Cotton, the Professor of Physiology in the Faculty of Medicine at The University of Sydney from the mid-1940s to 1955. 'Prof', as he was known, was the epitome of the absent-minded professor and his boundless enthusiasm made him appear somewhat eccentric at times. Cotton's research at Harvard University in the United States during the 1930s had been in cardiovascular physiology, which equipped him well for his important contribution to the Allied war effort during the Second World War. In 1941 at The University of Sydney, he developed the Anti-G (gravity) Suit which prevented fighter pilots from blacking out during steep dives when engaged in dog fights with the enemy, thus saving the lives of many young British, Australian, Canadian and later American pilots. As well as being an excellent academic, Cotton had been a New South Wales swimming champion in the 1920s and because of his personal experience in devising his own training methods, he had a strong interest in the physiology of training. He

Professor Frank Cotton, who held the Chair of Physiology in the Faculty of Medicine at the University of Sydney, was the father of sports science in Australia. (By courtesy of F. Carlile.)

applied these and other methods to swimmers, runners and oarsmen in the latter half of the 1940s and the early 1950s, with excellent results.

Cotton also developed talent identification tests for athletes and was famous for his bicycle and rowing ergometer testing. His young protege in the 1940s was Forbes Carlile, a lecturer in physiology at The University of Sydney. Carlile was interested in research in the physiology of training, but he also wanted to test the revolutionary training methods he and Cotton had devised.

In 1955 Carlile resigned from The University of Sydney to become a full-time coach. Fortunately, he did not forget his cutting-edge research on the stress of training, which he continued in his own privately-funded sports science laboratory.

The mid-1950s was an opportune time for Carlile to conduct this research. Several Australian coaches, notably Franz Stampfl and Percy Cerutty in athletics, and Frank Guthrie, Harry Gallagher, Sam Herford and Don Talbot in swimming, had devised very rigorous interval training regimes which were much more intensive than any training administered to athletes up to that time. The training maxim of the day was 'No pain, no gain', and Australian athletes and swimmers had moved to the top in international competition by the mid-1950s. These methods were obviously valuable for those individuals who could withstand the high levels of stress; however, many others were burned out and soon moved out of their sport. Fortunately, Carlile's research monitored the athletes' adaptation to intensive training and he generally endorsed the new training methods, but he added a note of caution, warning coaches that there was a 'fine line between training and straining' and that it was important not to overstress their charges. Further information on Forbes Carlile is presented in the following section.[3]

EARLY DEVELOPMENTS IN SPORTS SCIENCE

It took the formation of the Division of Physical Education at The University of Western Australia for the field of sports science to become systematically established in Australia. The writer took up duty as the head of this division in early 1968, establishing the first degree course in Australia for physical education majors early in the same year. A master's degree quickly followed and a PhD degree was granted soon afterwards. These programs and post-graduate degrees could not have been conducted without a competent staff, which gradually grew from 1968 onwards.[4]

The curriculum for the first bachelor's degree in Australia in this field included several sports science subjects, as did the first coaching accreditation course, which was mounted as early as mid-1969 at The University of Western Australia. This was conducted under the auspices of the National Fitness Council of Western Australia, mostly by personnel from The University of Western Australia. Those involved in the program included the writer and his colleagues Alan Morton, Brian Blanksby, Ken Fitch, Bruce Elliott and Frank Pyke, who later became professors, as well as Drs Gerry Jones, Richard Lockwood and Jeff Watson. Len Pavy, from the then Nedlands Secondary Teachers' College, also made a valuable contribution to the program.[5]

During the early 1970s, research in sports science gradually gathered momentum in the upgraded Department of Physical Education and Recreation at The University of Western Australia. Significant investigations were undertaken in swimming, rowing, rugby, track and field, squash and Australian (rules) football. The quality of the research was high for that era and, for the first time in sports science in Australia, the above staff had their work published in national and international refereed journals.[6]

THE ROLE OF THE AIS IN SPORTS SCIENCE

The big breakthrough in sports science outside the university sector took place when the AIS was opened in Canberra at the beginning of 1981. A Sports Science Unit was established early in the same year, with Dr Dick Telford, a talented exercise physiologist from Melbourne, as the first head of the unit. His great strength was that he understood the coaching field well, having been a very competent distance running coach in his own right. His offsider, a sports science technician, was a young runner named Robert de Castella, who later distinguished himself as a world marathon running champion. Upon his retirement from competitive sport, de Castella was to become the director of the institute.[7]

The demand for sports science services grew rapidly at the AIS as the coaches began to realise how valuable the input from the scientists was. Names such as Dr (now Professor) Allan Hahn *(see accompanying profile below)*, Drs Bruce Mason and Mario Lafortune and sports psychologist Jeff Bond, as well as Dick Telford himself, rapidly became well known in Australian sport. They were the 'quiet achievers' of the institute, because in most cases they worked behind the scenes in an athlete support role. This group serviced the athletes well, profiling them thoroughly, suggesting how their weaknesses could be strengthened and monitoring the athletes while they were in training or during competition. It was this very practical approach which enabled sports science to be established as an important ingredient in the preparation of elite athletes in Australia, as well as being an essential component in the area of talent identification.[8,9,10,11]

In order to expand the traditional role of the Australian Institute of Sport (AIS), the Sports Science and Medicine Centre was formed in 1991. This was done to enable AIS scholarship holders or other high-level athletes in the National Sports Program to receive medical or sports science assistance while in Canberra or during interstate or overseas competition. Rather than being a local service unit for just the institute's athletes, it assumed a national co-ordinating role. In addition to providing services for athletes, the centre commenced an applied research function and during the last decade has taken on several high-quality research and development projects.[12,13]

THE QUIET ACHIEVER

Professor Allan Hahn is an unassuming man and on first meeting one would never suspect that in his youth he was a competitive boxer or that he is now one of Australia's leading sports scientists.

Allan completed his post-graduate studies at The University of Western Australia in the early 1980s and, after a short stint at The University of Canberra, joined the AIS in 1984 as a senior research scientist. Ten years later he became Head of the Department of Physiology and Applied Nutrition and was awarded a Professorial Chair in 1998. While in the above positions he has published more than 100 research papers in national and international journals.

However, Allan Hahn is probably best known for his pioneering work, first in athletic profiling and then in talent identification, which he began with young rowers at the AIS in 1987. Since that time he has also worked with cyclists, swimmers and kayakists, both in identifying their talent and helping them to reach their ultimate performance.

He has also investigated the new field of micro-technology, which enables coaches and sports scientists to monitor an athlete's performance while in heavy training or competition. Allan has already investigated the advantages of this cutting-edge field, which will revolutionise both training and sport performance in the future. When asked recently whether Australia could afford to adopt this new technology, he said: 'It is essential that we enter this new field now, otherwise we will be left behind the more scientifically advanced countries in North America and Europe. And it will take us a long time to close the gap if we don't keep up with our competitors.'

Professor Hahn's total contribution to sports science in Australia over almost two decades has been immense. Australia's sportsmen and women are fortunate that he intends to continue in his present role for some time into the future.[14]

THE AUSTRALIAN ASSOCIATION FOR EXERCISE AND SPORTS SCIENCE (AAESS)

In contrast to other professional fields in Australia such as physiotherapy, exercise and sports science made a delayed entry into the professional arena. At the Bicentennial Sports Medicine Congress in Sydney in 1988, Professor Tony Parker, the then President of Sports Medicine Australia (SMA), convened a meeting to discuss the need for a professional body to represent the fields of exercise and sports science.

Several meetings were held at subsequent SMA conferences and in 1992 the organisation was formally constituted in Perth, with Professor Parker elected as the inaugural president, a position he held for eight years. This development was not without opposition, as both SMA and the Australian Council for Health, Physical Education and Recreation believed that their respective organisations should provide the vehicle for professional representation of exercise and sports scientists. A small steering committee, co-ordinated through The University of Wollongong by Tony Parker and Tom Penrose, concentrated initially on determining the criteria for membership and other essential functions of the new association, which developed rapidly over the next 11 years.

The goals of AAESS are to enhance the profession of exercise and sports science through advocacy; to clarify the role and responsibilities of practitioners in the field; to accredit graduates; and to protect the rights of professionals in this area. AAESS is currently implementing procedures for the accreditation of Australian university programs, as well as playing a crucial role in the formation of an international organisation which would co-ordinate exercise and sports science professionals around the world.[15]

SPORTS SCIENCE IN UNIVERSITIES, INSTITUTES AND ACADEMIES

Currently Australia has a great many well-trained sports scientists, both in its various university departments of human movement and the state institutes or academies of sport. At least 12 universities in Australia now have sports science units that are the equal of those in the better American or European universities. They have above-average research facilities and conduct high-quality post-graduate supervision, but their basic research is often limited because they have to rely mostly on university funding, which is not adequate for this type of investigation. This is because there is currently not a single funding body which has a category for either sports science or sports medicine in Australia.

The state institutes or academies of sport are in a similar situation. They have funds to carry out service testing and to develop databases for their athletes, but none of them can afford to conduct basic research in order to try to solve many of the more fundamental problems which arise in sport. This situation makes the establishment of a funding and co-ordinating body in sports science and sports medicine research imperative.[16]

SPORTS SCIENCE RESEARCH AT THE SYDNEY 2000 OLYMPICS

Because Australia has a competent group of applied sports scientists, it was chosen by the International Olympic Committee to gather data in the field of biomechanics on selected athletes before and during the Sydney 2000 Games. Professor Bruce Elliott, a well-known sports biomechanist from The University of Western Australia, was the supervisor of this project, which yielded some very valuable sports science data on elite athletes in eight sports and events. This is the first time that a project of this magnitude had been undertaken and research of this nature should now become an important component of all future Olympic Games.[17]

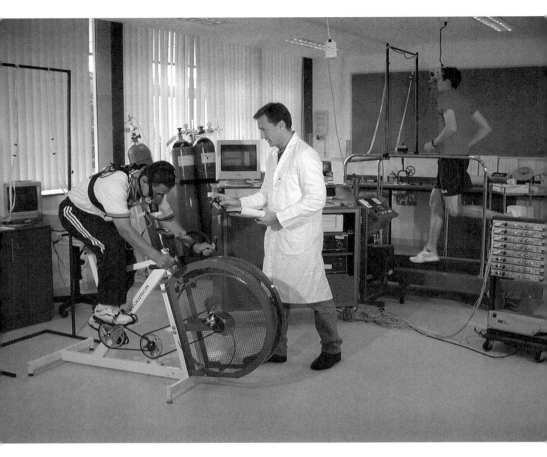

Part of the exercise physiology laboratory in the School of Human Movement and Exercise Science at The University of Western Australia. (By courtesy of the School of Human Movement and Exercise Science, UWA.)

AUSTRALIA'S INTERNATIONAL STATUS IN SPORTS SCIENCE

Australia is generally seen across the board as one of the top half-dozen nations in the world in the field of sports science. This is particularly so in two areas: the methodology for infusing sports science into coaching techniques; and the efficiency with which Australian sports scientists have been able to identify talent and monitor training. This country is therefore seen as being able to apply sports science knowledge to sport performance, and this has been invaluable to its elite performers.

However, Australia has been less successful in contributing to the international body of knowledge in sports science. There is a general research malaise in Australia and sports science is only one of many fields which have been neglected. A reasonable level of funding is required to significantly improve research output and better co-ordination is needed between the various groups which contribute to the field. This could be remedied by the establishment of an independent National Sports Science and Medicine Research Council, which would be best located in Canberra at the AIS. It could then act as a co-ordinating body with the AIS, the state and territory institutes or academies of sport and the various university schools of human movement and exercise science, as well as with industry.

In the recent past, approximately $2.5 million each year has been allocated to research and development in sports science and medicine by the Australian Sports Commission in this country.[18] However, for Australian sport to increase its body of knowledge in these related fields, to the point where it can positively benefit from this research within the next decade, at least $6 million (or approximately five per cent of the federal sport budget) needs to be spent annually from 2003 onwards. Australia's closest sporting competitors in Europe are already allocating at least five per cent of their sports budgets to research and development, which is two to three times more than Australia currently spends.

AUSTRALIAN SPORTS SCIENCE IN THE FUTURE

In the previous section, a case was made for the establishment of a National Sports Science and Medical Research Council to ensure that Australia can maintain its position with other top sporting nations. This council must lobby hard to develop the field of micro-technology in sport. This new technology measures biological and mechanical variables using instruments that are so small they can be worn very comfortably by the athlete, and which can monitor the above parameters during training or low-level competition without impeding performance.[19] The Director of the AIS, Michael Scott, who has had extensive experience in the latest developments in elite sports performance, recently predicted that current techniques used by high-performance athletes would be replaced by micro-technology as early as the Athens Olympics. In fact, he stated that 'Australia's 2004 Olympic team would be the first [Australian athletes] to wear the next-generation [of] performance monitors'.[20]

Even though many of the above technologies will be developed in partnership with micro-technology companies, a reasonable level of funding and scientifically-trained personnel will be required to trial and adapt the micro-equipment to the point where it can be of value in sport. If funding is not attended to shortly, Australia will miss the boat and wallow helplessly in the wake of its competitors.

SPORTS COACHING

As Australia's amateur sports system slowly evolved, it generally followed the British model, which was probably the best in the world in the 19th century and the first part of the 20th century. Coaching in this country was also modelled on British lines, with the majority of coaches serving an informal apprenticeship, often as assistant coaches. As sport became more specialised after the Second World War, Britain set up practically-oriented short duration coaching courses through several of its major national sporting organisations, as well as through the Rothmans' National Sports Foundation. The former development did not occur so easily in Australia, except in the sport of swimming, where regular coaching clinics were held in New South Wales from the early 1960s. The Rothmans' National Sports Foundation in Australia also mounted courses similar to those in Britain, and these were valuable for the sports which participated in those programs.[21]

At the same time as the post-World War II coaching programs were slowly evolving in Britain, the Eastern European countries were developing a much more centralised and professional sports system, an integral part of which was a specialised coach education program with a strong sports science base. It wasn't long before the Western Europeans were also on a similar track, but they were less professional about it. By the late 1960s and early 1970s Canada had a reasonably well-developed coach education program, but the United States relied on its tertiary education system to develop the majority of its coaches. In fact, the American system was, and still is, a good one, in that it used mainly trained physical education specialists, many of whom had also been very competent athletes. The sport of golf, however, had a different development in the United States, as it used its own well-trained professionals to coach the young trainees in its association.[22]

AUSTRALIA'S EARLY COACHING DEVELOPMENTS

Except for the Rothmans' National Sport Foundation and the coaching accreditation courses being run in Western Australia, the majority of Australian coaches came through an ad hoc apprentice system before 1982. Australia was also renowned for its tough 'blood and guts' coaches, particularly in the body contact sports, but coaches like Franz Stampfl and Percy Cerutty in athletics, Harry Hopman in tennis, Frank Guthrie, Harry Gallagher, as well as Sep Prosser and Don Talbot in swimming also trained their athletes very rigorously. Several coaches had seen military service in the Second World War and urged their athletes on as though they were in uniform. Punitive action was sometimes even taken with so-called 'slackers', who were ordered to do more push-ups or extra laps after training if the coach felt they had not put enough effort into the session. Some coaches, even at the top level in rugby league and Australian (rules) football, still subject their players to this type of discipline.[23]

AUSTRALIA'S COACHING SUCCESSES — WHY?

As Eunice Gill has pointed out, the Australian Coaching Accreditation Scheme is 'an outstanding example of the co-operation which is possible between government and sport'.[24] With around a quarter of a million coaches trained in Australia over the last 24 years, both young and not so young athletes are in good hands. This is largely because many of Australia's better coaches have a sound understanding of the biological and social science base which now underpins modern coaching. The Australian Coaching Council (ACC), whose first chairman was Paul Brettell, did an excellent job in guiding the early development of this program. Laurie Woodman, the former Director of the ACC, should also be congratulated for his role in developing the coaching accreditation courses; and Peter Corcoran, its long-standing chairman, as well as the many people who have been members of the council over the last 20 years, must also be acknowledged.

As well, several very competent people in the late 1940s and 1950s led the way with science-based coaching in Australia. Although Professor Frank Cotton did not actively coach, he and Forbes Carlile were the first scientists to develop a sports science-based philosophy of coaching in Australia. Carlile's wife, Ursula, has coached many international-level swimmers and was the first female selected by the Australian Swimming Union to coach the women's team for the 1972 Olympic Games in Munich.

Another coach who developed a science-based program was the swimming coach Harry Gallagher, who was responsible for the development of two of Australia's famous Olympians, Dawn Fraser and Jon Henricks. Gallagher had no formal training in the coaching field, but wisely sought advice from Frank Cotton, who helped him to apply some useful scientific knowledge to the training of his swimmers. Another very successful coach at an international level was Don Talbot. Don had first trained as a primary school teacher but, realising he needed a better scientific basis for his coaching, he completed a master's degree in Canada some time later.

The establishment of the AIS is another reason why coaching is so strong and so professional in Australia. Bob Ellicott, the Minister for Sport in 1980, when plans were being laid for the first year of operation of the institute in 1981, decided that Don Talbot would make a good executive director. His rationale was that Talbot would understand both high-level sport and those people who trained the athletes, namely the coaches.[25] Talbot's appointment was a good choice, as was the selection of the major coaches in the first four years. The first top-level coaches were Adrian Hurley (basketball), Wilma Shakespear (netball), Jimmy Shoulder (soccer), Kasuya Honda (gymnastics), Ray Ruffels (tennis), Kelvin Giles (track and field), Lyn Jones (weight-lifting) and Dennis Pursley and Bill Sweetenham (swimming). Later, other excellent coaches such as Richard Aggis (hockey), Warrick Forbes and Ju-Ping Tian (gymnastics), Pat Clohessy (track), Heather MacKay and Geoff Hunt (squash), Steve Foley (diving), Charles Turner (water polo), Rheinhold Batschi (rowing), Charlie Walsh (cycling) and Rodney Marsh (cricket) were appointed to the AIS coaching

THE CARLILE CONTRIBUTION

Forbes Carlile has been at the forefront of competitive swimming in this country for 55 years, and as one of his swimming guinea pigs, the writer was fortunate to know him in his early career.

Forbes was always fascinated by both science and sport, but in the post-World War II period there was no career pathway in sports science or scientific coaching. Therefore, in the tradition of a true pioneer, he forged his own path, conceiving a scientific coaching system for Australia from which many of our athletes have greatly benefited.

While a student at The University of Sydney, Forbes was a very good sportsman, first as a swimmer and rugby player and later as Australia's first Olympic modern pentathlon representative in 1952. Forbes had begun part-time coaching in the late 1940s with an experimental squad known as the Palm Beach Amateur Swimming Club, which gave him the opportunity to combine sports science with practical coaching. During the latter part of the 1940s and early 50s, he was a lecturer in the Department of Physiology at The University of Sydney, but resigned in 1955 when Professor Frank Cotton died. Carlile established his own sports science laboratory at Drummoyne Swimming Pool in Sydney, naming it 'The Frank Cotton Memorial Laboratory' after his mentor. He then set about conducting research in sports science, testing a large number of swimmers and many athletes from other sports.

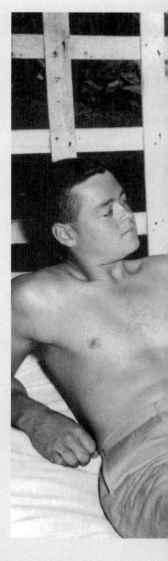

Forbes would be the first to say that he was very fortunate when a young female physical education graduate applied for a job at the Drummoyne pool in 1957. He and Ursula were subsequently married and have been a very effective coaching partnership for 45 years. Between them they have coached 16 Olympic medallists and world record-holders, becoming two of the most successful coaches in the history of Australian sport.

Forbes Carlile has not only been a very fine coach, but more importantly, along with Professor Frank Cotton, was a co-founder of Australian sports science.[26]

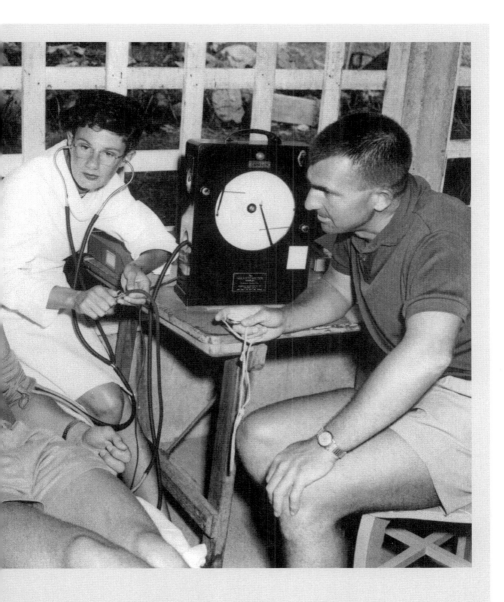

Forbes and Ursula Carlile, who became Australia's foremost scientific coaches, test Terry Gathercole, a former world breaststroke champion. (By courtesy of F. Carlile.)

staff. Many of them were influenced by the AIS sports science and medicine staff after co-operating with them for several years, and thus they gradually adopted a more scientific approach.[27]

The overall effect of the above coaches was very positive. The national sporting organisations were so impressed with the improvement of their athletes and the input of the AIS coaches that they began to lobby the Federal Government to provide not only national coaches, but also national directors of coaching, with the task of coaching the coaches. In very strong sports, the states with better-developed sports systems also started to press their state governments to assist with full-time professional coaching.

The Australian coaching system is fortunate to have many coaches who are well-trained but who still incorporate some of the toughness of the past into their coaching techniques. It seems that the most successful Australian coaches not only possess the positive characteristics of many of those mentioned above, but also have an inclusive style which leads to the development of an intrinsically motivated athlete.

THE CONTRIBUTION OF SPORTS MEDICINE

Although European medicine had been involved in the field of physical culture and its effect on the prevention of disease for more than 200 years, it was only in the early 20th century that the sub-discipline of sports medicine evolved to the point where an international body could be formed. This took place in 1928 when the *Fédération Internationale Médicine Sportive (FIMS)* was established in Europe, with 11 countries becoming foundation members.[28]

The federation grew steadily from its base in Europe and its focus at first was on the treatment of sports injuries and the application of medicine to physical activity and sport. As the field developed outside Europe, its main emphasis was on the treatment of sports injuries, particularly in the United Kingdom and the United States. However, it was not until 1954, as the Melbourne Olympics were approaching, that Australia had any affiliation with the world body or displayed any interest in this new field.

The Australian Sports Medicine Federation (ASMF) was officially founded in 1963, after various disputes between the state sports medicine associations had held up the establishment of a true national body for several years.[29] There were some disagreements over the status of the non-medical membership, but by 1970 the majority of members had agreed that a multi-disciplinary model was the most desirable one to adopt.

Barry Cohen was the first Australian politician to suggest in 1972 that the Federal Government should assist with sports medicine research in Australia,[30] and the Bloomfield Report in 1973 also recommended Australian Government support.[31] The next major development was the inclusion of sports medicine at the AIS, and Dr Ken Maguire, a well-credentialled sports medicine specialist from Perth, took up a position in early 1982. With the addition of the then

Dr Peter Fricker, who began by assisting Ken Maguire for several sessions a week, this small team set up the AIS Sports Medicine Centre.

From day one it functioned well, due mainly to the enthusiasm and dedication of the group. When Ken Maguire left to return to Perth in 1983, he was replaced by Peter Fricker on a full-time basis.[32] Sports medicine at the AIS has grown rapidly and has been a great`success story in which many people have participated. However, for this type of outcome to happen, a group must have positive leadership and this has been supplied by Professor Fricker, who has made an outstanding contribution to the AIS and also to Sports Medicine Australia. He received an Order of Australia award for his services, both to the institute and to sports medicine in Australia, in the Queen's Birthday honours list in 1993.

SPORTS MEDICINE IN AUSTRALIA

Since 1963, sports medicine in Australia has operated under the aegis of the Australian Sports Medicine Federation, which now has the operative title of Sports Medicine Australia (SMA). It is currently a professional body of 3250 members representing several disciplines, who focus on sports medicine from different specialised perspectives. For the first 20 years, the federation concentrated almost entirely on the treatment of sports injuries, but in the early 1970s its membership broadened to include physiotherapists, dentists and sports scientists. In recent years dietitians, sports psychologists and podiatrists have been encouraged to become members and have greatly broadened the field's focus in this country.[33]

With such a breadth of expertise, SMA has been active both in the political arena and in adopting various positions on controversial and important issues. In Chapter Two of this book, the crucial lobbying role played in 1972 by the then senior executive of the federation was explained in detail. There is no doubt that this group had an important role in the setting up of the first Australian Government Ministry for Recreation *(see Appendix A)*. Sports Medicine Australia has also initiated up-to-date policies which have been crucial in the areas of drugs in sport, the prevention of cardiovascular disease, safety in children's sport, sports competition during pregnancy and the regulations preventing players from continuing to participate with open wounds. There are several other initiatives currently being pursued.

Volunteering has been crucial to the contribution sports medicine makes to sport in Australia. SMA is an excellent example of a highly professional non-government agency which operates on a voluntary basis, except for a handful of professional administrators who are responsible for implementing the policies of its council. Since this body was formed, well over a million Australians have received free medical treatment and a great deal of valuable advice from SMA doctors. These volunteers provide a free medical service for several thousand sports teams each week and are present in a voluntary capacity at numerous sporting venues on a weekly basis around Australia. This dedicated service began in this country and can only be found in a handful of Commonwealth countries which have followed Australia's lead.

Few Australians would be aware that Sports Medicine Australia has also qualified more than 42 000 sports trainers in its courses since 1983. These volunteers administer first aid and treat sports injuries at the many thousands of locations where sport is played in Australia each week. The members have demonstrated their professionalism and dedication to the welfare of their fellow Australians for almost 40 years, and SMA now ranks with the Australian Surf Lifesaving Movement, the Sea Rescue Service, the rural fire services and the state emergency services as outstanding examples of voluntary community service.

AUSTRALIA'S INTERNATIONAL REPUTATION IN SPORTS MEDICINE

As with the field of sports science, sports medicine in Australia has a very good international reputation, and this has resulted from the way in which knowledge in this field has been skillfully applied to Australian sportsmen and women, as Australian doctors and physiotherapists practising in sports medicine are regarded as very competent practitioners. They have embraced the Australian sports ethos, as they feel that they are an integral part of sport in this country. Furthermore, the sports medicine service which was offered to athletes at the Sydney Olympics was second to none. The feedback given by the visiting coaches and their athletes who received assistance at the Olympic Village Polyclinic (Sports Medicine Centre) was very positive, and they left Australia with nothing but praise for the treatment and advice they had been given.

However, sports medicine must not rest on its laurels, as it is not enough to only apply existing knowledge to the field. Little systematic research has been done in Australia in sports medicine, apart from the AIS Sports Science and Medicine Centre, The University of Western Australia, where Professors Fitch and Morton have been very productive, and Monash University, where Dr Barry Oakes has conducted some high-quality research. Sports Medicine Australia needs to lobby the powers that be to improve Australia's research output and to rectify this situation as soon as possible.

In addition, Australian sports medicine specialists should by now have full consultant status. The existing College of Sports Physicians, led at various times by Drs Bruckner, Creighton, Fricker and Steinweg, has done an exceptional job, often in a hostile environment with opposition coming from other medical specialists as well as the Federal Government. However, it is high time for fully qualified sports medicine specialists to practise in this field and significant lobbying needs to be done in the next half decade to achieve that outcome.

LEADERS IN AUSTRALIAN SPORTS MEDICINE

During the 40-year history of SMA in this country, there are many individuals without whose leadership Australia would not have gained its worldwide reputation in sports medicine.

One of the earliest members to have a significant impact on the development of the field was Dr Brian Corrigan, a rheumatologist from Sydney and national president in the early 1960s, who also held several offices in New South Wales. Mr Howard Toyne, an orthopaedic surgeon from Melbourne and a treasurer of *FIMS*, held various offices in Victoria for many years and was national president in the early to mid-1970s. The writer was the first non-medical national president in 1972-73; and Professor Ken Fitch of Perth served as the national secretary for eight years and the national president for two years in the late 1960s and 1970s, making an outstanding contribution. He has been profiled on the following page.

Other pioneers were Dr Geoff Vanderfield from New South Wales, who was very active in the 1970s; Dr Kevin Hobbs of Queensland, national president in the mid-1970s and founder of the sports trainers' program; and Dr Jack Refshauge from Victoria, who became an Australian president and later a vice-president of the international body. Others to make their mark were Dr Bill Webb from New South Wales, a very active president; Dr Brian Sandow, a former president and the head doctor of the Australian Olympic Team on many occasions; and Professor Tony Parker, a sports scientist from Queensland who became the second non-medical doctor to be elected president of the federation in the mid-1980s. He was very successful in developing the non-medical sub-disciplines of SMA.

Professor Peter Fricker of the AIS has been a major contributor to the development of sports medicine as an educator, researcher, author and clinician. He will long be remembered for the way in which he has integrated sports medicine into the AIS program, establishing it as a vital part of the Australian sports system.

The current patron, Sir William Refshauge, deserves a special mention. This outstanding former high-ranking soldier and Commonwealth Director-General of Public Health is an excellent role model for every member of Sports Medicine Australia and has been an inspirational patron during his long term of office.

A SPORTS MEDICINE PIONEER

Professor Ken Fitch, a former sprinter and Australian (rules) footballer, is a member of a select band of pioneers of Australian sports medicine, having spent 48 years giving exemplary service to the Australian community.

As a young registrar, Ken became convinced that exercise was a valuable therapy for patients with musculoskeletal and cardiovascular disorders. In order to better understand many of the unanswered questions in the field, he has devoted almost half a century to research, authoring more than 100 academic papers and co-authoring several books. Much of this work was done in the Department of Human Movement and Exercise Science at The University of Western Australia, where he was a sports medicine consultant and later an adjunct professor.

As well as pursuing his research with vigour, Professor Fitch also became a highly reputed sports medicine physician, accompanying several Olympic teams overseas. He was the team doctor for the West Coast Eagles for 15 years and Director of the Royal Perth Hospital's Sports Medicine Clinic, while still conducting a busy private practice. Professor Fitch also spent several years in various official capacities in sports medicine in Western Australia, before serving as national secretary for eight years and two years as the SMA president.

Ken's competence was recognised by the International Olympic Committee, who invited him to join their Medical Commission in 1985. He is currently Deputy Chair of the World Anti-Doping Agency and a member of several other national and international sports medicine committees.

Finally, Ken Fitch's service to research, his patients, his profession and to all the young doctors he has assisted over many years has been acknowledged by several honours, the highest of which is his 1979 Order of Australia award.[34]

Professor Ken Fitch, a pioneer of Australian sports medicine, has devoted almost half a century to research and development in this field. (By courtesy of Ken Fitch.)

CHALLENGES TO SMA IN THE FUTURE

During the last 40 years, Sports Medicine Australia has been a very positive contributor to the development of the Australian sports system. In its short history, its members have strongly supported many health initiatives and given caring treatment to a large number of Australians. SMA's status in this country has never been higher and its lobbying capacity never greater. It is time, therefore, to strike while the iron is hot in order to implement the following initiatives:

- to lobby the Federal Government to establish a National Sports Science and Medicine Research Council;

- to approach the major entities who comprise the Australian sports system to enlist their help in lobbying the appropriate government agencies, with a view to establishing a full medical specialty in sports medicine.

If SMA continues to perform as well as it has in its short history and if the above goals can be gradually achieved, it will provide a more informed body of knowledge which will improve the performance and participation levels in sport throughout Australia. In addition, it will produce more highly-qualified sports medicine doctors, who will ultimately improve patient care in this country.

RECENT DEVELOPMENTS IN SPORTS STUDIES

Since the early 1930s, the field of sports studies as it relates to social history and sociology has been systematically studied in the United States. However, there was no national academic or professional body formed until 1973, when the National American Society for Sports History (NASSH) was set up.

Formalisation of the United States society took place only four years before the first Sporting Traditions Conference was held in Australia in 1977 at The University of New South Wales. Several years later, the Australian Society for Sports History (ASSH) was formed at the fourth Sporting Traditions Conference held in Melbourne in July 1983. Its objectives were to promote research into sports studies in Australia and to organise meetings and publish materials which generate interest and scholarship in the field. In 1984 the first journal was published, entitled *Sporting Traditions*, which has carried a wide range of articles relating to Australian sports history and is highly rated when compared to similar international journals.[35] In addition, several sports historians have authored various books in the field and Walla Walla Press, Australia's only dedicated sports history publisher, has produced several highly specialised books in this area.

A critical analysis of papers presented at the biennial Australian Sporting Traditions Conference, articles published in the society's journal and several books relating to Australian sports history indicate that ASSH is alive and well. There is no doubt that Australia needs an active group of social scientists who can provide a critical and reflective view of Australian sports culture so as to identify areas of weakness in the system. They can also reflect on the social utility of sport and its value to Australian society.

Several pioneers have collectively spent many thousands of hours establishing the sports history field in Australia and should be mentioned in this work for their efforts. Dr Colin Tatz was the inaugural president of ASSH while Dr Wray Vamplew was the first editor of *Sporting Traditions*. Significant contributions have been made by Professors John Daly, Max Howell, and Brian Stoddart, as well as Dr Murray Phillips and Associate Professors Ian Jobling, Ed Jaggard and Richard Cashman, who is the current President of the Australian Society for Sports History.[36]

NATIONAL SPORTS ORGANISATIONS

There are currently 120 national sport and recreation bodies in existence in Australia, each one of which has a club network co-ordinated in each state or territory by a state sports organisation. In some cases the national body is still known as an 'association' or 'federation', but they are now generally referred to as national sports organisations (NSOs).

Each of the state organisations represents the clubs in its state or territory at the national level and together they make up the NSO, which is the peak body for that particular sport throughout Australia. Each national body is incorporated and represents its members in several forums, both inside and outside Australia. Currently there are about 50 major NSOs with over 3.6 million members in total, as well as 70 smaller ones with about half a million members. [37]

The management of the modern national sports organisation is far superior to that of several decades ago, especially in the larger ones, some of which have more than a quarter of a million members. The ten largest national sports organisations are listed in Table 6.1 below. [38]

Table 6.1
The ten largest National Sports Organisations in Australia

Sport	Registered members
Golf	492 629
Basketball	456 191
Australian football	448 410
Netball	338 212
Soccer	334 547
Bowls	329 894
Cricket	311 932
Tennis	200 907
Rugby league	140 780
Rugby union	136 000

SOURCE Adapted from Sport 2000 Task Force — R. Oakley Chair (1999) 'Shaping Up — A Review of Commonwealth Involvement in Sport and Recreation in Australia', Commonwealth of Australia, Canberra, pp.113-114.

The majority of the national sporting organisations in Australia are partially funded by the sports commission and are mostly run by capable professional managers. Because they control competition at the national level, they are generally efficient and provide positive leadership for their constituents. Australian standards are currently high in a range of sports; therefore their senior officers and officials often represent their organisations internationally on the world bodies of their respective sports.

To enable the reader to understand how these organisations function, five of them are discussed briefly in the remainder of this chapter. Those described below have been chosen because they are unique to Australia, because they have obtained good results at the international level, or because they represent a wide spectrum of age groups and genders.

AUSTRALIAN RUGBY UNION (ARU)

The ARU is the smallest of the four football codes currently played in Australia with approximately 136 000 registered players. However, its growth rate in the last 12 months was almost 12 per cent.[39] In comparison to other national sports organisations in this country, it is only a middle-sized association, but it performs well above its numerical strength because it is well managed. This is demonstrated by a comparison with the number of registered players of the countries in the northern hemisphere against which Australia competes so successfully. The British Isles have 5.7 times more registered players and the English Rugby Union has almost four times as many players as Australia. In the southern hemisphere region, South Africa has double the number of registered players, whereas New Zealand has only recently dropped slightly behind Australia.

The World Cup victory in 1991 gave rugby union the impetus and the drive to plan a very professional development program. It was put into practice with the arrival in 1995 of the new managing director, John O'Neil, who was formerly the Chief Executive of the Colonial State Bank in New South Wales. By professionalising the ARU, the management of rugby in this country has become more efficient and the appointment of competent staff since that time has had a positive effect on its development. The 1995 change from amateur to professional status also gave rugby a significant boost, as did the gaining of TV rights in conjunction with the Super 12 series and the Tri-Nations Tests.[40] Now that Australia has been awarded the 2003 Rugby World Cup Tournament, the third-largest world championship in existence, further growth seems assured.[41]

The ARU has one of the most efficient coaching development programs in Australia. A great deal of credit must go to Dick Marks, Brian O'Shea and David Clark, all of whom played a significant role in setting up the early coaching program. Warren Robilliard, the current Coach Education Manager, has recently been the major force behind this program, which commences with *mini rugby* and continues to the Australian Coaching Council's Level III course.[42] Level III coaches have the opportunity to be selected to attend the Australian Rugby Coaching Academy at Camp Wallaby to improve their coaching skills with international players; and the elite level of coaching, which has a strong sports science and sports medicine basis, is also developing rapidly.

From a development viewpoint, Australian Rugby has a well-defined pathway through which its players can rise to the elite level. It begins with such programs as *try rugby, mini rugby, midi rugby,* and *Walla rugby*, followed by school, junior and senior rugby, the AIS development unit, Super 12 rugby, then to full international level. George Gregan is an example of an Australian player who has progressed along such a pathway, and his profile appears at the end of this section.

The opportunities this program has offered young players in the last decade have seen Australia's international performances skyrocket, especially when Rod McQueen took over as the ARU's head coach. In the recent past, the World Cup, the Tri-Nations Championship, the Bledisloe Cup, the series against the British Lions and the Mandela Challenge Plate[43] were all won by Australian teams. The Wallabies' future performances should continue at a similar level, as the head coach, Eddie Jones, has an enviable record. The Wallabies have also been a great credit to Australia by demonstrating outstanding levels of sportsmanship and fair play, especially when under intense pressure on the field. They have been led in recent years by captains of the quality of Andrew Slack, Nick Farr-Jones, John Eales and George Gregan, all of whom have been fine role models for young Australians; and the administrators, coaches and players of this prestigious national sports organisation have done Australia proud.

SURF LIFE SAVING AUSTRALIA (SLSA)

Surf lifesaving was founded in Australia early in the 20th century and is unique among the world's sporting associations, as historically it has had a two-fold mission. The first is humanitarian, in that its function is to save lives; and the second is to stage competitions in events designed to assist surf lifesavers to improve their rescue skills.

The first club in Australia was formed at Bondi, Sydney in 1906 and was known as the Bondi Surf Bathers' Life Saving Club.[44] In 1907 The Surf Bathing Association of NSW was formed and finally in 1922 the Surf Life Saving Association of Australia came into existence.[45] Since that time, more than 100 countries have modelled their systems on Australia's and there are now 22 countries participating in international competitions. There are 101 000 members belonging to 274 clubs around this country, and members of the SLSA have performed more than 460 000 rescues since 1906.[46] All active members must pass demanding practical and theoretical examinations leading to the award of the Bronze Medallion, and these members are also obliged to donate their time to carry out surf patrols. In fact, they are not allowed to take part in surf competitions unless they perform their voluntary duties.

THE RUGBY GENERAL

George Gregan is currently one of the most effective players in world rugby. Born in Zambia in 1973, George moved to Australia at the age of one and completed his schooling and university studies in Canberra.

His introduction to rugby was at St Edmunds College in the ACT, which has a long tradition of developing elite young players. From school he went on to represent Australia in the Under 19 team in 1992 and the Under 21's in 1994, then broke into Test rugby when he played against Italy at Ballymore in 1994. He had won a scholarship to the AIS in 1993 and 1994 which helped him to hone his already considerable skills. Since that time, George has played 82 games for the Wallabies, as well as 79 for the ACT Brumbies in the Super 12 competition.

One of the world's great tactical half-backs, Gregan is known for his exciting attacking play as well as for his spectacular defence. His ability to scrag-tackle players 30 or more kilograms heavier than himself is legendary.

George has made a smooth transition from vice-captain to captain of the Wallabies since the retirement of John Eales. He was fortunate to be an understudy to Eales over a four-year period and has now matured to the point where he is a tenacious and capable leader of his team. In the year 2001, he was awarded the International Rugby Players' Association Player of the Year award and shortly afterwards he won the inaugural Rugby Medal for Excellence, which recognised his outstanding performance both on and off the field. George will be an inspiring mentor for the younger players who are to be absorbed into the Wallaby team in preparation for the Rugby Union World Cup this year.[47 48]

The rugby 'general', George Gregan, directs play from the base of the scrum while representing Australia against the New Zealand Maori team in Perth in 2002. (Newspix.)

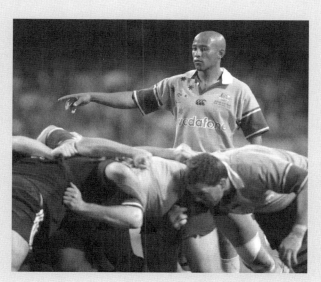

Several surf ski champions have become prominent Olympic kayak paddlers. Clint Robertson, an Olympic K1 gold medallist, has also won the Australian surf ski championship on ten occasions. (By courtesy of Harvie Allison.)

The sport aspect of surf lifesaving is highly competitive. Many of Australia's Olympic swimmers have also been outstanding performers in the surf and some surf ski paddlers have crossed sports to become successful Olympic kayakists. Several ironmen and ironwomen have participated in similar events away from the surf and have also competed with distinction in international triathlons. Each year, the Australian Surf Lifesaving Championships, currently held in south-east Queensland, draw at least 7500 competitors from around Australia.[49]

The events in which the participants compete are surf swimming, ski and board paddling, surfboat rowing, ironman and ironwoman contests, various rescue events and beach events. Some 50 000 people attend the national championships, complementing a big television audience. In addition to club, branch, state and national championships, Australian surf teams have been competing internationally since 1937, when the first competitive tour to New Zealand took place.[50] Since that time many Australian teams have competed with distinction in other countries which have adopted the Australian system.

Australian surf lifesaving has always lived up to the SLSA motto of 'vigilance and service'. This is very much in keeping with the volunteer ethic, which has become a part of the Australian way of life for over a century.

THE PROFESSIONAL GOLFERS' ASSOCIATION OF AUSTRALIA (PGA)

The PGA of Australia was founded in 1911, just after the Australian Open Golf Championship was held at Royal Sydney Golf Club. The association was formed as a direct result of the poor treatment the professionals had received from the club during this tournament.[51] Members of the PGA took around 70 years to gain total acceptance by some of the more conservative amateur golf clubs and associations, but fortunately the days of regarding the 'pro' as little more than a tradesman are long gone. The modern professional is now well accepted by the private clubs, resorts and public courses as a well-informed and essential member of the organisation.

Today the PGA rates as one of Australia's outstanding professional sports associations. Since it corporatised in the late 1980s and introduced professional management to establish its programs, it has gained a reputation around the world for its positive impact on the development of golf in Australia.

In the last two decades, this association of 1600 members has developed an outstanding Professional Development Program (PDP) for its own fully-qualified professionals.[52] The excellent course for its 300-plus trainees annually can be completed over a three-year period, either through the PGA Academy of Golf,[53] or in the Bachelor's Degree of Business with an emphasis on golf, which is run at Griffith University on the Queensland Gold Coast.[54]

Stemming from the above training has been the delivery of a sound golf education program, not only for the 1.4 million Australians who play golf each year,[55] but also for the many junior golfers who participate in the development programs operated by PGA professionals. Golf academies for juniors, such as the Graham Marsh Golf Foundation, which was founded in Western Australia by Graham Marsh and the writer in 1978, the Jack Newton Golf Foundation and the Greg Norman Golf Foundation, have all attracted many young players to the game. The recently founded Schweppes PGA Junior Golf Program is expected to do likewise.

The expert coaching by PGA professionals of Australia's junior golfers at the club, district and state levels has been particularly impressive. The state institutes or academies of sport and the AIS, whose coaches are PGA members, have also played an important role in golf development. These programs have 'put the icing on the cake', so to speak, enabling Australia's young amateur players to reach the international level. In recent years about 20 Australian professional golfers are regularly playing the men's and women's tours in the United States and a similar number are qualified for the European and Japanese tours. There are also many impressive performances taking place in the junior ranks and dozens of young amateur players with scratch handicaps or better are spread throughout the country. Just as impressive for their age, and with low handicaps, are the sub-juniors in many club programs.

The recent history of the PGA of Australia has been a great success story. Peter Thompson, the former five times British Open Champion and a past president of the association, was an inspiring leader; and Neville Wilson, the current president, has been a tireless worker for his organisation. Don Johnson will also be remembered for his pioneering spirit in the early development of the PGA, now capably led by Max Garske as its CEO and Ian Robilliard as its chief of operations.

AUSTRALIAN SWIMMING

Although the first recorded swimming championship in Australia took place in 1846 at Robinson's Baths in the Sydney Domain, it wasn't until the second half of the 19th century that recreational swimming slowly developed in the various colonies, with competitive swimming only becoming popular in the 1890s. Harbour or river baths were first developed in the Sydney region and the coastal rock pools were constructed some time later. The other colonies developed similar facilities to those in NSW, generally ten to 15 years later.

It should not be surprising therefore that Australia has a rich swimming history which has been building up for more than 100 years. Almost all Australians have had some experience with the aquatic environment and a brief history of Australia's swimming exploits has already been covered in Chapter One of this book. National performances have ebbed and flowed for more than a century, since the first Amateur Swimming Association was formed in 1892 in New South Wales.

The main reasons for the variable performances of Australia's elite swimmers were related to the development of facilities and levels of coaching. Australia had reasonably good aquatic facilities for the era of the late 1800s and the first 30 years of the 20th century, because the pools located along the coast and in the rivers were used to good effect. However, this country began to fall behind the United States and Western Europe once filtered and heated pools were constructed there during the 1930s and late-1940s. At the same time there was a steady development of coaching systems overseas, particularly in the United States and Europe.

After the Second World War, and especially in the 1950s and early 60s, Australian swimmers performed very well internationally until sophisticated high school and university programs and facilities became fully operational in the United States. At the same time, the Europeans were steadily recovering from the war and rapidly developing their sports programs as well as their facilities. Because Australia had performed poorly internationally in the 1970s, pressure was applied late in that decade for better facilities. The 80s saw rapid swimming facility development in Australia and coaching education gradually improved. The AIS had begun operations and the state institutes and academies of sport had been evolving rapidly; by the early 1990s they had become an integral part of the swimming system. In addition, Australian Swimming has been ably led by Craig McClatchy, Terry Gathercole and more recently John Devitt. The latter two had been Olympic champions in their own right and were able to give constructive leadership as presidents.

The recent developments in coaching have probably been more responsible than any other factor for propelling Australia to the top as a swimming nation. Don Talbot was appointed head coach in 1989 and quickly moulded the coaches, sports scientists and all those associated with the sport into a close-knit group. It was a unified team in every respect, known as 'Team Talbot' as the Sydney 2000 Olympics approached.[56]

This team approach has not only paid off with magnificent results in the pool, as demonstrated again at the 2001 world championships, but has produced a group of outstanding young ambassadors for Australia. Many young role models have emerged from the Australian swimming team and it is hoped that other young Australians will continue to emulate them.

Head swimming coach Don Talbot climbs from the pool after being thrown in by his winning Australian team — often referred to as 'Team Talbot'. (Newspix.)

AUSTRALIA'S LATEST 'SUPERFISH'

Currently Australia's greatest sportsman, and regarded as one of the best athletes of all time, Ian Thorpe has been a phenomenon since the age of 14, when as a 400m freestyle specialist he became the youngest male to qualify for any Australian swim team. That was for the 1997 Pan Pacific Championships in Japan, where he won two silver medals and the enduring adulation of the Japanese fans. Shortly after, he won over Australian crowds by donating his prizemoney of $25,000 to charity when he became the first swimmer to break a world record at the new Sydney Aquatic Centre.

He then won two gold medals at the World Championships in 1998 and four gold medals at the Commonwealth Games in Kuala Lumpur, before entering the Sydney Olympics with the hopes of the nation behind him. There he suffered his only defeat in a long-course 200m or 400m freestyle event since he became a senior swimmer, to Dutchman Pieter van den Hoogenband in the 200m freestyle, but still came away with three Olympic gold medals and two silver. His greatest performance, however, was at the 2001 World Championships in Japan, where he won an unprecedented six gold medals. He followed that up with another six golds and a silver at the 2002 Commonwealth Games in Manchester. Still only 20 years old, Thorpe has already broken 21 world records. As a result of these outstanding performances, he received the Young Australian of the Year award in 2000 and the World's Most Outstanding Athlete award for 2002.

Thorpe is from Sydney and belongs to the SLC Aquadot Club in Sutherland, where he was coached by Doug Frost until 2002 and is now under the tutelage of Tracey Menzies. He was awarded a swimming scholarship by the NSW Institute of Sport shortly after it commenced in 1996, which he still holds.

What is most admirable about this young man is his concern for other people, particularly those who have some form of disability. He has created the Ian Thorpe Foundation for Youth Trust, which supports various disadvantaged young people around Australia. He is also an erudite speaker who ably represents Australia worldwide, and whose positive attitude is an inspiration to many of his peers.

Ian Thorpe portrays the very best features of a wholesome young Australian and he must be applauded for his positive and resolute example to us all.[57] [58]

NETBALL AUSTRALIA

Netball is one of Australia's major sporting success stories of the last two decades. Having first been played in England well over a century ago, the sport arrived in Australia soon after that time and developed steadily. Since 1975 the federation has grown by 50 per cent and it is now one of Australia's largest sports associations, with approximately 340 000 registered members.[59]

Netball Australia has catered for junior players in the schools and the community since its inception. In recent years it has embraced the modified game of *netta* and many of its members have qualified as junior coaches through the Australian Coaching Council courses. The selection of netball to become one of the eight inaugural sports at the AIS in 1981 gave the game a significant boost around Australia. Wilma Shakespear as head coach, ably assisted by Gai Teede, moved the game to the next level, as they were both high-profile coaches and charismatic role models for young women. In 1990 netball formed a national league which enjoys a high level of performance and draws good crowds around Australia. Internationally, Australia has won many world netball titles in the last two decades and has been the top nation in the world for most of that time. Australia again retained its number one world ranking, defeating a greatly improved New Zealand team two matches to one in a Test series in 2001, as well as winning the gold medal at the Manchester Commonwealth Games in 2002.[60]

Netball is also a great participant game and the various state sports organisations have developed more than 300 regional associations. The game attracts junior players from seven years of age right up to veterans or seniors in their 50s or older. All the states have well-developed netball centres, where large numbers of teams can compete simultaneously, as for example in Perth and Fremantle, where approximately 9000 players compete each Saturday during the season. Fortunately, netball is still mainly an outdoor sport, well suited to the Australian climate, and this has enabled facility costs to be kept at a minimum, helping to make it a low-cost game for the players. There are now competitions for mixed teams of male and female players, as well as for handicapped participants at various levels.

Netball is well coached and managed throughout Australia and its top competitors are fine role models for younger players.[61]

UNREGISTERED SPORT PARTICIPATION

At the beginning of the 21st century, about 7.5 million Australians participated in sport each year in this country. This includes the previously-mentioned 4.1 million members of the national sports organisations, while the remaining 3.4 million play informal or recreational sport.[62] The latter groups often use municipal facilities like tennis courts, outdoor fields, swimming pools, golf courses or commercial facilities such as squash courts, skating rinks or bowling alleys. As the local sports clubs which make up the state sporting organisations have minimum standards for their sports, many Australians use these facilities to develop their skills in a sport before becoming a club member and taking part in regular competition. Coaches are available at many of these venues to teach the basic skills. Other individuals are simply content to use the available facilities to play recreational sport with their friends in a less formal atmosphere.

NATIONAL LEAGUES AND SPONSORSHIP

Sara Brown, in her doctoral thesis on the development of national leagues in Australia, suggests that the last 20 years have seen major changes in organised sport in this country. She asserts that 'the most important of these has been the emergence of sporting leagues which have created national competitions'.[63] Most sports administrators would partially agree with her claim, as the establishment of the national leagues has certainly been one of the major developments in Australian sport.

An examination of the evolution of competitive sport in Australia shows that serious high-level competitions have been in place for at least 120 years. Competition was very informal in the first half of the 19th century and consisted mainly of 'pick-up' matches or 'friendlies', which were also common in England at that time. Competitions were gradually established on a home and away basis in various cities and country districts and cricket matches were often staged over two successive Saturdays.[64]

After the colonies had been granted responsible government from 1851 onwards, the rivalry between the states became intense. Organised leagues were set up for Australian football in Victoria and South Australia in 1877 and in Western Australia in 1885. In fact, these state bodies established their leagues well before the British soccer associations were formed in England in 1888 or in Scotland in 1892.[65] The first inter-colonial cricket match was played between Tasmania and Victoria at Launceston in 1851[66] and this was followed by a New South Wales versus Victoria game in the 1856-57 season, with regular matches being played each year from then on. At a later time, the Sheffield Shield inter-colonial competition commenced between the then colonies of New South Wales, South Australia and Victoria, in the 1892-93 season. Other sports which introduced inter-colonial contests during the 19th century were rowing, bowls, rugby, soccer, cycling and athletics. At the time of Federation in 1901, the inter-colonial competitions became interstate contests and official Australian championships were inaugurated at that time.

The 1970s and early 1980s saw the development of truly national competitions with elite-level sports clubs entering the leagues. Some sports such as Australian football and rugby league were very strong in two or three states where they had several high-level teams, while weaker states had formed just one or two. In order to manage these leagues, a national administrative body was established. From time to time, friction has occurred between these bodies and the national sports organisation responsible for that particular sport, but generally they have had good relationships.

The first inter-colonial cricket
match held between New South
Wales and Victoria in January
1857 at the Domain field, Sydney.
(By permission of the National
Library of Australia — see
Appendix H for photo credits.)

However, the whole question of commercial versus community interests as
they relate to national leagues was tested in the acrimonious Super League affair,
which raged for several years in the mid to late-1990s. Rupert Murdoch, through
his company News Limited, established a new rugby league competition with the
primary purpose of providing content for his pay television interests and set
about contracting teams and players for the new league. This move split the code,
taking established players away from the Australian Rugby League, but after a
period of two years and with poor attendance at the games, the new league
proved not to be a viable option. A deal was then struck between News Limited
and the Australian Rugby League to combine both groups. Strict limits were
placed on the number of teams in the new competition and some old and well-
established clubs were not included in the newly formed National Rugby League.

They were expected to merge with other clubs which had already been chosen to join the new organisation. South Sydney (the 'Rabbitohs'), one of the original clubs in the first competition held in Sydney in 1908, challenged this ruling, finally winning an appeal to the Federal Court of Australia. The well-publicised challenge was mounted by the club president, George Piggins, and the club members and supporters, several of whom were well-known Sydney identities. The whole affair was a victory for 'people power', with News Limited losing a considerable amount of money and prestige, and it threw into sharp relief the clash between sport as a commercial enterprise and sport as a community-based activity. At this point, it would appear that the majority of people concerned with sport in this country want to see the situation remain by and large as it is.[67]

The existence of the national leagues in Australia is now dependent upon exclusive television rights and sponsorship, and lucrative contracts have been drawn up between the sports and the various television networks. Sometimes the sport has amended some of its rules in order to make the game more attractive for viewers, while in other cases the fixtures have been re-scheduled to attract larger spectator audiences in Sydney and Melbourne. Brown states that 'in accommodating television, sport essentially transformed itself into a "packageable" commodity to be bought and sold by television stations, sponsors and entrepreneurs'.[68]

Overall, the development of national leagues has been a positive step in fostering high-level competition in Australia. The sports of Australian (rules) football, basketball, netball, surf lifesaving, cricket, hockey, water polo, soccer and rugby league have benefited from national leagues, while rugby union is now in an international-provincial league known as the Super 12 series.

CONFEDERATION OF AUSTRALIAN SPORT (CAS)

In Chapter Two of this work, several of the past actions of the Confederation of Australian Sport were discussed in relation to the turbulent period of the Fraser Government. Such lobby groups tend to form when governments are antagonistic to developments for which there is strong public support, and this was the case in the establishment of the confederation.

CAS was founded in Melbourne at the meeting of high-level sports admini-strators on 3 November 1976. Wayne Reid was elected president, Sir Arthur George vice-president and Gary Daly became the honorary secretary/treasurer. Some funding was available from private donors and those NSOs which became members paid a fee of $25. Within six months the confederation produced a white paper on 'The Financial Plight of Australian Sport', the information coming from the 68 affiliated bodies which had become members.[69] This paper stated the financial needs of sport accurately, but there was some suggestion of inconsistencies in the report, which somewhat detracted from its effectiveness.

The confederation then prepared a well-presented 'Master Plan for Sport'.[70] This contained a series of recommendations which would have greatly assisted

Australia's sport development at that time. However, for reasons still unknown both to the writer and to various sports officials, the plan was never acted upon by the Fraser Government.

The effectiveness of the confederation seemed to ebb and flow through the 1980s. After five years in existence and much persistent lobbying, a review was completed in which a long list of achievements was claimed.[71] However, as mentioned earlier, CAS clashed strongly with the Interim Committee for the Australian Sports Commission after allegedly lobbying the Opposition to 'torpedo' the Australian Sports Commission Bill. The attempt failed because the Australian Democrats' support in the Senate allowed it to be passed on 31 May 1985 and proclaimed on 1 July 1985.[72]

In the early years of the sports commission, the confederation was a constant critic of its programs. The continual discord caused several of the constituent members to leave the confederation, making it a less effective body than it had previously been. The confederation worked hard in the early days of its existence to assist sport development in Australia, but some of its efforts appear to have been negative and misplaced in the latter part of the 1980s, thus diminishing its effectiveness. In 1989, Greg Hartung became president and oversaw several positive initiatives, enabling the confederation to better represent its constituency to the government. Since the mid-1990s it has shifted its focus from sport per se towards the sports industry and has recently changed its name to Sports Industry Australia.[73] This move could be a positive one for Australian sport, especially since the Australian Sports Commission sees a definite role for this organisation in helping schools, sports clubs, local government and private businesses to increase their input into Australian sport.

THE AUSTRALIAN OLYMPIC COMMITTEE (AOC)

Australia has had a long association with the Olympic Games, having joined the International Olympic Committee as a founding member in 1894 under the umbrella of Australasia. A meeting had been set up by Baron Pierre de Coubertin to review the principles of amateurism and his proposal to revive the ancient Olympic Games led to their commencement in Athens in 1896.[74] Australia is one of only two countries which can claim the distinction of having competed in every summer Olympic Games since Athens. There is no doubt that this country's very long association with the Olympic movement was one of several factors which helped Australia to win the bid for the Sydney 2000 Games.[75]

Australia's performances at most of the 24 Olympic Games thus far have been well above average, especially considering the fact that Australian athletes competed out of season for all but two of them. In addition, until regular air travel began in the late 1960s, it was necessary for competitors to spend between three and six weeks on board a ship before arriving at a Games venue either in Europe or North America. Since 1896, Australia has averaged 12th place in the medal count, and at the 2000 Olympics this improved to fourth.[76]

The Australian Olympic Federation (AOF) was the peak Olympic body in Australia from 1923 until 1990, but before that time it operated under several names.[77] The AOF and its predecessors coped well when Australia had an amateur sports system, with dedicated officials such as Julius ('Judy') Patching, Syd Grange, Phil Coles and Kevan Gosper, who worked hard for the Olympic movement. However, there is no doubt that the AOF has benefited from becoming a more professional body in recent years and the election of John Coates to the presidency in 1990 placed an exceptional administrator into the chair — one who had the foresight to lead the newly constituted AOC into the 21st century.

PLANNING FOR SYDNEY 2000

Under Kevan Gosper's competent leadership in 1988, the AOF had embarked on a policy of making a serious bid for an Olympic Games to be held in Australia in 2000. Previous bids had come from Brisbane and Melbourne and these were mainly driven by the cities involved. Under John Coates' direction, an impressive strategy document with Sydney as the host city was completed by March 1991. The Australian Olympic team's good performance in Barcelona almost certainly added weight to the bid. The decision was made in Monte Carlo on 23 September 1993 and announced by the then IOC President, Juan Antonio Samaranch. His long-awaited announcement — 'And the winner is ... the, uh, the winner is Sydney' — was to change the face of Australian sport forever.[78]

After the host city announcement, the enormity of the project sank in. It was fortunate that, as President of the AOC, John Coates was in a position to oversee the total project, covering the multitude of variables which needed to be addressed before September 2000.

On the performance side, he had already developed an Olympic Co-operation Agreement with the AIS in August 1987, and with their continued co-operation and that of the sports commission, the preparation of Australian athletes was smoothly executed.[79] The majority of the build-up towards Sydney 2000 will be discussed in Chapter Seven.

AUSTRALIAN COMMONWEALTH GAMES ASSOCIATION (ACGA)

The first official games for Commonwealth athletes were held in conjunction with the Coronation of King George V in London in 1911. They were called the Festival of Empire and competitors in the four sports of athletics, swimming, boxing and wrestling from Great Britain, Canada, South Africa and Australia were invited to participate. Even though the above Festival proved to be popular, it was not until 1930 that another similar event was to be held. Because Canada had won the medal tally in 1911, Hamilton in Ontario was chosen as the venue of the first official British Empire Games. From that time on, the Games have been held every four years, except during the Second World War. The name has changed several times, but the most recent title of Commonwealth Games seems likely to be retained.[80]

In the 1930s only seven or eight sports were admitted, but by 2002 19 sports were included in the program. The Games have now been held on 17 occasions and Australia has won the medal tally ten times, being runner-up on three other occasions. The 2002 Commonwealth Games were in Manchester, England, where the home nation performed much better than in previous years, as it is currently spending large sums of money in a concentrated effort to upgrade its sports system.[81] [82]

The Australian Commonwealth Games Association has become a much more professional body of late, largely because of the appointment of Perry Crosswhite as the chief executive officer in 1998. Crosswhite is not only a three-time former Olympian, but is also one of Australia's most capable sports administrators.

STATE SPORTING ORGANISATIONS

These bodies have already been mentioned because of their relationship to their national sporting organisations and also because they play a co-ordinating role in their respective states. Almost all of the state organisations employ professional sports managers in the capital cities to conduct their day-to-day business and to implement the policies of their board or executive committee.

STATE SPORTS FEDERATIONS

Western Australia was the first state in Australia to have an official committee to represent the above-mentioned state sporting organisations. A sub-committee of the National Fitness Council of Western Australia had been formed as early as 1950, under the title of 'Associated Sporting Committee'.[83] In late 1975 the writer and Jack Evans proposed that this committee be upgraded to 'The Western Australian Sports Federation'. This happened in 1976, with Evans as its first chairman, before he later became a Federal Government senator representing Western Australia.[84] [85]

The federation's function was to act as the peak body for sport in the state and also to collectively represent the interests of the various state associations and federations to the government. It was a very effective body, with the Western Australian model now replicated in all the states of Australia.[86]

THE ROLE OF PRIVATE SCHOOLS

Australia's private schools were set up on the English model and the more traditional ones have always fostered competitive sport, especially the British sports and games. The original Great Public Schools (GPS) in Sydney have the distinction of forming the first inter-school competitions in Australia and similar schools in the other capitals set up almost identical models as those centres became more populous. Many of the traditional male single-sex private schools have a long history of elite sport competitions, but inter-school sport is more low-key in the co-educational private schools which have been established mainly in the last two decades. The greatest developments in inter-school sport in the last 25 years have been in the girls' independent schools, where levels of competition are now quite high.

The private schools tend to be particularly strong in the traditional sports of cricket, rugby, Australian (rules) football (especially in the southern states), rowing, swimming, tennis, athletics, hockey and netball. There is no doubt that the private schools still play an integral role within the Australian sports system, contributing greatly to the development of many young athletes. However, there are signs that change may be on the way. Some private school teachers in Queensland have requested additional remuneration for their participation in extra-curricular activities and sport is one of the activities included in their claim.

THE IMPORTANCE OF NON-GOVERNMENT SPORTS SERVICES

As with the government sports services, the non-government sector is crucial to the operation of sport in Australia. However, in this part of the system almost all the members of the associations or federations are volunteers. It is therefore important for each organisation to have a professional staff to co-ordinate the volunteers' activities so as to provide specialised expertise and continuity from year to year. Some government assistance is necessary to provide this expertise and to bolster the funds raised from memberships, sponsorship and other fund-raising activities. The Sport 2000 Task Force quoted a figure of 1.7 million Australians involved in the non-government sports services sector. However, this number is slowly diminishing, for reasons which will be discussed in Chapter Eight.[87]

Chapter Seven
A professional sports system in place

The Howard Government — 1996-

After winning a total of 41 medals at the 1996 Atlanta Olympics and gaining second place in the Paralympics, Australia had a sports system that had developed to the point where only fine-tuning was needed. The Howard Government was elected in 1996 and, not wanting to upset the momentum which had been achieved in the first half of the 1990s, guaranteed that funding would remain unaltered until the end of the Sydney 2000 Games. The new Coalition Government commenced its term on a very positive note and was fortunate to have the help of Jim Ferguson as Executive Director of the Australian Sports Commission. Ferguson's aim in the early 1990s had been to set up a national sports network which incorporated the states and territories, and he did this with thorough strategic planning and positive diplomacy. This plan had been successfully implemented just before the new government came to office, so that all the Howard Government needed to do was to keep the system in balance until the Sydney Olympics commenced.

The lead-up to Sydney 2000
INTEGRATION OF THE ASC, AIS AND AOC PROGRAMS

Even though the Australian Sports Commission, the Australian Institute of Sport and the state or territory institutes or academies were well co-ordinated by 1996, it was necessary for the Australian Olympic Committee to co-operate closely with the above bodies in the latter part of the 1990s. The AOC president, John Coates, whose profile appears below, realised that his committee needed a better funding base so that it could become a more equal partner. In the 1991 contract for Sydney's endorsement to host the 2000 Olympics, he had ensured that provision was made for the NSW Government to pay the Olympic committee a sum of money to cover part of the expenditure of staging the Games. The figure agreed upon was $60 million, to assist in the preparation and participation of the Australian team.

Over the four years leading up to the Sydney Olympics, the above money, added to the fundraising achieved for the team, enabled the funding of several crucial new programs which were to significantly improve Australia's

THE MAN BEHIND SYDNEY 2000

John Coates first came to prominence in Australian sport with his appointment as manager of the Australian rowing teams at the 1975 world championships and 1976 Montreal Olympics. Soon afterwards he was elected Honorary Secretary, and then President, of the Australian Rowing Council. It was during the ten-year period of Coates' office that the Australian men's eight won the world rowing championships for the first time, laying the foundations for what has become Australia's third most successful medal-winning Olympic sport behind swimming and cycling.

John has been a member of the executive of the Australian Olympic Committee since 1982 and its president since 1990. This was a period of great change in the Australian Olympic movement, with a strong emphasis on athlete support programs and high-performance development. As chef de mission of our teams from 1988 in Seoul up to 2004 in Athens, he has been instrumental in bringing a new professionalism to Australia's Olympic involvement.

As a Director of the Australian Institute of Sport from 1985 and deputy chairman from 1986 until 1989, John was in a strong position to influence the direction of the Federal Government's elite funding for sport. And when the AIS was incorporated into the Australian Sports Commission, John became deputy chairman of the new body from 1989 until 1998.

As Senior Vice President of SOCOG and chairman of its key sports commission, John Coates, more than any other individual, was responsible for bringing the 2000 Olympics to Australia and later for their stunning success. He has been acknowledged for his invaluable contribution to Australian sport and the Olympic movement by being made a Member (AM) and then an Officer (AO) of the Order of Australia. During the Sydney Olympics John was awarded the International Rowing Federation's Medal of Honour; and at the spectacular Closing Ceremony, he was presented with the Olympic Order in Gold, the highest recognition the Olympic movement can bestow.[1]

performance. These included grants of $10.7 million to the member national sporting associations; $18.2 million for a medal incentive scheme for a four-year period leading up to the Games for athletes and their coaches; $7.5 million to likely medal-winning sports for special projects and equipment; $20.6 million for the 1998 Nagano and 2000 Olympic teams; and $1.7 million for Australian athletes who won medals at the Sydney Games. These funds, combined with the Olympic Athlete Program, the *'Maintain the Momentum'* funding and the state and territory institute and academy programs, enabled an integrated build-up to take place during the run-up to Sydney 2000.[2]

THE 1998 COMMONWEALTH GAMES

The Australian team produced its best overall performance ever at the Commonwealth Games held in Kuala Lumpur in 1998, with a total of 198 medals, 80 of them gold, 61 silver and 57 bronze.[3] Australia had sent 324 athletes to the games, 299 (92 per cent) of whom held either shared scholarships with the AIS and the state or territory institutes or academies of sport, or were past or current AIS scholarship holders.[4]

INTERNATIONAL TRIUMPHS IN 1999

Since the Barcelona Olympic Games in 1992, Australia's performances had continued to improve in both Olympic and non-Olympic sports. Of course, Australia's international successes in the former were closely related to the increased money and expertise provided by the Olympic Athlete Program. The non-Olympic sports also improved towards the end of the decade, as the entire sports system was running very efficiently by that time.

In 1999 Australia won 12 world championships in team sports and 21 in individual sports. Appendix C gives details of the successful teams, competitors and events in which they competed. In addition to the above senior championships, a large number of Australian junior teams and individuals either won or gained places in world championships as the century drew to a close. One of the most noteworthy achievements was by the Australian Under 17 soccer team against Brazil in the world championship on their opponents' home territory. In that game the Australian Joeys were only beaten 5-4 in a penalty shoot-out.[5][6]

PRE-OLYMPIC GAMES ORGANISATION

The organisation of the Olympic Games in Australia was a Herculean task, partly because of Australia's three-tiered system of government. Fortunately there had been strong support from the government of New South Wales ever since the original bid. In fact, there were two changes of government after Sydney became the host city, as the Greiner Coalition Government in New South Wales was replaced by the Carr Labor Government at the state level, and the Howard Coalition Government replaced the Keating Labor Government in 1996 at the federal level. Nevertheless, the above transitions took place in a true spirit of co-operation, as all leaders were aware that the reputation of the nation was on the line.

With a lead-up period of almost seven years, the various planning committees started soon after the games were allocated to Sydney. Not only had new facilities to be planned and constructed, but transport, communication and the security systems all needed fine-tuning, as did quarantine and immigration services. Along with 15 000 athletes from more than 200 countries, approximately half a million people were to come in and out of Sydney before, during or after the Olympic and Paralympic Games.[7]

In the four years leading up to Sydney 2000, there was outstanding co-operation between the Australian Olympic Committee (AOC), the Australian

Sports Commission (ASC) and the 28 national sports organisations (NSOs) whose athletes were to participate in the Olympics, as well as the state or territory sports institutes or academies. John Coates of the Olympic committee and Jim Ferguson of the sports commission were generally responsible for the co-ordination of the above sporting bodies.

In the early stages of the Olympic Athlete Program, the AOC had taken the decision to select for Atlanta all the Australian athletes who qualified, with a view to fielding a full team at the Sydney Games. This was a wise move, as it gave many of the younger competitors experience at a high level. There were in fact 632 Australian athletes competing in Sydney, compared with 424 in Atlanta and 290 in Barcelona.

While a large number of dedicated people worked steadily in the background to organise the 2000 Olympics and Paralympics, there were problems which from time to time cast aspersions on the Sydney Organising Committee for the Olympic Games (SOCOG). The major one was caused by the controversial Olympic ticketing program; there was a public outcry when it was revealed that some tickets were being held back from general sale and directed to the corporate sector. This was later rectified and the vast majority of tickets were sold to the public. Other controversies to emerge during the lead-up to Sydney 2000 included the dismissal of several chief executive officers, until Sandy Holloway filled the position, in which he performed very creditably; the resignations of several SOCOG chairmen; and Michael Knight's appointment as the SOCOG president while he was also the Minister responsible for the Olympic Games in the Carr Government. The Phil Coles episode was raised by several newspapers, who alleged that, as an IOC member, Coles had accepted favours during the bid for the Salt Lake Winter Olympics in 2002. The Australian public had also been prepared for some minor hiccups as a result of the ABC television satire, *The Games*, in which John Clarke and Brian Dawe brilliantly lampooned the organisation leading up to Sydney 2000. However, everything came together on schedule and the many thousands of individuals involved in the largest peace-time operation ever undertaken in this country were poised to produce the greatest Olympics staged in the 104-year history of the modern Games.

The Sydney 2000 Olympics

THE TORCH RELAY

For many Australians, the torch relay was the official lead-up to the opening of the Games. The torch was first transported from Olympia in Greece and its 27 000 kilometre journey around Australia began at Uluru in the Northern Territory, finishing in Sydney 100 days later. The staging of the torch relay gave millions of Australians the opportunity to see the thousands of runners carrying the torch throughout the country. By the time it approached Sydney, Australians were well and truly in the mood for the Games to begin.

Andrew Gaze as flag bearer leads the
Australian team into the Olympic
Stadium at the Sydney 2000 Olympics,
followed by Chef de Mission John
Coates and Deputy Chef de Mission
Peter Montgomery. (By courtesy of
Sport the Library.)

Cathy Freeman stands in the 'ring of fire' after lighting the Olympic flame at the Sydney 2000 Olympic Games. (By courtesy of Sport the Library.)

THE OPENING CEREMONY

On the day of the Opening Ceremony the torch was on its final journey through Sydney and was timed to arrive at the Olympic site in Homebush that evening.

In the meantime, Stadium Australia had been steadily filling up to its capacity of 110 000 spectators. Following the arrival of the Governor-General, Sir William Deane, the national anthem was sung and the Games of the XXVII Olympiad began. With the crack of their whips, 120 stockmen and women spurred their horses into the Olympic Stadium to welcome the world to Sydney.[8] The 12 697 performers, backed up by 5000 behind-the-scenes staff, proceeded to thrill the audience with one of the greatest outdoor productions ever staged.[9] The seven themes portrayed interwove history with Australia's aspirations for the future and Ric Birch, the director of ceremonies, David Atkins, the artistic director, and their colleagues produced an unforgettable performance celebrating the triumph of the human spirit.[10] [11]

The parade of athletes followed, then short addresses were given by Michael Knight, the Minister for the Olympics, and Juan Antonio Samaranch, President of the International Olympic Committee. Then the Governor-General, Sir William

Deane, officially opened the Sydney 2000 Games. This was followed by the Olympic flag ceremony and the oaths on behalf of the competitors and the judges. Finally, because it was the 100th anniversary of the participation of women in the Olympics, Australia's famous female Olympians passed the torch from one to another as they jogged around the track. Dawn Fraser, Shirley de la Hunty, Shane Gould and Raelene Boyle began the sequence; then Raelene pushed Betty Cuthbert, who was seated in a wheelchair while holding the torch aloft. It was then passed to Debbie Flintoff-King and finally to Cathy Freeman at the foot of the cauldron. The very popular Indigenous Australian sprinter grasped the torch, ascended the stairs and lit the flame, signifying that the Games had begun.

The Opening Ceremony was hailed by the Australian and foreign press alike as the most spectacular Olympic Games opening ever staged. It will certainly become the 'gold standard' for future Games Opening Ceremonies.

AUSTRALIA'S RESULTS

The details of individual and team performances have been well documented in several excellent publications which appeared soon after the Games. Even though the Australian team fell just short of the medal target of 60, the results were still outstanding, with 58 medals, including 16 gold, 25 silver and 17 bronze. The above medal return was considerably better than at Atlanta, where the total had been 41 medals, with nine gold, nine silver and 23 bronze.[12] Medals were also gained across the board in 20 sports compared to 14 in 1996; and Australia had 128 athletes in the top eight places compared with 94 in Atlanta. These were very good results for the host country; the next major challenge for Australia in Olympic sport will be to consolidate a position among the top five nations in the medal tally when competing outside Australia in 2004.[13]

THE CLOSING CEREMONY

The closing ceremony was another memorable celebration and *The Australian* newspaper in its *Closing Ceremony Souvenir,* entitled 'Simply the Best', said this on the front page: 'Australia bid farewell to the Olympics last night in a celebration that saw the athletes of the world unite after 16 days of hope, anguish, joy and despair. The Games that began with Cathy Freeman standing in a fiery lake ended with a river of fire. Sydney never missed a beat. And it won the ultimate praise from Juan Antonio Samaranch for producing the "best Games ever".'[14]

After the spectacular Closing Ceremony at the Olympic Stadium, the action moved from Homebush Bay to the Sydney Harbour Bridge with a succession of fireworks which flashed down the Parramatta River into Sydney Harbour. In a spectacular finale lasting for 20 minutes, a dazzling display of fireworks lit up the bridge and the surrounding foreshores, watched by an estimated 1.5 million people. As the final barrage went off and the cheering slowly abated, Australians were left to reflect upon a celebration the like of which had never been seen in this country.[15]

LEFT The record-breaking 4x100 metre freestyle gold medallists at the Sydney Olympics. Left to right: Ashley Callus, Chris Fydler, Michael Klim, Ian Thorpe. (By courtesy of Sport the Library.)

ABOVE The final of the men's eight oar rowing championship, which was held at the International Regatta Centre during the Sydney 2000 Olympics.

REACTIONS TO THE OLYMPICS

THE AUSTRALIAN SPECTATORS

It was easy to gauge the reaction of the huge crowd to the Sydney Olympics. On the day of the Opening Ceremony, the torch had moved off from the Sydney Town Hall just before dawn to complete its circuit of the north shore, the northern beaches and Sydney Harbour, and everywhere it was greeted by euphoric crowds of several hundred thousand spectators. It finally reached Stadium Australia to thunderous applause, just as the evening ceremonies were about to begin. The electric atmosphere engendered by the opening of the Games was to continue for the next 16 days at the main site at Homebush, the other Olympic competition sites and at various venues around Sydney, where large viewing screens had been erected.[16]

At any one time during the Games, Olympic Park at Homebush attracted approximately 400 000 people, with several hundred thousand others distributed between the surrounding competition sites or at the above-mentioned viewing spots around Sydney. Because the transport services functioned so efficiently and the volunteers were so welcoming and helpful, the spectators were able to keep their sense of enjoyment to the fore. Even walking the extra few hundred metres for the sake of better crowd control, or standing in a line for short periods at peak times, was accepted with good grace.[17]

There was an obvious outpouring of nationalism during the games period, not only at the events but with anything related to the Games. Hundreds of thousands of caps, hats, T-shirts and such were worn by Australian and overseas spectators and the local crowd supported their athletes with great fervour — but also barracked loudly for representatives from other countries. For example, Ivan Pedroso from Cuba started a rhythmic clap while contesting the long jump final, inviting the crowd to join in. Australia's competitor, Jai Taurima, also received enthusiastic support and finally gained a silver medal behind Pedroso.[18] Many similar incidents took place, the most memorable perhaps being the swim by Eric 'The Eel' Moussambani of Equatorial Guinea. He struggled to complete his solo swim after his opponents were disqualified, but received spontaneous encouragement worthy of any winner. Nor was Eric's situation an isolated incident, as rousing cheers were given to some distance runners who had been lapped by their competitors, or who were well behind the field as they crossed the finishing line. Many Australians will recall the cheers at school athletic carnivals for those competitors who gallantly completed their long-distance races at the tail of the field.

The biggest support for the athletes came from the self-appointed cheerleaders, who were at the various sites, leading the rousing 'Aussie, Aussie, Aussie, Oi, Oi, Oi' refrain. This started on the first day of competition in several places and spread like wildfire to virtually all the venues.

THE AUSTRALIAN OLYMPIC TEAM'S REACTION

The very thorough preparation of the entire Australian team had enabled them to feel relaxed and confident during the competition period. The preparation was aided by several initiatives of the Australian Olympic Committee and the various national sports organisations in the long lead-up to the Games. First, the entire team had experienced a great deal of foreign competition in the previous two to three years and were reasonably familiar with their opponents. They were also at ease with their coaches, sports science and sports medicine personnel, as well as their team managers and assistants. The individual teams were also strongly encouraged to support their own peers and other Australian athletes competing in different sports, and they did this with great enthusiasm. And finally, their

Australia's silver medallist, Jai Taurima, acknowledges the crowd's enthusiastic support in the men's long jump event at the Sydney 2000 Olympics. (By courtesy of Sport the Library.)

accommodation in the Games Village was both comfortable and in close proximity to the events held in the Olympic Precinct at Homebush. Because of the very careful early planning, most of the other competition sites were reasonably close at hand and the efficient transport system made training and competition relatively accessible. This was in contrast to some previous Olympics, where long journeys and traffic jams caused frustrating delays. There is no doubt that the Australian team members were very happy with their preparation and voiced their satisfaction to their coaches and managers, as well as to the press.

WHAT THE JOURNALISTS SAID

Both the Australian and the foreign press were full of praise for Sydney, the various venues and the high quality of the competition. Many of the press showed great interest in the positive behaviour and good humour of the spectators, commenting very favourably on the 47 000 volunteers at the Olympic sites as well as the 8000 volunteers who assisted with the essential services around Sydney. There was also the regular staff, who worked overtime to keep Sydney transport running so efficiently for the huge influx of people over a short period of time. It was as though the media had discovered a dimension wider than the sports and events that were part of the Games, and were intent on delving deeper into the basic nature of Australian people. They were also impressed with Australia's outstanding Olympic results and interested in how this had been achieved in a country with such a small population. Because there was so much interest in this topic, it will be covered more fully in a later section in this chapter, as it has a strong link with Australia's early sporting history as described in Chapter One.

OPINIONS OF SIGNIFICANT OTHERS

At events like the Olympics, there are always high-profile people whose expert opinions are sought by the press, and some of these reactions to Sydney 2000 appear below:

- *Steve Cram — former world 1500m champion:* 'I have been to many championships as both an athlete and as a commentator now, and I can honestly say I've never known an atmosphere like this. To have more than 100 000 people here just for the morning qualifiers is just incredible, and the place simply lit up with flashbulbs when Cathy Freeman stepped out on the track in the evening. I haven't seen a stadium or crowd like it — it was something really special.'[19]

- *Sebastian Coe — former world and twice Olympic 1500m champion:* 'That was the best night of athletics I've ever seen in my life ... It was incredible. I couldn't sleep. I've been up talking about it for hours. Britain has suffered from sporting sclerosis for the past 30 years. An institute of sport like the one in Australia is vital. I don't care where it goes as long as it's a centre of excellence. It's got to be one big mother of a centre, aspirational and inspirational, where kids want to be.'[20]

- *Maurice Greene — winner of the men's 100m sprint, Sydney 2000:* 'The Australian crowd was great. They came out in large numbers and showed us a lot of love.'[21]

- *Marion Toler — mother of Marion Jones, winner of the women's 100m and 200m events, Sydney 2000:* 'My family and I are visiting Australia for the Olympic Games and especially to support my daughter, Marion Jones, as she makes her bid for gold. The purpose of this letter, however, is to express my thanks to the people of Australia for your support for my daughter ... Above all, I wish to thank you for the sportsmanlike attitude displayed at every meet and spirited cheers for Marion when she won the 100 metres and 200 metres, even though Australian athletes had been defeated in these heats. Thank you, Australia, and thanks for loving my daughter Marion.'[22]

The Sydney 2000 Paralympics

THE LEAD-UP

After the euphoria of the Olympics died down and athletes, officials and visitors returned to their home countries, life returned to normal in Australia rather quickly. So as to stimulate people's interest in the Paralympics, the press covered various aspects of the forthcoming Games in the week preceding their Opening Ceremony. Several pertinent articles appeared in the Australian press, describing the difficulties faced by a large number of disabled athletes. This example expressed the widely-held sentiment: 'Anyone who gets to the Paralympic Games as a competitor can lay claim to the title of champion before even one event is held — because each competitor represents a triumph over adversity. If the Olympics are about striving for perfection in a range of physical activities, the Paralympics could be said to be about conquest over imperfection through the indomitability of the human spirit. The athletes who will compete at the Sydney Paralympics have already shown that they have exceptional qualities of character simply by getting there. They have refused to allow their spirits to be crushed by disabilities that might appear to others to be insurmountable obstacles to sporting achievements. When they take to the various arenas at the Paralympics, they will display sporting abilities developed in the face of daunting handicaps. They deserve to be applauded for their abilities, instead of the focus being on their disabilities. And they should be valued for the inspiration they can provide for everyone who has ever been tempted to give in to life's difficulties.'[23] Australians were encouraged to see the Paralympic Games in a new light and became more receptive to them. By the time the Games began, there was a heightened level of interest, anticipation and compassion.

THE PARALYMPICS BEGIN

The Paralympics Opening Ceremony was held on 18 October, after a break of two and a half weeks. During that time the Olympic Precinct, the village and the facilities had received a hurried facelift and were prepared for competition or last-minute training. Karen Richards, the director of ceremonies, with $5 million or ten per cent of the budget of the Sydney Olympic Games, had developed an Opening Ceremony with a theme depicting 'a story told through song'. It was both colourful and inspiring and proved very suitable for the occasion. One hundred and ten thousand spectators filled the stadium and the Games were again opened by the Governor-General, Sir William Deane. Four thousand athletes from 128 countries paraded around the track, accompanied by 2000 team officials. Tracey Cross delivered the athlete's oath and Louise Sauvage lit a small fire in the arena, setting off a chain of flame which leapt up the grandstand to light the cauldron at the top. The Games were ready to begin.[24][25]

AUSTRALIA'S RESULTS

The first two days of competition were rather quiet, with the venues only half full. Then suddenly the spectators began to appear in much greater numbers and the 15 000 volunteers were very much in demand to assist with crowd control. Forty thousand school children began to arrive each day, with a final total of 320 000 attending; and as the Games progressed the venues became more crowded, especially for the finals. Overall, 1.1 million spectators attended the Paralympics and the ABC ratings rose well above their normal level. It was estimated that 4.2 million people in Australia watched the Opening Ceremony and that the television audience during the Paralympics Games period averaged 500 000 viewers per night.

Australia's performance in the 18 sports was again outstanding. In the four years since Atlanta there had been spectacular improvements in almost all the events and in Sydney no less than 347 world and 262 Paralympic records were broken. Australia topped the medal tally with a record of 149 medals, 63 of them gold, 39 silver and 47 bronze. Great Britain was second with 131 medals and the United States third with 110. In fact the medals were spread across more countries at these Games, indicating that many other nations are taking the Paralympics seriously and preparing their athletes more thoroughly.[26]

The spectacular Closing Ceremony was more than a salute to the Paralympic Games. *The Australian* newspaper stated that the director of ceremonies, Karen Richards, had 'wanted a circus, a dance party, a spectacle that was relaxed and casual, [and] a chance for the athletes to let their own hair down'. She certainly achieved her aim in fine style.[27]

REACTIONS TO THE PARALYMPICS

The public's reaction to the Paralympic Games was very positive. The organisation had been superb and as the athletes and officials left Australia, they were most laudatory with their praise. The spectators, at first reticent, had quickly warmed to the spirit of the occasion and Lois Appleby from the Sydney Paralympic Olympic Commission summed it up by saying: 'I think the numbers have been great [but] it's the enthusiasm of the crowds that has just been sensational.'[28]

The journalists also praised the Games, particularly the athletes themselves. It was as though they had suddenly awakened to the fact that disabled sports people can also be top performers, and that as athletes they must be given every opportunity to pursue their sport with the same resources as able-bodied competitors. *The Australian* newspaper, especially Shelley Gare, wrote some

Neil Fuller of Australia, on the far left of the photo, won four gold medals in amputee running events at the Sydney 2000 Paralympics. (By courtesy of the Australian Sports Commission.)

highly informative articles; and the ABC, with Karen Tighe as anchor, also did a superb job. One editorial aptly summed up the event: 'The Sydney Paralympic Games were the biggest, best and most popular ever held. Australians have cause to glow with pride at their unqualified success. Many of the intangible barriers that sometimes separate disabled people from the mainstream of society were broken as huge international audiences marvelled at superb feats of athleticism. Australians also have cause for pride at the dominance of home-grown athletes in competition. The Australian Paralympic team easily topped the list of medal winners with a total haul of 149, including 63 gold. But perhaps the most compelling reason for pride is that this performance reflects a compassionate society that is prepared to give people a fair go.'[29]

The final of the women's 800 metre wheelchair event at the Sydney 2000 Paralympics, which was won by Australia's greatest athlete with a disability, Louise Sauvage. (Getty Images.)

Post-Games assessments

As the Olympics and then the Paralympics concluded, there was a spontaneous assessment of their impact by various commentators and journalists. Most reports on the performance of the Australian Olympic athletes were positive, as many journalists had not expected Australia to win the 60 medals forecast before the Games and had suggested a figure closer to 50. There is no doubt that 58 medals and fourth place on the medal tally were outstanding achievements for a country with Australia's population.

Paul Kelly of *The Australian* newspaper made a number of observations with which other press and television journalists later concurred. After talking to many business people and journalists, Kelly claimed that the universal reaction was not only that the facilities were outstanding and the Games well planned and organised, but that there was also plenty of sport drama. He claimed that the Games had been a triple success for Australia as the nation's best sporting performance at an Olympics; as an organisational triumph; and as an occasion to improve this country's international image. As he said: 'The crowds have been vast, good-humoured and generous ... There has been a distinctively Australian character to the Olympics, typified by the volunteers ... [and] Australia had "delivered" on the world's biggest event.'[30]

Other commentaries related to Australia's place in the world and the way in which it perceived itself following the Olympics. In an editorial concerning how the Games portrayed Australians, the editor of *The West Australian* newspaper asserted that this nation had 'thrown off' the cultural cringe and that 'self-consciousness has become self-confidence'. He also stated that 'few could doubt that it was a celebration staged by a nation that is confident in its abilities and increasingly secure in its identity.'[31]

The assessment of Australia's performance in the Paralympics was similar to that of the Olympics, although in the case of the Paralympics, Australia's effort in topping the medal tally brought accolades from an even wider range of individuals. Many Australians were not aware that a disabled sports program had been steadily building up since 1983 at both the state and federal levels. The sports commission had become very supportive of the program in the early 1990s and in 1994, when Sydney was awarded the Paralympic Games to follow the Olympics, federal money was made available for athlete preparation and to organise and administer the Games.

As the preparation for the Paralympics progressed on many fronts, it tended to be overshadowed by the Olympic Games. But it was fortunate that the press steadily warmed to it and was very laudatory, both in regard to the performances of our athletes as well as the smooth conduct of the Games.

Australia's social ambience during the Games

In Chapter One of this book, various social dynamics relating to early Australian sport were discussed. There is no doubt that sport has had a significant effect on the evolution of this nation, just as this country's development appears to have influenced the evolution of sport itself. After more than two centuries of European settlement, the Olympic Games revealed two major social traits which have appeared from time to time, but which had been less visible in Australia since the Second World War. It was as though the nation needed significant events of both the proportions and intensity of the Olympic and Paralympic Games for these characteristics to burst out of their cocoon.

NATIONALISM

There was certainly an outpouring of nationalism, which slowly built up during the torch relay, reaching a crescendo at the Opening Ceremony of the Games. This was to last until the end of the Closing Ceremony, then abate until the Paralympics commenced. At no time during the Paralympic Games did it reach the level of the Olympic Games, but nevertheless Australians were very proud of their disabled athletes and of the way in which the Games were conducted.

In the context of nationalism, almost every journalist who wrote about the spectators at the various venues mentioned the exhilaration of the crowd. It was as though Australians lost their inhibitions and let themselves go in support of their athletes. Senior politicians and even the Governor-General were seen joining in the 'Mexican wave'. Many dignitaries spontaneously joined in the chanting, waving their arms or punching the air when Australians won or were placed in an event.

Two of many overt displays of spontaneous nationalism characteristic of the crowd are described below. The first took place at Circular Quay, where several thousand people were watching the swimming finals on the big viewing screen. When Susie O'Neill won her event and was presented with her medal, the spectators rose to their feet as one and proudly sang the national anthem.[32] The other occasion took place in a railway carriage which had stopped at signal lights on the way back to Central Station from the Olympic site. It was late at night and the carriage was crowded, as a large crowd was returning from at least eight venues at Homebush. Suddenly a young man shouted from the back: 'The Australian girls have just won the water polo.' A spontaneous cheer went up and someone led the carriage in an 'Aussie, Aussie, Aussie' chant. This was followed by another loud cheer as hats or caps were thrown into the air. A spectator from the United States sitting across from the writer said in a strong Southern drawl: 'Ah just love the way you Aussies root for your teams!'

As the Games drew to a close, many local and overseas journalists wrote about the close bond between Australian spectators and their teams and the nationalistic fervour of the crowds. Tony Barrass, in an article headlined 'Glorious Games a Sign of our Nationhood', wrote that in the past Australia had sometimes 'struggled with its identity and place in the world, [but] seems at long last to be at peace with itself.'[33] The editor of *The West Australian* declared: 'It was said of the Sydney Olympics that they would give Australia a nation-defining moment in its history. The extent to which that has proved to be true will be debated by historians and social commentators for years to come. What can be asserted now with a high degree of confidence is that the Olympics have prompted Australians to seek insights ... [into] the character of their nation – and people have liked much of what they saw. Certainly, there are flaws to be seen, but also much that is admirable.'[34] Finally, a quote from an article by David Malouf seems appropriate. After claiming that sport was the biggest single factor in Australia's move towards Federation, he states: 'We came late to nationalism.

Given the terms in which national feeling was being argued elsewhere, in blood and soil notions of ethnic exclusivism or mystical notions of brotherhood and death, it was both original and far-sighted of us to settle so early for sport, which was to become 100 years later one of the world's universal religions, as a way of defining ourselves and channelling national feeling. To this extent the Sydney Olympics really was the apotheosis of Australia's national achievement and the revelation, to ourselves as much as to others, of an achieved national style. That was, in many ways, our real celebration of Federation.'[35]

SOCIAL COHESION

As was pointed out in Chapter One, the colony of New South Wales had a difficult start and the various early governors had to work hard to neutralise the many sources of conflict in the new colony. Because of the oppression experienced by the convicts, the emancipists and their children, a strong sense of mateship, co-operation and a 'them and us' attitude to the authorities developed. This was later reinforced by the privations suffered by those who joined the Gold Rush, settled the outback or went to war in the late 19th or early 20th centuries. It seems that the hardships which the early generations of Australians endured fostered a caring attitude towards their friends, beneath an often rough exterior. Garvin gives an insight into this in his description of life in the bush for many Australian settlers: 'Survival meant mastering many skills and explains why, like in so few other countries, you needed bush camaraderie. When fire, flood or any difficulty arose you needed a mate to stand beside you – and you had to be prepared to stand with your mate when hardship hit him.'[36]

As the Games drew to a close, several commentators remarked on the displays of social cohesion which had surfaced on many occasions during the Games. An article by Bob Carr, the Premier of New South Wales, which appears in Appendix D,[37] pointed out that a 'socially co-operative society' had been basically responsible for the success of the Sydney 2000 Olympics. In a perceptive article in the *Sydney Morning Herald* concerning the behaviour of Australians during the Games, Robert Manne asserted that: 'If the Sydney Olympics are any guide, the health of both the family and civil society are, in contemporary Australia, far more robust than is commonly supposed.'[38]

Because social cohesion was so evident during the Games, *The Australian* newspaper devoted Part 4 of its post-Games publication, entitled 'Lessons from the Olympics', to a discussion of social capital and how it manifested itself in a positive way during the period of the Olympic and Paralympic Games. The authors of the articles in this supplement were Michelle Gunn and Martin Stewart-Weeks. Gunn suggested that 'Sydney dropped its guard during the Games and social capital soared'. At a later time she commented that 'Sydney wasn't a city known for its friendliness ... but then something happened. The rules of public engagement changed' and people treated each other with a more caring attitude. This was exemplified by the 50 000 *(sic 55 000)* Olympic and services volunteers, whose behaviour, combined with the goodwill of the residents of Sydney, created a feeling of trust and an harmonious social environment, even though such values had been widely considered to be in decline in the current economic rationalist agenda.[39]

Martin Stewart-Weeks also stated in his article that 'we saw people working together, we saw trust and respect and we saw that sense of shared purpose and common focus which is what community is. And we liked it!' However, he went on to warn of the danger of complacency, asking: 'Are our stocks of social capital robust enough to extend that spirit of trust and co-operation for a common cause in which we took such delight for three weeks? ... The biggest fear is that we are losing our capacity for community even as we work out that we need it now more than ever. It doesn't have to be that way, but we will have to work harder to make sure it doesn't happen.'[40] This erudite article by Stewart-Weeks is reproduced in Appendix E.

Reflections

It is clear, from the above observations relating to the 2000 Olympic and Paralympic Games, that Sydney was a triumphant culmination of almost 200 years of evolution of the Australian sports system. Furthermore, it was obvious that most Australians were very happy with their teams' performances. And they were proud of the positive social environment engendered by the Games.

That Australia has been able to rise from its harsh beginnings to the point where it is now regarded, by and large, as a fair and just society, says a great deal about the way in which this country has evolved. Sport has been able to play an important role in this evolution and our forebears must be gratefully acknowledged for their foresight, wisdom and perseverance in this process.

Chapter Eight
The future — where
to from here?

After the Sydney Olympics

In the period following Sydney 2000, as the year drew to a close, many Australians reflected that it was as though the Olympics had been a dream rather than a reality. It is normal after the Olympics for a decline to occur both in spectator interest and sports sponsorship. John Coates, the current President of the Australian Olympic Committee, has recently commented on this phenomenon on two occasions.[1 2] Other factors contributing to the drop-off in interest were the retirements of some athletes after the Games and the reduction in training and competition schedules by others.

Avoiding a post-Olympic slump

THE PRE-GAMES PERIOD

THE OLYMPIC LEGACY

The way in which the Australian Sports Commission and the Australian Olympic Committee integrated their programs was discussed in the section on the lead-up to Sydney 2000 in Chapter Seven. John Coates was able to obtain $60 million as an endorsement for Sydney's candidature in the 2000 Olympics in 1991, and in 1996 he also managed to obtain an additional $88 million, which was placed into the Australian Olympic Foundation. These funds enabled the first Australian Youth Olympic Festival to be held at the Sydney Olympic venues in 2001 and it is planned that this festival will be held every two years from that time on. In addition, a large team of Australian athletes will be able to compete every fourth year in the East Asian Games, which are held in the year following the Olympics. These two sports festivals will help to give Australian athletes valuable international competition between Olympic Games.[3]

THE SPORTS REPORTS

Two reports had been initiated before the Sydney Olympics in 1999. The first one was produced by the Australian Sports Commission and was a comprehensive and visionary document entitled 'The Australian Sports Commission — Beyond 2000'. In the Foreword of this report, Peter Bartels, the respected chairman of the commission, stated: 'While we are confident that the Olympics will provide a pinnacle of Australian sporting success, they are by no means the end of the line.

The Olympics can, and must, be used as a springboard to even higher levels of sporting achievement and to further enhancement of our sports system.'[4] The other document was initiated by the government in the form of a white paper for the future development of sport and recreation in the post-2000 period. This was entitled 'Shaping Up — A Review of Commonwealth Involvement in Sport and Recreation in Australia'. The then Minister, Jackie Kelly, established a Sports 2000 Task Force chaired by Ross Oakley to carry out the above investigation.[5]

THE POST-GAMES PERIOD

In an attempt to combat any lingering post-Olympic complacency, John Coates released the '2004 Olympic Medal Plan'[6] shortly after the conclusion of the Paralympic Games. This challenging report, in which the Federal Government was requested to provide realistic support for Australia's Olympic athletes up to June 2005, was submitted to the government in early November 2000.

The second post-Games document was not a report as such, but rather a special supplement developed by the Australian Sports Commission for *The Australian* newspaper (17 November 2000) and was a timely publication, informing the public of the sports commission's future directions. The lead article by the chairman, Peter Bartels, entitled 'It's Time to Get Active and Change — Sport in the 21st Century', was one of the most important statements made in regard to national sports policy in the last decade. It signalled a directional change in the Australian Sports Commission's philosophy, which will devolve and modernise the sports system. The positive effect it will have in the future is discussed later in this chapter.[7]

Finally, the Australian Sports Commission produced its 'Strategic Plan 2002-2005' in 2002, which outlines its major directions and the strategies it will use to achieve them. By clearly enunciating how the commission will interface with the wider community in further developing all aspects of sport in the country, the ASC sent a positive message on the way all Australians can benefit from its many and varied programs.[8]

Post-Olympic performances

WORLD CHAMPIONSHIPS

In 2001, Australian athletes won 13 world championships in team sports and 26 in individual events.[9] [10] [11] [12] The majority of these were in the non-Olympic categories, demonstrating that Australia was also doing very well in the other international sports in which it competes. This was an even better result than in 1999, when Australian athletes won 12 world team championships and 21 individual championships. Many of the non-Olympic sports are not big budget items, so Australia is certainly 'getting its money's worth' by funding them.[13] The above results contradict negative statements made by several sports administrators concerning this country's 2001 international performances. Some journalists also appear to have made similar criticisms without checking the facts about these results, which appear in Appendix F.

THE GOODWILL GAMES

It was the Cold War that originally inspired Ted Turner to initiate the Goodwill Games and they appeared to fulfil a useful purpose until the Iron Curtain collapsed at the end of the 1980s. In recent times their critics have regarded them either as an anachronism or as an expensive international sports festival whose standards have slowly deteriorated. For either or both of these reasons, a decision has been made to discontinue them. With 47 countries competing in Brisbane in early September 2001 and a large number of invited elite athletes attending, perhaps 50 per cent of the events could be regarded as 'international' as far as world standards are concerned. Australia won 29 gold medals, and 75 medals in total; Russia was second with 24 gold and 71 medals overall. Even though several of their Olympic gold medallists did compete, the USA was criticised for not sending its strongest team. Australia's performance was generally rated as good, despite the fact that in several events where gold medals were won, the standards were not truly international.[14]

THE 2002 'MEDAL TALLY'

The Australian Olympic Committee examined the 2002 performances of Australia's Olympic athletes, comparing their results with those of athletes from other countries who had competed internationally in the same events in that year. If the Olympics had been held during 2002, the projected medal tally for Australia would have been approximately 46 (14 gold, 18 silver, 14 bronze), in comparison to the Sydney 2000 total of 58 medals (16 gold, 25 silver, 17 bronze). This estimate would have placed Australia fourth in the medal tally, behind the United States, Germany and Russia, and in the same position as the Sydney 2000 Games.[15] However, if China had sent her top teams to several world championships, they might well have gained more medals and been placed fourth, just ahead of Australia. John Coates was quoted as saying that he did not believe the Australian team would maintain its position in the top four nations at the 2004 Games in Athens.[16] His statement was mainly based on the AOC's 2004 Olympic Medal Plan, which states in the specific Objectives for 2004 that Australia aims 'to place ... within the top five nations on the total and gold medal counts'.[17]

THE SALT LAKE CITY WINTER OLYMPICS AND PARALYMPICS

Australia had not fared well in previous Winter Olympics, despite a steady improvement in several of the events during the 1990s. However, Australia's overall performances in 2002 in Salt Lake City were better than ever before, with two gold medals being won by the team. Stephen Bradbury won the gold medal in the 500 metres speed skating event after a spectacular collision eliminated all

Michael Milton's brilliant skiing
performances won him four gold
medals at the 2002 Winter
Paralympic Games in Salt Lake City.
(By courtesy of the Australian
Sports Commission.)

his rivals in the final; and Alisa Camplin, whose profile appears below, was the
other gold medallist in the aerial skiing event. In addition to Australia's excellent
Winter Olympic performance, the outstanding achievements of Michael Milton in
the 2002 Paralympic Games must be mentioned. Milton won four downhill skiing
events in Salt Lake City, adding to his previous total of six gold medals won in
Paralympic Winter Games and World Championships since 1992. The AOC's
Olympic Winter Institute is now in full operation and with additional funding
from the AIS and the ASC, Australia's results should steadily improve over the
next few years.

SOARING TO GOLD

Alisa Camplin sprang on to the world scene at the Salt Lake City Winter Olympics as she soared to success as an aerial skier. It seemed as though she had come from nowhere, but in fact Alisa had been pursuing her Olympic dream through a variety of sports. She began with running, collecting 15 Victorian state age-group medals in little athletics, and went on to win several state titles in gymnastics.

Various injuries saw her ambitions thwarted one by one, until, almost by accident, she was 'discovered' at a Melbourne ski show by Geoff Lipshut, who later became coach of the Australian Winter Olympic Institute. Alisa was studying information technology at university at the time, and in order to pay for her lift tickets at the week-end, she was working at various part-time jobs and coaching gymnastics through the week.

She was fortunate to be in the same squad as the world champion, Jacqui Cooper, with whom she has maintained a friendly rivalry for several years. Jacqui became her 'standard', as Alisa doggedly trained to catch up on her late start in this challenging sport. Despite further injuries such as broken ribs, collarbones and micro-fractures of her feet, she persisted with a gruelling schedule of mental and physical training.

When Jacqui Cooper crashed out of competition, Alisa, then 27, had the maturity and skill to step up onto Jacqui's pedestal. The phenomenal jump which won her the gold medal at Salt Lake City surprised everyone except her coach and those who had been aware for many years of Alisa's ability and tenacity. Cheerful, plucky, modest, yet mentally strong, Alisa Camplin is the epitome of an Australian athlete who has somehow managed to succeed despite daunting obstacles and great personal sacrifice.[18] [19] [20]

Alisa Camplin demonstrates the form that won her the gold medal in the women's aerial event at the 2002 Winter Olympics in Salt Lake City. (Newspix.)

THE 2002 COMMONWEALTH GAMES

Before the Games took place, there was a great deal of speculation as to whether the Australian team could maintain its supremacy by winning the medal tally for the fourth consecutive time. It was clear after the fifth day of competition that this would happen and that the anticipated challenge from England would not occur in 2002. Australian won 206 medals, 82 of them gold, 62 silver and 62 bronze, which was eight more than in Kuala Lumpur in 1998. England won 165 medals, 54 of them gold. This was a much better performance than in Kuala Lumpur, where their medal tally had totalled 136, including 36 gold. There is no doubt that the recently developed sports system in Britain is starting to pay off, and this subject will be discussed more fully later in this chapter.[21]

The most encouraging aspect of the Australian team's performance was the high standard of many of the younger athletes, several of whom surpassed their highly-rated senior team members. The men's and women's cycling teams were both outstanding, while competitors in boxing, weight lifting, shooting and squash improved their performances. Australian athletes again demonstrated their tenacity and ability to rise to the occasion at the Manchester Games, and several of their feats are recorded in the profile outlined below. Performances in non-Olympic sports and at the Manchester Games also indicate that Australian athletes are likely to maintain their 2001 record in the various world championships to be held in the next few years.

Australia and New Zealand battle it out during overtime in the 2002 Commonwealth Games netball final. (Getty Images.)

THE TENACITY OF THE AUSTRALIAN ATHLETE

Australia's sportsmen and sportswomen are tenacious opponents, especially when representing their country in international sporting contests. They also have a reputation for responding well to pressure, and this was again evident at the 2002 Commonwealth Games in Manchester, and graphically illustrated in the following examples:

- *Ian Thorpe* won six gold medals and one silver against high-level competition, with one world record and another near-record.[22]

- *The Australian men's cycling team* won eight gold medals in eight events, despite some of its members having just competed in the gruelling 3500 kilometre Tour de France; and several of these performances were either world or Commonwealth records.[23] [24]

- *Margaret Hemsley* displayed great fighting spirit when she crashed on the wet road after leading the 93 kilometre road race by more than 300 metres 14 kilometres from the finish line. She courageously re-mounted her bike and finished in 12th place, despite a broken collarbone and a badly lacerated elbow.[25]

- Australia's top walkers showed dogged determination in all the events they entered. By decisively winning the 20 kilometre walk, *Jane Saville* atoned for her nightmare disqualification at the Sydney Olympics when she was close to the finish and leading the field.[26] And *Nathan Deakes* won the 20 kilometre and 50 kilometre double, with only 38 hours between the events. Despite suffering severe cramps midway through the longer race, he persevered to the end, breaking the Commonwealth record by 17 minutes.[27]

- Three Australian women in their thirties gained the first three places in the women's marathon. The Australian newspaper's headline 'MARATHON MAMAS' said it all, as *Kerryn McCann* and *Krishna Stanton*, the gold and silver medallists, each have a small child.[28]

- It took a nail-biting sudden-death play-off between traditional rivals New Zealand and Australia to determine the *women's netball* result, with Australia finally snatching victory. And this occurred only one day after the *Australian rugby union* team performed a similar feat to retain the Bledisloe Cup against New Zealand in Sydney.[29]

TEAM COHESION PAYS DIVIDENDS

The importance of teamwork was brilliantly illustrated to both spectators and television viewers during the 2002 Commonwealth Games in the 188 kilometre road racing event.

In order to psych up for their race the following day, Stuart O'Grady, Baden Cooke, Michael Rogers, Cadel Evans, Brad McGee and Nathan O'Neill volunteered to be bike handlers for the Australian 4000 metres pursuit team, which managed to win the gold medal in world record time.

With their team-mates' victory of the previous evening fresh in their minds, the road racing team planned a tactical race in an effort to ensure the best possible result for at least three of the six-man team. For four and a half hours they virtually played with the rest of the field, allowing several breakaways to tire themselves out as they sat in their slip-streams before sprinting past them. At the 120 kilometre mark they attacked with such velocity that only seven other riders could stay in the bunch with them. In a demonstration of true team spirit, the six riders decided that Stuart O'Grady, who had performed with distinction in the Tour de France just a week beforehand, was the fittest among them, so they sent him on his way after a steep hill climb.

Sixteen seconds ahead at the bottom of the hill, O'Grady outpaced the pack while the other five Australian riders continued to protect his lead. Cadel Evans and Baden Cooke were then dispatched, crossing the finishing line to win the silver and bronze medals behind O'Grady.[30][31]

FUTURE SPORTING POTENTIAL

Currently Australia has numerous junior athletes who have excelled internationally. The wealth of potential is obvious in the following list:

- *Liesel Jones* — a young swimmer who has already won a silver medal in breast-stroke at the 2000 Olympics, as well as in the 2001 world championships.[32] She also won two gold medals at the 2002 Commonwealth Games in Manchester.

- *Sarah Lauren* — a 15-year-old gymnast who won two gold medals at the Commonwealth Games in Manchester.[33]

- *Rick Kulacz* — a 17-year-old golfer who won the International Federation of Junior Golf World Title with a six under par score of 282 in Mexico. Rick was then one of the youngest golfers in the field.[34]

- *Hussy Hussein* — a young flyweight boxer who has won the vast majority of his professional fights by knock-out. Currently he is a WBO title contender.[35]

Holly Grima, a member of the Australian Opals, is one of this country's most talented young basketball players. (By courtesy of the Australian Sports Commission.)

- *Alex Brosque* – an outstanding young national league soccer player, already in demand from overseas clubs.[36]

- *Jana Pittman* – a young 400 metre hurdler whose performance at the Commonwealth Games in Manchester was outstanding.[37]

- *Philippe Rizzo* – the first junior male gymnast to win a major international open event, and this was achieved at the 2001 Goodwill Games. He followed up that success by winning three gold medals at the Manchester Commonwealth Games. Rizzo's profile appears below.[38]

- *Shane Watson* – an outstanding junior cricketer, both as a batsman and a bowler, who was chosen in the Australian cricket team to tour South Africa in 2002.[39]

- *David Barnes* – an archer who recently defeated the 2000 Olympic gold medallist, Simon Fairweather, and whose scores currently place him in a medal-winning position at the Olympic level.[40]

- *Holly Grima* – a 19-year-old basketballer from the AIS who has already played for Australia. Her team was third in the world championships in late 2002.[41]

THE GYMNASTIC RIZZOS

Philippe Rizzo is the first male gymnast in the history of the sport in Australia who has an excellent chance of winning an Olympic medal.

Philippe is from a gymnastic family, as his father represented France in the Rome Olympic Games in 1960 and his brother Blaise is a former Australian gymnastics champion. André Rizzo, Philippe's father, continued to compete for five years after Rome, then migrated to Australia in 1970. Ten years later he set up the Australian Gymnastics Academy in Belmore in Sydney, and Kerschler has said in an interesting article that 'Philippe learnt the sport while he was still in nappies sitting on the rubber mats' in his father's Sydney gymnasium. At the age of 15 Philippe gained a scholarship to the AIS, where he has trained for the last six years.

Rizzo has risen to prominence very rapidly, representing Australia in the 2000 Sydney Olympics at 19 years of age. In the World University Games in 2001 he won a gold medal on the high bar with an impressive score of 9.812, repeating the victory at the Goodwill Games. In the same year he also won the silver medal in the high bar event at the World Gymnastic Championships at Ghent in Belgium, and has the distinction of being the first Australian ever to win a medal at that level.

This outstanding young gymnast won three gold medals at the 2002 Manchester Commonwealth Games in impressive style and looks set to improve these exceptional performances as he matures over the next few years.[42 43]

International competition in gymnastics is very intense, but Australia's triple Commonwealth Games gold medallist, Philippe Rizzo, appears set to reach the top. (By courtesy of the Australian Sports Commission.)

In addition to the above high-profile juniors, several other Australian athletes are currently demonstrating their talent in the national and international arenas. Many of them have recently reached the top and are expected to remain at that level for several years because they are still relatively young for their sport. Brad McGee, whose profile appears below, is a good example.

Problems ahead for Australian sport

The steady resurgence of Australian sport after the low point of the Montreal Olympics was hardly noticed by most of our international rivals until the early 1990s. Australian performances gradually improved, with some advance notice being given at the Barcelona Olympics in 1992. However, it was not until 1994, after the Games had been awarded to Sydney, that other countries began to realise that Australia was the 'big sleeper' in international sport, and that it was shaping up to be a major sporting power by the turn of the century.

Within six months of the Sydney 2000 Olympics announcement, various sporting contingents began to arrive in Australia's eastern states to make arrangements for accommodation and training. While in Australia, many of the foreign delegations were impressed when they visited the AIS in Canberra and several of the state institutes of sport. However, it was not until Australia's excellent performance in Atlanta in 1996 that this country's sporting potential was fully recognised, and it was realised that a unique professional sports system had been created in the southern hemisphere. Moreover, there were several aspects of it that some countries wanted to adopt.

Threats from other countries

Because the Australian system was proving to be so successful, it was only a matter of time before rival countries began to examine it in detail. However, they could only learn so much from external observation, so they soon began to invite Australian administrators, coaches and sports scientists to consult and lecture. The next step, which occurred shortly after the Sydney Olympics, was to offer contracts to some of this country's high-profile specialists, usually at much higher salaries than they had been receiving in Australia.

Several countries such as South Africa, France and Canada have recently hired Australian sporting personnel, but the most demand has come from the United Kingdom. For well over a century Australians have maintained a love/hate relationship with Britain in regard to sport. During that time, Australia, with approximately 30 per cent of the British population, has been successful in at least 60 percent of the major Australia-United Kingdom sporting competitions. Especially during the last decade, Australia has been the more dominant country in both Olympic and non-Olympic sports, and informed individuals from the United Kingdom have attributed much of this success to the effectiveness of the Australian sports system.

THE CYCLING 'IRON MAN'

Brad McGee is one of Australia's great sportsmen. Born in Bankstown, Sydney, in 1976, McGee started cycling at ten and by the age of 17 had won gold and bronze medals at the World Junior Cycling Championships.

After completing his HSC in 1993 he took up a scholarship at the Australian Institute of Sport. There he honed his skills to the point where he became a top international rider, winning two gold medals at the 1994 Commonwealth Games and another two in 1998. In 1996 at the Atlanta Olympics he won two bronze medals, having taken a gold medal at the world championships in 1995.

In 1997 Brad turned professional and began road racing in Europe in the big league, with back-up from the NSW Institute of Sport from 1998. He had three victories in 1999, returning to compete in the Sydney 2000 Olympics only 24 hours after completing the Tour de France. Despite having to deal with a broken collarbone, which had a plate fastened to it with seven screws, he managed to win two Olympic bronze medals. In 2001 and 2002 he won four stages in European cycle tours, gained two second places and won Stage 7 of the 2002 Tour de France. Having survived a heavy fall in Stage 11 of the Tour, he flew to the Manchester Commonwealth Games, where he won two gold medals just 48 hours after finishing the arduous 3273 kilometre French event. His time in the 4000 metres individual pursuit was a Commonwealth record and would have won him the past two world championships. In late 2002, in the World Track Cycling Championships in Copenhagen, Denmark, he rode another outstanding race, winning the gold medal in the men's 4000 metres individual pursuit.

As well as being a tenacious competitor and a popular team member within the cycling community, Brad is also a very positive ambassador for Australian sport in general.[44] [45]

Brad McGee is currently one of the world's top cyclists, both on the road and on the track, as well as being one of the most tenacious competitors Australia has produced. (Newspix.)

THE BRITISH CHALLENGE

For at least 30 years there have been calls in the United Kingdom to develop a modern sports system, and John Major was the first Prime Minister to officially acknowledge the need. However, he was unable to establish any such system because the Conservative Government failed to retain office in the 1997 elections. When the Blair Government came to office, it announced that it would help sport to develop along similar lines to several European countries, as well as Australia.

After a slow beginning, the new Labour Government in the United Kingdom has generously funded sport through a national lottery. In the first year of the program to June 2000, one billion pounds, or $A2.6 billion, were allocated to modernise their system.[46] Since that time their yearly budgets have been substantial and their forward funding for the Athens Olympics is generous. As just one example, the UK Sports Institute has already been set up and several satellite centres of excellence are currently being established throughout the country.[47]

In the near future there are two threats which an invigorated British sports system will pose for Australia. The first is that this country will lose even more of its capable and experienced personnel, as large amounts of money have recently been paid for the services of Australian managers, coaches and sports scientists. Approximately 30 high profile Australians were contracted to UK sport, some of the more notable being David Moffett (who was CEO of Sport England and who has recently moved to a similar position with the Welsh Rugby Union), Wilma Shakespear (CEO of the English Sports Institute), Rod Marsh (Director, English Cricket Academy), Ian Robson (CEO of 'Sport Scotland') and Bill Sweetenham (National Performance Director of Swimming).[48] The Australian press has made much of this, some even suggesting that 'defections' from Australian sport will continue for several years. Such headlines as 'BRITISH SPORT THE AUSTRALIAN WAY',[49] 'OUR BLOODLESS COUP OF BRITAIN MAY BE JUST BEGINNING',[50] 'WAKE-UP CALL',[51] 'ENGLISH CASH TO TEST OUR MEDAL METTLE',[52] 'MARSH SWITCHES ALLEGIANCE TO OLD FOE'[53] and 'THE POMS' REVENGE'[54] are just some that have appeared in Australian newspapers in recent times.

The second threat to Australia's sports supremacy will be the large amount of money the British are currently investing in their national sports organisations. In some cases this is four times as much as Australia spends on the equivalent sport and is accompanied by a concerted effort to encourage juniors to join various sports associations.[55] They already have in place an active talent identification program and are attracting young second-generation migrants from the Caribbean, Africa and the sub-continent, who excel in several Olympic and high-profile non Olympic sports. It is now well documented that these races possess certain physical characteristics that give them a performance advantage in several sports over athletes of Anglo-Celtic origin.[56] Furthermore, these young people, like Australia's 'currency lads' of the early 1800s and the African-Americans in the United States in the 1970s and early 1980s, will try to use high-profile sport in the United Kingdom as a pathway to social equality and financial security. With these groups moving into a much more professionalised sports system and on sheer numbers alone, Britain is likely to become a strong sporting nation.

Some Australians are blasé about this, but they may not be aware that since the early 1960s the British sports system has been one of the most antiquated in the developed world, which gives it enormous room for improvement. Furthermore, any student of history will be aware that the British are a resolute people who could rise to the occasion and acquit themselves well, particularly if they fully embrace the present challenge. However, there are several major problems that Britain will need to overcome if she wishes to become a world sporting power:

- The country will need to establish a 'sport culture' in which participation and elite sport have equal status. Several commentators believe that there is currently too much emphasis on the former.

- Mark Peters, a very experienced sports administrator and currently Executive Director of the Australian Sports Commission, believes that Britain has yet to establish well-defined athlete development pathways similar to those which have been so successful in this country.[57]

- David Moffet was a former Executive Director of New Zealand Rugby Union, then of the Australian National Rugby League. He then became the CEO of Sport England before taking a similar position with the Welsh Rugby Union. He was quoted in *The Guardian* newspaper as saying: 'British sport would never enjoy long-term success because of red tape and an unwillingness to change [and that it] is like a convoluted bowl of spaghetti [with] too many governing bodies and committees.' Moffet further suggested that Britain would need to move quickly to overhaul several other countries including Australia.[58]

Unless the above changes occur, the United Kingdom will not fully reap the rewards one might expect from the large amounts of money currently being spent to modernise its sports system.

CHALLENGES FROM EUROPE

Australia has three other major European competitors in Germany, France and Italy. Although all three countries were defeated in the medal count at the Sydney Olympics by Australia, Germany has now fully unified the former East and West German sports systems into one very functional and devolved unit, and the world can expect some excellent performances from them in the near future. In fact the Australian Olympic Committee's 2002 medal assessment indicated that Germany has already moved ahead of Australia, now occupying second place on the notional Olympic medal tally, with 56 notional medals in comparison to Australia's 46.[59] As for the other two countries, France has a well devolved and functional sports system and will steadily improve its international performances over the next few years; and Italy is in a similar position. Australia will need to perform at its very best to remain among the top five nations of the world in the Olympic sports in the foreseeable future.

ASSISTANCE TO OTHER COUNTRIES

The Australian sports system has been so visible during the late 1990s, and then further showcased by Sydney 2000, that as well as the high-profile people mentioned above, a large number of other experienced Australian sports managers have been lured overseas to assist in the organisation of several future international sports festivals. For example, approximately 60 former employees of the Sydney Organising Committee for the Olympic Games worked in the team that successfully mounted the Commonwealth Games in Manchester. Australians are already very visible in Athens, assisting in the preparation of the 2004 Olympics; and large numbers are preparing to leave for China, as that country looks to Australian expertise to advise on many aspects of the 2008 Beijing Olympics.

Issues within Australia

As previously mentioned, the Australian Sports Commission is currently considering various changes which could affect the future development of sport in Australia. The writer spoke on this subject with the executive director of the commission, Mark Peters, who made the following points during the discussion.[60]

SOCIAL ISSUES

In recent years there have been various social changes which could ultimately affect the sports system if they are not carefully considered:

- The first and most obvious change has taken place within the traditional Australian family structure. No longer do the vast majority of children come from a single-income or two-parent family, where there was strong motivation from one or both parents, encouraging children to join sports clubs. Within that family structure, one parent or the other was usually available to assist the team or club in a volunteer capacity, but in the single-parent family this is now less likely.

- Another factor is the declining birth rate in Australia. This phenomenon will see a reduction in the number of children taking part in modified, junior and eventually senior sport, thus placing pressure on both the financial and volunteer resources of club sport.

- Risk management issues are now playing a part as far as volunteers are concerned. The Australian Bureau of Statistics recently released information indicating that from the 1.7 million volunteers in Australia who played a vital role in sport up to 1997, there has been a decline of 321 000 individuals (a 19 per cent drop) over the last five years.[61] One of the main reasons for this appears to be an increase in litigation, which has only recently become a major financial issue in this country. Smaller sports clubs have found that insurance premiums have risen exponentially and on their meagre budgets they can no longer afford coverage for their coaches and officials.[62]

- Associated with the decrease in volunteer numbers is the problem of education of voluntary coaches and officials. Many parents now feel that they do not have enough basic knowledge of sports and games to coach them competently, even at the modified and/or junior level.

- Another factor is the gradual change which has taken place in Australia's migration program over the last two decades. Instead of the Europeans who arrived in large numbers in the 50s, 60s and 70s, the mix has recently shifted to one in which more people are coming from Asia and the Middle East. The children of the post World War II migrants readily joined sports clubs, whereas there has not necessarily been the same traditional or cultural motivation to participate in sport among the more recent arrivals.

When asked whether the changes mentioned above can be solved by our current system, both Mark Peters and John Coates stated that Australia will need to develop different strategies to foster sport and physical activity among the youth of the future. They believe that several modifications need to be made to the Australian sports system in the near future, particularly for junior sport.[63] [64]

COMMERCIAL VERSUS COMMUNITY INTERESTS

There are two additional and related issues that could have an effect on the delicate balance of the current sports system. The first is the clash between commercial and community interests in sport. With more money available through television and sponsorship, there is a tendency for those who stand to gain commercially from sport to develop the former at the expense of the latter. A good example of this was the Super League affair, which was discussed in Chapter Six. It will therefore be important for federal and state governments, as well as the national and state sports organisations, to monitor the balance between commercial and community interests in sport.

The second issue concerns the ratio of professionals to volunteers to actually manage grassroots sport in the future. If sport has too many professionals, there is the risk that they will steadily replace the volunteers and this creates two problems. Not only will the cost of sport *per se* rise steeply for both the competitors and the taxpayer, but the nation will also lose even more of its volunteers, thereby decreasing its current stocks of 'social capital'. Until recently Australia was able to build up and utilise a large number of volunteers, but both governments and sporting organisations need to decide on the future ratio of professionals to volunteers in the sports system and then develop strategies to maintain a balance between the two.

PHYSICAL FITNESS AND OBESITY

It is now common knowledge that fitness levels, particularly in children, are slowly declining in Australia and that obesity is on the rise. This is an insidious problem which all Western democracies face and it is basically linked to an inappropriate diet and lack of exercise. In fact, many of society's most debilitating (and increasingly prevalent) diseases are highly correlated with a lack of regular physical activity.[65] This trend, which can be directly linked to increasing levels of technology, could be gradually turned around if a cohesive program were to be delivered to the children of Australia at an early age. The youth and adults of this country could also profit from sustained and well run community health and fitness programs.

FUNDING

Funding for sport in Australia comes from several sources, the main one being private citizens, who contribute approximately $4.15 billion per year. The three tiers of government also contribute, as do the corporate sector and the Australian Olympic Committee. The total sport and recreation budget at present is approximately $6.1 billion, with the Federal Government allocating $146 million per year, the state governments combined contributing approximately $349 million per year, and local governments allocating approximately $1.1 billion per year. The remainder is made up from the corporate sector, the Australian Sports Foundation and the Olympic committee ($308 million).[66] Even though there has been a small rise in the Federal Government's projected funding for the next four years, there has been a marked decline in contributions from the corporate sector and this is currently causing considerable concern at the elite level. Details of the total budget can be found in Table 8.1.

When one examines the Australian sports budget, it is obvious that the Federal Government's contribution is minimal by international standards and that of the private citizens is very considerable. The Federal Government will need to consider increasing its funding to keep Australia's elite performances at a high level. It must also offer matching funds to the states in order to counter the low levels of physical fitness and high levels of obesity discussed above.

Table 8.1
Funding sources for sport and recreation in Australia

Sources	$Million	$Million Total
COMMONWEALTH GOVERNMENT		
Australian Sports Commission	137.0	
Australian Sports Drug Agency	4.6	
Dept of Industry Science and Resources	2.0	
Other departments	2.1	145.7
STATE SOURCES		
Sport and recreation appropriations	194.6	
Gaming sources	87.5	
Health promotion sources	2.7	
Other — special events and projects	63.9	348.7
LOCAL GOVERNMENT		
Facilities	340.0	
Programs	787.0	1127.0
PRIVATE SOURCES		
Corporate sector	282.0	
Australian Olympic Committee	20.0	
Australian Sports Foundation	6.0	308.0
PARTICIPANTS		
Cost of sport and recreation to the private citizen		4146.0
	Total	$6075.4

SOURCES Adapted from Sport 2000 Task Force — R. Oakley, Chair (1999),
'Shaping Up — A Review of Commonwealth Involvement in Sport and Recreation
in Australia', Commonwealth of Australia, Canberra, p.67.
Peters, M. (2002) Updated budget figure for the Australian Sports Commission —
personal communication with the author.

Strategies for the future

Current changes to the sports system

Since its inception, the Australian sports system has passed through two distinct phases. The first was the steady evolution of an amateur system which was unco-ordinated and which lasted in this country until early in 1973. This particular model was common in Europe until the end of World War II. However, it started to change in Eastern, then later in Western, Europe in the postwar period, gradually becoming one in which the central government exerted a controlling influence. From early 1973 until 2000, Australia steadily adopted this model, to great effect. However, at the turn of the century, the Australian Sports Commission flagged the introduction of a third developmental phase, which was characterised by less central control. This commenced in November 2000 when the commission's chairman, Peter Bartels, announced several new policy directions to be pursued by the commission.[67] These are briefly stated below:

- Provided that the national sports organisations operate within the framework of their strategic plans, they will be able to carry out their various functions independently of the sports commission, in order to increase their administrative efficiency. This policy will even extend to the granting of a one-line budget appropriation from the commission. This partial devolution from the central controlling body changes the relationship between government and non-government sporting bodies and will raise issues of power, control, autonomy and accountability in the future. However, this should not be a concern for either party, as each national sporting organi-sation will eventually make the transition and will be the stronger for it.[68]

- The sports commission will in the future place an emphasis on additional programs, to be conducted in conjunction with the national sports organisations, in order to improve the levels of sport participation and physical fitness in the local communities and also as a base from which high-performance sport can be developed. A good example of this is the new community *Target Sports Program*, which national sports organisations and the sports commission share. Nine sports, namely Australian football, basketball, gymnastics, athletics, baseball, softball, golf, surf lifesaving and rugby union are currently in the program, and tennis was the latest sport to join in May 2002. Tennis Australia plans to attract 33 000 children from the age of seven into this low-key skills-oriented program.[69]

- The ASC will continue to work closely with Sports Industry Australia (formerly the Confederation of Australian Sport) to ensure that their industry operatives, including schools, community clubs, local governments and private enterprise, can maximise their input into Australian sport at all levels. Rather than relying only on the traditional sport model of the clubs, there are many other community agencies which can share in the enhancement of the existing programs. One partially untapped source to date is the private provider, which can act as a delivery channel for sport to improve the quality and quantity of services around Australia. It is the commission's aim to foster these alternative delivery services, so as to increase participation and performance levels in this country.

- In the past the AIS was mainly a full-time residential establishment for scholarship holders. In the future it will change to cater for a mix of full-time and part-time residential and camp-based programs, giving it the flexibility it needs to better serve high-performance sport. This is a welcome change in policy which will enable the institute to be utilised by a larger clientele in the future.

- The commission is to place an emphasis on research in the fields of sports science and sports medicine, as well as on social science as it relates to sport. The former two are reasonably well developed, but better co-ordination and co-operation is needed between the sports system and the universities. However, one of the attractive aspects of this new policy is that for the first time Australia will investigate the social ramifications of sport and recreation from an Australian perspective, rather than relying on foreign data, which may not necessarily apply to this country. The development of research in the cultural and social aspects of sport in Australia is essential and the Commission is to be applauded for this important initiative.

The above modifications are vital, as they grant more autonomy to the national sports organisations, most of which are now ready for it. The less developed NSOs will be assisted by the commission to gradually adopt a more independent mode of operation and, in addition, business and industry will be approached to play a more active role in developing sport and recreation at all levels. The AIS will also become a much more flexible organisation and sports-related research will be positively encouraged for the first time in Australia's sporting history.

These welcome changes will devolve a good deal of the responsibility for the future development of sport back to its grassroots, which should be the ultimate aim of all community development. This means that the centrally-driven model of the last three decades will be slowly phased out and the sports commission will play the role of a catalyst with the various entities which make up the sports system. If this transition can be achieved, then Australia will have progressed to the next level of its sports development.

Possible modifications for the future

It is important to acknowledge that the vast majority of the sports system's current programs are functioning efficiently. Many of them have been in place for a long time and have served sport well; therefore they should not be tampered with. In section two of this chapter, several social issues were mentioned which might lead to a decrease in performance and participation levels in the future. However, if the following recommendations are introduced, they may counter these trends.

- Some children, because of their family structure, do not have as much access to sport as other young Australians. The federal and state governments should develop introductory programs through their sports organisations to help these children to experience both recreational and competitive sport. This is already being done in some European countries through after-school programs, in which children are taught basic skills, before joining in weekend sport when their skill level improves.

- The declining number of volunteers has already been mentioned. In a recent article, Dortch stated that in the last five years almost 70 000 coaches and 116 800 referees or umpires had dropped out of sport.[70] The reasons given for this rapid attrition were: busy lifestyles; Australia's ageing population; fear of abusive players; and lack of insurance cover in case of litigation. Affirmative action will need to be taken, as the system cannot afford to lose coaches and officials at that rate. Anecdotal evidence indicates that both these groups require more education and support, so as to feel secure and confident to perform their roles. They also need to be covered by public risk insurance in case of litigation, which is becoming much more common.[71]

- Another figure given by Dortch was that 134 400 sports administrators have dropped out of sport since 1997,[72] particularly since the implementation of the Goods and Services Tax. It has been stated that not only are former club treasurers having problems with the complexity of the new system, but that secretaries have reported an increase in paperwork from regulatory bodies for the completion of more complex returns. Affirmative action is needed to streamline accounting procedures and offer more sophisticated training courses for potential treasurers and amateur sporting club office-holders. It may be possible also for the state sports organisations, through their clubs, to consider the granting of a modest honorarium to the individuals concerned, to cover at least some of their incidental expenses.

- Recent migrants are not yet joining junior sports clubs at the same rate as other young Australians, even though some of them are already being steadily inculcated into the Australian way of life. For example, Bradley[73] reports that there are now 208 junior rugby league teams in the Canterbury Bulldogs' district in Sydney and that some of these teams consist largely of young migrant girls and boys. North[74] suggests that Hazem El Masri, the Canterbury player of the year in 2000, is probably responsible for much of the Muslim interest in the above competition. Affirmative action is needed to motivate young migrant children to participate in sport and to assist their successful young athletes to become good role models for their local communities.

LOW FITNESS — HIGH OBESITY

As previously mentioned, Australia has still not addressed in a systematic way the steady decline in fitness levels or the increase in obesity among the Australian population. Politicians, physical educators and some members of the medical profession have discussed this topic for at least 30 years, but no sustained educational program for children or adults has yet been established in an effort to counteract these trends.

There are two possible solutions to this problem, outlined below:

• State Education Departments should all be strongly encouraged to upgrade primary school health and physical education programs by providing trained health and physical education teachers in this specialist field. The debate as to whether this is possible or not from a financial viewpoint should cease, because Australia cannot afford not to have it. With the rapidly escalating health-care costs in recent years, the Federal Government must immediately act as a catalyst with the states to develop this preventive medical program.

• The federal and state governments should develop a community health and fitness program which targets youth and adults and which is modelled on the successful *Life Be In It* program of the late 1970s.

ELITE SPORT

In a recent letter to the Federal Minister for Sport, John Coates emphasised that two major problems facing our elite athletes are direct athlete assistance and additional financial support for coaches. European nations, especially the United Kingdom, are generously supporting performance-based incentive schemes for their top athletes and coaches in the four-year period leading up to the Athens Olympic Games. This has been done by linking the athletes' and coaches' personal funding to their current success in international competitions. Australia introduced a similar incentive scheme for the first time in the run-up to Sydney 2000, but this support has greatly diminished since that time. This is currently Australia's biggest weakness and urgent funding is needed to rectify the deficiency.[75]

FUTURE FUNDING

In order to increase funding to cater for the fine-tuning of existing programs and to establish the others mentioned above, additional sources of finance will need to be found. Unlike the Western European countries, Australia has never had a national lottery to assist in the funding of sport and culture, because state rights currently preclude this. The establishment of such a source of revenue would be a good solution, but is not a viable option in the immediate future. Therefore, urgent action should be taken to raise additional funding for various needy areas within the system. The total federal and state sport and fitness budgets are currently under-funded by approximately $60 million per annum, or around ten per cent, and must be topped up to a level which will enable Australia to function on equal terms with other Western democracies.

The way forward?

Readers will already have appreciated that, by and large, this nation's sports system is running reasonably smoothly. However, Australia cannot rest on its laurels and needs to act to shore up some of the small cracks which are starting to appear in the structure. The structural modifications and the additional funding mentioned above would improve the current system and would lead to the evolution of the next stage of the Australian sports system.

It is important to remember that Australian sport has undergone a transformation over the past 200 years from a simple localised amateur system to a highly centralised and professional one which is basically responsible for new performance standards in this country. Its development has become more complex as it integrated its policies at both the federal and state levels. The high point of the process was undoubtedly reached at the Sydney Olympics and Australia's sports system is now both widely admired and increasingly copied.

However, nothing ever stands still, especially when a more democratic process is embarked upon. In the future many new initiatives will evolve, bringing greater devolution, decentralisation and democracy to Australian sport. More responsibility and authority will be vested in the national sports organisations as well as the state or territory sport entities and there will be a greater focus on new ways to build grassroots participation. The next phase of the sports system's evolution will be a more complex network of resources and expertise combined with a high degree of autonomy, but with a strong commitment to high standards.

This evolution should not be construed as a swing of the pendulum back to the unstructured amateur approach of the past. Nor is it about abandoning the gains this country has already made in terms of its investment in sport. Rather, the new way forward will be for the Federal Government, through the Australian Sports Commission, to play the role of a catalyst. What does this really mean? It means retaining a role not so much as a driver or controller of the system, but rather as a smart and strategic investor in it.[76]

If Australia adopts the above approach, young Australians will continue to achieve at the elite level, and at the same time, the citizens of this nation will be able to use sport as a pathway to better personal health and well-being.

References and notes

CHAPTER ONE
AUSTRALIA – A SPORTING NATION

1   Garvin, M. (1987) *Us Aussies*, Hayzon, Sale, pp.26-27.
2   Molony, J. (2000) The Native-Born: *The First White Australians*, Melbourne University Press, Carlton South, p.51.
3   Hughes, R., (1987) *The Fatal Shore*, Alfred A. Knopf, New York, p.356.
4   Cunningham, P. (1827) Two Years in New South Wales, in Garvin, M., op. cit., p.33.
5   Garvin, M. (1987) op. cit., p.31.
6   Ibid., p.46.
7   Ibid., pp.42-82.
8   Jacques, T. and Pavia, G. (1976) Introduction to Elford, K., Sport in Australian Society: A Perspective, in *Sport in Australia*, McGraw-Hill Book Co., Sydney, p.33.
9   Elford, K. (1976) Sport in Australian Society, in Jacques T. and Pavia, G. (eds) (1976) op. cit., pp.35-36.
10 Ibid., p.36.
11 Ibid., pp.41-42.
12 Molony, J. (2000) op. cit., p.123.
13 Elford, K. (1976) op. cit., p.33.
14 Snyder, E. and Spreitzer, E. (1978) *Social Aspects of Sport*, Prentice-Hall Inc., Englewood Cliffs, New Jersey, p.13.
15 Garvin, M. (1987) op. cit., pp.121-122.
16 Mandle, W. (1973) Cricket and Australian Nationalism in the Nineteenth Century, *Journal of the Royal Australian Historical Society*, Vol. 59, Part 4, pp.237-241.
17 Ibid.
18 Chan, G. (2000) Battlefield or Cricket Pitch: The Test of a Nation, *Review, The Weekend Australian*, 28-29 October, pp.6-7.
19 Headon, D. (2001) Personal communication with the author.
20 Malouf, D. (2001) Here We Are, Against the Plan and Against the Odds, Centenary of Federation Commemoration, *The Australian*, 1 January, pp.12-13.
21 Nash, M. (2001) *Cargo for the Colony*, Navarine Publishing, Woden, ACT. p.8.
22 Elford, K. (1976) op. cit., p.34.
23 Molony, J. (2000) op. cit., p.196.
24 Dunstan, K. (1973) Our Sporting Obsession, in Jacques, T. and Pavia, G. (eds) (1976), op. cit., p.8.
25 Elford, K. (1976) op. cit., pp.37-38.
26 *Bell's Life* (1845) Sydney, 6 September.
27 *Sporting Times* (1848) Sydney, 15 July.
28 Mandle, W. (1973) op. cit., p.242.
29 Garvin, M. (1987) op. cit., p.13.
30 Dunstan, K. (1973) op. cit., p.13.
31 Waters, E. (1963) Recreation, in The Pattern of Australian Culture, in Jacques T. and Pavia, G. (eds) (1976) op. cit., p.110.

32 Dunstan, K. (1973) op. cit., p.7.
33 Mandle, W. (1985) Origins, in *Australian Sport: A Profile*, Australian Government Publishing Service, Canberra, p.4.
34 Garvin, M. (1987) op. cit., p.123.
35 Dunstan, K. (1973) op. cit., pp.11-13.
36 Sport 2000 Task Force – R. Oakley, Chair (1999) *Shaping Up – A Review of Commonwealth Involvement in Sport and Recreation in Australia*, Commonwealth of Australia, Canberra, p.89.
37 Ibid.
38 *Sydney Morning Herald* (2000) *Volunteers' Souvenir Edition*, Sydney, 6 October, p.2.
39 Ibid.
40 Mandle, W. (1985) op. cit., p.3.
41 Molony, J. (2000) op. cit., p.123.
42 Australian News and Information Bureau (1962) Sport: A Reference Paper, in Jacques, T. and Pavia, G. (eds) (1976) op. cit., p.76.
43 Ibid.
44 Molony, J. (2000) op. cit., pp.74-75.
45 Vamplew, W. (1994) Australians and Sport, in Vamplew, W. and Stoddart, B. (eds) (1994) *Sport In Australia: A Social History*, Cambridge University Press, Melbourne, pp.7-10.
46 Ibid.
47 Mandle, W. (1985) op. cit., pp.9-10.
48 Cashman, R. (1994) Cricket, in Vamplew, W. and Stoddart, B. (eds) (1994) op. cit., p.60.
49 Mandle, W. (1973) op. cit., p.233.
50 Fitzsimons, P. (1999) *Everyone and Phar Lap: Face to face with the best of Australian sport*, Harper Sports, Sydney, pp.12-13.
51 Ibid., p.6.
52 Vamplew, W. (1994) op. cit., p.3.
53 Tomkins, J. (2002) Oarsome Foursome Official Website – http://www.oarsomefou rsome.com.au/OF_bio.yel.htm
54 Mandle, W. (1985) op. cit., p.5.
55 Vamplew, W. (1994) op. cit., p.3.
56 Fitzsimons, P. (1999) op. cit., pp.44-74.
57 Molony, J. (2000) op. cit. pp.123-125.
58 Ibid.
59 Cliff, P. (1999) *A Sporting Nation: Celebrating Australia's Sporting Life*, National Library of Australia, Canberra, p.50.
60 Mandle, W. (1985) op. cit., pp.4-5.
61 Garvin, M. (1987) op. cit., p.122.
62 Mandle, W. (1985) op. cit., p.7.
63 Cliff, P. (1999) op. cit., p.55.
64 Mandle, W. (1985) op. cit., p.7.
65 Australian News and Information Bureau (1962) op. cit., p.76.
66 Mandle, W. (1985) op. cit., p.7.
67 Turner, I. (1979) The Emergence of 'Aussie Rules', in Headon, D. (ed) (2001) *The Best Ever Australian Sports Writing: a 200 year collection*, Black Inc., pp.265-270.
68 Mandle, W. (1985) op. cit., p.7.
69 Hickie, T. (1998) 1863 And All That, in Headon, D. (ed) (2001) op. cit., pp.379-381.

70 Mandle, W. (1985) op. cit., p.9.

71 Cliff, P. (1999) op. cit., p.42.

72 Gatt, R. (2001) Ruling Body Pins Financial Hopes on Levy Boost, *The Australian*, Sydney, 12 December, p.22.

73 Cunneen, C. (1979) The Rugby War, in Headon, D. (ed) (2001) op. cit., pp.313-318.

74 Sport 2000 Task Force – R. Oakley, Chair (1999) op. cit., p.113.

75 de Groot, C., with Webster, J. (1991) *Pro Golf: Out of the Rough*, Professional Golfers' Association of Australia, Cattai, pp.12-13.

76 Mandle, W. (1985) op. cit., p.9.

77 Australian News and Information Bureau (1962) op. cit., p.78.

78 Carlile, F. (2002) Personal communication with the author.

79 Mandle, W. (1985) op. cit., p.10.

80 Phillips, M. (2000) *From Sidelines to Centre Field: A History of Sports Coaching in Australia*, UNSW Press, Sydney, p.15.

81 Bloomfield, J. (1961) *Know-how in the Surf*, 2nd ed., Angus and Robertson, Sydney pp.2-4.

82 Maxwell, C. (1949) *Surf: Australians Against the Sea*, Angus and Robertson, Sydney, pp.14-15.

83 Vamplew, W. (1994) op. cit., p.10.

84 Cunneen, C. (1979) op. cit., pp.313-325.

85 Mandle, W. (1985) op. cit., pp.7-8.

86 Bloomfield, J. and Thompson, G. (1990) *Current Developments in Sport and Human Movement*, Course Notes for HM 684, The University of Western Australia.

87 Ibid.

88 Dunstan, K. (1973) op.cit., pp.14-16.

89 Cashman, R. (1994) op.cit., p.63.

90 Bloomfield, J. and Thompson, G. (1990) op. cit.

91 Luck P. (1999), *This Fabulous Century*, New Holland Publishers (Aust), Sydney, p.248.

92 Franks, W. (1995) Test Cricket in Stalag 344, in Headon, D. (ed) (2001) op. cit., pp.516-520.

93 Fitzsimons, P. (1997) Keith Miller, in Headon, D. (ed) (2001) op. cit., pp.523-526.

94 Maxwell, C.B. (1949) op. cit., pp.287-302.

95 Sarsfield, R. (1999) *The Olympic Games*, Dorland Kindersly, London, pp.242-268.

96 Australian News and Information Bureau (1962) op. cit., p.81.

97 Cashman, R. (1994) op. cit., p.63.

98 Australian News and Information Bureau (1962), op. cit., p.77.

99 Kinross-Smith, G., Lawn Tennis, in Vamplew, W. and Stoddart, B. (1994) op. cit., pp.139-142.

100 Australian News and Information Bureau (1962) op. cit., p.77.

101 de Groot, C., with Webster, J. (1991) op. cit., pp.50-56.

102 Australian News and Information Bureau (1962) op. cit., pp.78-79.

103 Sarsfield, R. (1999) op. cit., pp.261-264.

104 Ibid., p.264.

105 Vamplew, W. (1994) op. cit., p.18.

106 Waters, E. (1963) Recreation, in Jacques, T. and Pavia, G.(eds) (1976) op. cit., pp.104-120.

107 Dunstan, K. (1973) op. cit., pp.14-16.

108 Polack, J. (2002) http://www.cricket.org/link_to_database/PLAYERS/AUS/W/WAUGH_ SR_02001795/CV, 5/11/2002.

109 *Inside Edge* (2002) King Ricky, Year Book 2002, pp.95-99.

110 Ramsey, A. (2002) Captain Punter Playing for Big Stakes Now, *The Weekend Australian*, Sydney, 14-15 September, p.45.

111 Polack, J. (2002) ACB Web Site (2002) CV of Adam Gilchrist.

112 Cashman, R. (1994) op. cit., p.64.

113 Sarsfield, R. (1999) op. cit., pp.270-277.

114 Ibid., pp.270-281.

115 Cliff, P. (1999) op. cit., pp.95-96.

116 Australian News and Information Bureau (1962) op. cit., pp.85-86.

117 Sarsfield, R. (1999) op. cit., pp.283-296.

118 Howell, M. and Van Vliet, M. (1963) *Physical Education and Recreation in Europe*, Fitness and Amateur Sport Directorate, Department of National Health and Welfare, Ottawa.

119 Parr, D. (1976) How the East Germans Go About It, *AAP-Reuter, West Australian*, Perth, 3 August.

120 Molyneaux, D. (1962) *Central Government Aid to Sport and Physical Recreation in Countries of Western Europe*, University of Birmingham, Birmingham.

121 Ministère de l'Education Nationale, Secrétariat D'Etat A La Jeunesse et Aux Sports, (1965) Institut National des Sports, Paris.

122 Humphries, R. (1976) Mass Sport Secret of GDR Success, *Melbourne Age*, Melbourne, August.

CHAPTER TWO
BEGINNING A PROFESSIONAL SPORTS SYSTEM

1 Rees, J. (1972) On the Way to Unfitness, *The West Australian*, 26 September.

2 Gray, R. (1979) *The First Forty Years: The National Fitness and Community Recreation Councils of Western Australia 1939-1978*, Department of Youth, Sport and Recreation, Perth, pp.4-7.

3 Snedden, B. (1972) Letter to K.D. Fitch, Secretary of the Australian Sports Medicine Federation, 9 November.

4 Gray, R. (1979) op. cit., pp.35-46.

5 Wilson, K. (1969) Sport Looks for Leadership, *The Independent*, 28 September, pp. 44-46.

6 Graham, H. (1972) Letter to J. Bloomfield, 13 July. See Appendix G.

7 Bloomfield, J. (1971) Letter to R. Healy, 29 January. See Appendix G.

8 Healey, R. (1971) Letter to J. Bloomfield, 19 February. See Appendix G.

9 McLaren, G. (1971) *Hansard – Questions*, Australian Government Publishing Service, Canberra, 14 September, p.665.

10 Anderson, K. (1971) Creation of a Ministry of Sport. Answer given to Senator G. McLaren, 2 December to a Question Without Notice. Reply supplied by the Prime Minister, the Rt Hon. W. McMahon. See Appendix G.

11 McLaren, G. (1972) *Hansard – Questions*, Australian Government Publishing Service, Canberra, 26 September, p.1145.

12 Bloomfield, J. (1972) The Conservation of Man, *Proceedings of the Conference on the Human Consequences of Technological Change*, The University of Sydney, 25 August, pp.8-12. See Appendix G.

13 Cohen, B. (1972) MP: More Sport in Politics, *The West Australian*, 6 September.

14 Bloomfield, J. and Fitch, K. (1972) A Request to the Federal Government of Australia to Establish a Ministry for Recreation and Sport. (Appendix A).

15 Replies by letter, telegram and telephone were counted in mid-January 1973. They are now in the author's sports archives.

16 Bloomfield, J. (1972) Recreational Planning in the Perth Region, *ANZAAS Conference Proceedings*, 24 June, p. 6. See Appendix G. (Letter from J. Bloomfield to H. Graham dated 27 June 1972 accompanied the above ANZAAS paper.)

17 Graham, H. (1972) op. cit.

18 Gray, R. (1979) op. cit., pp. 76-79.

19 Stewart, F. (1978) Curriculum Vitae.

20 Bloomfield, J. (1969-2002), Personal Sport Archives, Perth.

21 Bloomfield, J. (1973) *The Role, Scope and Development of Recreation in Australia*, (White Paper), Report to the Commonwealth Government of Australia, Canberra.

22 Bloomfield, J. (1972) op. cit. (The Conservation of Man)

23 Bloomfield, J. and Fitch K. (1972) op. cit.

24 Information on Government Assistance to Sport (1974) — The Department of Tourism and Recreation, Commonwealth Government of Australia, Canberra.

25 Dempster, G. (2001) Personal communication with the author.

26 Dixon, B. (2002) Curriculum Vitae, Melbourne.

27 Coles, A. (1975) *Report of the Australian Sports Institute Study Group*, Department of Tourism and Recreation, Australian Government Publishing Service, Canberra.

28 The following Federal Budget allocations show reductions until 1979. Labor's last budget was $ 8.3 million in 1975-76. The next three budgets of the Liberal-Country Party Government up to 1978-79 show reductions:1976-77 — $7.6m, 1977-78 — $5.6m and 1978-79 — $5.8m. The source for the above figures is: Interim Committee for the Australian Sports Commission (1984), *Report to the Minister for Sport, Recreation and Tourism*, Australian Government Publishing Service, Canberra, March, p. 24.

29 Liberal-Country Party (1972) Youth, Sport, Leisure and Recreation Policy, Canberra. See Appendix G.

30 *The Australian* (1976) Final Medal Standings, 2 August.

31 Ibid.

32 MacDonald, B. (1976) Australia's Golden Days Have Gone, *The West Australian*, 23 July.

33 Newman, A. (1976) Our Olympic Flops will Continue Unless ..., *The West Australian*, 17 September.

34 AAP (1976) Angry Athletes Tell P.M. to be More Liberal, *The West Australian*, 26 July.

35 Davies, J. (1976) Only Mandrake Can Help Us, *Daily News*, 21 July.

36 MacDonald, B. (1976) Canadians Turn Tables on Us, *The West Australian*, 29 July.

37 Kaye, R. (1976) Britain Has a Dig, *The West Australian*, quoted directly from the *Guardian*, 29 July.

38 O'Neill, G. (1976) Fraser Orders Olympic Inquiry, *The Australian*, 27 July.

39 Hollingworth, M. (1976) Fraser Steps into the Games Debate, *The Australian*, 26 July.

40 *The West Australian* (1976) Government Sounds a Warning, 27 July.

41 Lang, B. (1976) Experts Blast Government on Sport, *Daily News*, 26 July.

42 Daly, J. (1976) Courageous Amateurs Must Fail, *The Australian*, 3 August. See Appendix G.

43 Daly, J. (2002) Curriculum Vitae, Adelaide.

44 O'Reilly, D. (1976) Finance? You're On Your Own, Sport, *The Australian*, 5 August.

45 Ibid.

46 *The West Australian* (1976) Government Accused Over Projects, 30 August.

47 *Daily News* (1976) Sport Should Get More Aid, Say 70 Percent, 30 August.

48 O'Neill, G. (1976) op. cit.

49 *The Australian* (1976) Sport Lottery Plan: Government's 'New Idea' to Raise Finance, 29 July.

50 Ellicott, R (2001) Personal communication with the author.

51 *Daily News* (1976) Governments Urged to Look to Sport, 10 September.

52 The Editor (1977) Sports Plan, *The West Australian*, 17 February.

53 Bloomfield, J. and Thompson, G. (1990) *Current Developments in Sport and Human Movement, Course Notes for HM 684*, The University of Western Australia, Section E, p.8.

54 Confederation of Australian Sport (1977) *The Financial Plight of Sport in Australia*, Canberra, May.

55 Hartung, G. (1977) Thousand to One - Sport is the Poor Relation, *The Australian*, 27 April.

56 Hartung, G. (1977) No Money, No Medals, Sports People Tell Government, *The Australian*, 1 June.

57 Hartung, G. (1978) Sport in Critical Position PM Told, *The Australian*, 10 October, p.3.

58 Hartung, G. (1977) Sportsmen Strike Gold in Federal Lobby Game, *The Australian*, August.

59 Bloomfield, J. and Thompson, G. (1990) op. cit., Section D, p.12.

60 Ibid., Section D, p.13.

61 Ibid., Section D, pp.4-6.

62 Ibid., Section D, p.11.

63 Ibid., Section D, p.8.

64 Ibid., Section D, pp.9-10.

65 Ibid., Section D, p.17.

66 Deeley, P. (1977) Aussie Sport on the Slide, *Weekend News*, quoted directly from the *London Observer*, 22 October.

67 Hartung, G. (1978) op. cit., 10 October, p.3.

68 *The West Australian* (1978) Government Policy on Sport Attacked, 25 October.

69 Bloomfield, J. (1978) *The Development of Sport in Western Australia* (White Paper), The Government of Western Australia, The Community Recreation Council of Western Australia, November.

70 Confederation of Australian Sport (1980) *The Master Plan for Sport*, Melbourne, March.

71 Bloomfield, J. (1973) op. cit.

72 Coles, A. (1975) op. cit.

73 Daly, J. (1991) Quest for Excellence – The Australian Institute of Sport, Australian Government Publishing Service, Canberra, p.18.

74 Ibid., p.19.

75 Bloomfield, J. (1969-2002) op. cit.

76 Ibid.

77 Gordon, H. (1994) *Australia and the Olympic Games*, University of Queensland Press, St. Lucia, pp.323-331.

78 Bloomfield, J. (1969-2002) op. cit.

79 Daly, J. (1991) op. cit., p.23.

80 Australian Institute of Sport (1981) *First Annual Report*, Canberra, pp.47-48.

81 Bloomfield, J. (1969-2002) op. cit.

82 Australian Institute of Sport (1981) op. cit., p.7.

83 Hobson, R. (2001) Personal communication with the author.

84 Bloomfield, J. (1969-2002) op. cit.

85 Ibid.
86 Australian Institute of Sport (1981) op. cit., pp.11-13.
87 Bloomfield, J. (1969-2002) op. cit.
88 Hurley, A. (2002) Curriculum Vitae, Newcastle.
89 Daly, J. (1991) op. cit., p.180.
90 Bloomfield, J. (1969-2002) op. cit.
91 Daly, J. (1991) op. cit., p.31.
92 Bloomfield, J. (1969-2002) op. cit.
93 Ellicott, R., (2001) op. cit.
94 Daly, J. (1991) op. cit., pp.35-40.
95 Ibid.
96 Australian Institute of Sport (1983) *Second Annual Report 1982-83*, Canberra, pp.27-52.
97 Daly, J. (1991) op. cit., pp.39-40.
98 Australian Institute of Sport (1983) op. cit., p.18.
99 Australian Sports Commission (1991-92) *Annual Report*, Canberra, pp.12-13.
100 Bloomfield, J. (1969-2002), op. cit.
101 Ibid.
102 Blanksby, B. and Thompson, G. (1981) *The Development of Sport in Victoria* (Green Paper), The Government of Victoria — Ministry for Youth, Sport and Recreation, Melbourne, April.
103 Blanksby, B. and Thompson G. (1981) *A Proposal for the Development of a Victorian Sports Assembly and a Sports House* (Green Paper), The Government of Victoria — Ministry for Youth, Sport and Recreation, Melbourne, June.
104 Thompson G. (1982) *New Directions in Sport — A Structure and Context for the Development of Sport in Victoria* (White Paper), The Government of Victoria — Ministry for Youth, Sport and Recreation, Melbourne, January.
105 Nunan, M. (2001) Personal communication with the author.
106 South Australian Sports Institute (1983) *First Annual Report 1982/1983*, Adelaide, pp.2-21.
107 Bloomfield, J. Chairman (1983) *Report of the Sport Development Working Party* (White Paper), The Government of Western Australia — Ministry for Sport and Recreation, November.
108 Foreman, W. (2002) Personal communication with the author.

CHAPTER THREE
EVOLUTION OF THE SPORTS SYSTEM

1   Brown, J. (2001) Personal communication with the author.
2   Brown, J. (1983) *Sport and Recreation: Australia on the Move*, Australian Government Publishing Service, Canberra, December, pp.1-29.
3   Brown, J. (2001) op. cit.
4   Brown, J. (1983) op. cit., pp.1-29.
5   Daly, J. (1991) *Quest for Excellence — The Australian Institute of Sport*, Australian Government Publishing Service, Canberra, p.37.
6   Ibid., p.43.
7   Ibid., p.44.
8   Ibid., p.44. Dr Miller's statement from the *Canberra Times*, 18 August 1983.
9   Bloomfield, J. (1969-2002) Personal Sport Archives, Perth.
10 Daly, J. (1991) op. cit., p.45.
11 Bloomfield, J. (1969-2002) op. cit.

12   Australian Institute of Sport. (1983-84) *Annual Report*, Canberra, p.85.

13   Ibid., p.18.

14   Ibid., p.26.

15   Ibid., p.25.

16   Bloomfield, J. (1969-2002) op. cit.

17   Australian Institute of Sport. (1983-84) op. cit., p.85.

18   Brown, J. (2001) op. cit.

19   Bloomfield, J. (1969-2002) op. cit.

20   Daly, J. (1991) op. cit. p.60.

21   Bloomfield, J. (1969-2002) op. cit.

22   Sarsfield, R. (1999) *The Olympic Games*, Dorling Kindersly, Sydney, pp.316-320.

23   Daly, J., op. cit., pp.63-65.

24   Bloomfield, J. (1969-2002) op. cit.

25   Daly, J. (1991) op. cit., p. 66.

26   Ibid.

27   Kitney, G. (1985) Sports Institute Cries Foul Play, *National Times*, 26 April - 2 May.

28   Bloomfield, J. (1969-2002) op. cit.

29   Australian Institute of Sport (1985-86) *Annual Report*, Canberra, pp.10-24.

30   Bloomfield, J. (1991-2002) op. cit.

31   Mandle, W. (1985) Sporting Print, *Canberra Times*, Canberra, 15 September.

32   Hurst, M. and Anderson, K. (1985) Leaked Papers Expose Sports Spend-Up, *Daily Telegraph*, Sydney, 18 November, p.1.

33   Hurst, M. and Anderson, K. (1985) The Sporting Life, *Daily Telegraph*, Sydney, 19 November, pp.10-11.

34   Hurst, M. (1985) Coach: Why I Quit AIS; and Hawkins, T., Hurst, M. and Anderson, K., Probe Ordered, *Daily Telegraph*, Sydney, 20 November, p.1.

35   Hurst, M. and Anderson, K. (1985) Officials will Probe AIS Reports, *Daily Telegraph*, Sydney, 21 November, p.2.

36   Conkey, H. (1985) Minister Rejects Sport Institute Inquiry, *Canberra Times*, Canberra, 21 November.

37   Waterford, J. (1985) AIS Weakness Shown in Reports, *Canberra Times*, Canberra, 21 November, p.3.

38   Hawkins, T. (1985) Report Confirms AIS Over-Spending: We Were Right, *Daily Telegraph*, Sydney, 29 November, p.1.

39   Hawkins, T. (1985) A Whitewash: Opposition, *The Canberra Times*, Canberra, 29 November, p.2.

40   Ibid.

41   Cheffers, J. (1989) *Raw and Resilient: An Account of Australian Sport Seen Through the Eyes of the National Institute of Sport's Executive Director*. Report to the Trustees of Boston University and President John R. Silber, on Dr John Cheffers' activities during his leave of absence in Australia, May 1984 - September, 1987, pp.15-376.

42   Brown, J. (2001) op. cit.

43   Ibid.

44   Bloomfield, J. (1969-2002) op. cit.

45   Wilson, C. (2002) Luc Back Where it Started, *Canberra Times*, 31 January, p.20.

46   New York Knicks (2002) Player Profile – Luc Longley.

47   Colman, C. (2002) Dreaming of Boom Times, *Daily Telegraph*, 15 June, p.69.

48   Australian Institute of Sport (1985-86) op. cit. pp.58-90.

49   Australian Institute of Sport (1986-87) *Annual Report*, Canberra, pp.24-48.

50 Australian Institute of Sport (1985-86) op. cit., pp.3-7.

51 Australian Institute of Sport (1986-87) op. cit., p.2.

52 Bloomfield, J. (1969-2002) op. cit.

53 Gosper, R. and Bloomfield, J. (1987) *Olympic Co-operation Agreement Between the Australian Olympic Federation Inc and the Australian Institute of Sport*, Melbourne, August.

54 Australian Institute of Sport (1987-88) *Annual Report*, Canberra, p.53.

55 Australian Institute of Sport (1987) *Strategic Plan 1988 and Beyond*, Canberra, pp.3-30.

56 Australian Institute of Sport (1987-88) op. cit., p.53.

57 Bloomfield, J. (1969-2002) op. cit.

58 *Four Corners* (1987) The Winning Edge, Australian Broadcasting Commission — Video Tape, Sydney, 30 November (Video currently available at The University of Western Australia, Reid Library).

59 The two field athletes were Sue Howland and Gael Martin; the head coach was Kelvin Giles.

60 Daly, J. (1991) op. cit., p.115.

61 The three weight-lifters were Paul Clarke, Dallas Byrnes and Stan Hambessis. [Daly, J. (1999) op. cit., p.174.]

62 Daly, J. (1991) op. cit., p.116.

63 Daly, J. (1991) op. cit., p.180. See Appendix G.

64 Brown, J. (1983) op. cit., p.20.

65 Interim Committee for the Australian Sports Commission (1984) *Report to the Minister for Sport, Recreation and Tourism*, Australian Government Publishing Service, Canberra, March, p.14. See Appendix G.

66 Ibid., pp.iii-131.

67 Australian Sports Commission (1985) *Australian Sports Commission — An introduction to its role, objectives and activities*, Australian Government Publishing Service, Canberra, p.7.

68 Ibid., p.8.

69 Hartung, G. (2001) Personal communication with the author.

70 Australian Sports Commission (1985) Legislation and Parliamentary Debates, The Australian Sports Commission Bill 1985, Second Reading Debate — Senate, Senator Jack Evans, 31 May 1985. See Appendix G.

71 Brown, J. (1982) The ALP Sport and Recreation Policy, Canberra.

72 Brown, J. (1983) op. cit., pp.1-29.

73 Hartung, G. (2002) Curriculum Vitae, Canberra.

74 Sports Commission (1985) *Australian Sports Commission — Strategic Plan: a Summary*, Management and Planning Section, Canberra, pp.2-4.

75 Australian Sports Commission (1986) *Australian Sports Commission — Strategic Plan 1986-87 to 1988-89*, Australian Government Publishing Service, Canberra, pp.3-79.

76 Stewart-Weeks, M. (2002) Personal communication with the author.

77 Bloomfield, J. (1969-2002) op. cit.

78 Blanksby, B. and Thompson, G. (1981) *The Development of Sport in Victoria* (Green Paper), The Government of Victoria — Ministry for Youth, Sport and Recreation, Melbourne, April.

79 Blanksby, B. and Thompson, G. (1981) *A Proposal for the Development of a Victorian Sports Assembly and a Sports House* (Green Paper), The Government of Victoria — Ministry for Youth, Sport and Recreation, Melbourne, June.

80   Thompson, G. (1982) *New Directions in Sport — A Structure and Context for the Development of Sport in Victoria* (White Paper), The Government of Victoria — Ministry for Youth, Sport and Recreation, Melbourne, January.

81   Bloomfield, J. (1983) *Report of the Sports Development Working Party* (White Paper), The Government of Western Australia — Ministry for Sport and Recreation, November.

82   Lockwood, R. (1983) *Development of Sport and Recreation for Disabled People in Western Australia*, The Government of Western Australia — Ministry for Youth, Sport and Recreation, October.

83   Aitken, J. (1987) *Country Sport Report: Enquiry into Country Sport in Western Australia*, The Government of Western Australia — Ministry for Sport and Recreation, March.

84   Rate, Y. (1984) *Women in Sport in Western Australia,* The Government of Western Australia — Ministry for Sport and Recreation, December.

85   Douge, B. (1987) *Junior Sport Report — Focus on Children*, The Government of Western Australia — Ministry for Sport and Recreation, May.

86   South Australian Sports Institute (1983) First Annual Report — 1982-83, Adelaide.

87   Nunan, M. (2001) Personal communication with the author.

CHAPTER FOUR
CONSOLIDATION OF THE SPORTS SYSTEM

1   Brown, J. (1982) The ALP Sport and Recreation Policy, Canberra.

2   Brown, J. (1983) *Sport and Recreation: Australia on the Move*, Australian Government Publishing Service, Canberra, December, pp.1-29.

3   Bloomfield, J. and Harris, A. (1988) *A Case for Additional Funding to Further Develop Sport in Australia*, Australian Sports Commission and the Australian Institute of Sport, Canberra, August, p.5. See Appendix G.

4   Ibid.

5   House of Representatives Standing Committee on Finance and Public Administration. Chairman, Mr S. Martin, MP (1989) *Going for Gold!*, The Parliament of the Commonwealth of Australia, Canberra, March.

6   Richardson, G. (1989) Australian Sport — The Next Step, an address by Senator Graham Richardson at the launch of the future elite sport program held at the AIS in Canberra, 21 August.

7   Richardson, G. (1989) Australian Sport — The Next Step, *Media Release*, Canberra, 21 August.

8   Australian Sports Commission (1988-89) *Annual Report*, Canberra, pp.31-32.

9   Richardson, G. (1989) *The Australian Sports Kit*, Ministry for the Arts, Sport, the Environment, Tourism and Territories, Commonwealth of Australia, Canberra.

10   Australian Institute of Sport (1988) Inquiry Into: *The Use by Australian Sportsmen and Sportswomen of Performance Enhancing Drugs and the Role Played by the Commonwealth Agencies,* Canberra, July. (Submission to the Senate Standing Committee on Environment, Recreation and the Arts.)

11   Bloomfield, J. (1969-2002) Personal Sport Archives, Perth.

12   Australian Sports Commission (1988-89) op. cit., pp.32-33.

13   Interim Report of the Senate Standing Committee on Environment, Recreation and the Arts (1989) *Drugs in Sport*, Australian Government Publishing Service, Canberra, pp.75-191.

14   Second Report of the Senate Standing Committee on Environment, Recreation and

the Arts (1990) *Drugs in Sport*, Australian Government Publishing Service, Canberra, pp.41-391.

15 Daly, J. (1991) *Quest for Excellence — The Australian Institute of Sport*, Australian Government Publishing Service, Canberra, pp.166-167.

16 Coates, J. (2001) Personal communication with the author.

17 Australian Sports Commission (1989-90) *Annual Report*, Canberra, p.iii.

18 Ibid., pp.iii-iv.

19 Australian Sports Commission (1989-90) op. cit., p.iv.

20 Editorial (1990) *Canberra Times*, 4 February.

21 Australian Sports Commission (1992-93) *Annual Report*, Canberra, pp.17-79

22 Farmer, P. and Arnaudon, S. (1996) Australian Sports Policy, in Chalip, L. et al (1996) *National Sports Policies: An International Handbook*, Greenwood Press, London, p.10.

23 Australian Sports Commission (1992-93) op. cit., pp.7-9.

24 Australian Sports Commission (1991-92) *Annual Report*, Canberra, pp.7-9.

25 Australian Sports Commission (1992-93) op. cit., pp. 10-11.

26 Ferguson, J. (2001) Personal communication with the author.

27 Australian Sports Commission (1992-93) op. cit., p.3.

28 Australian Sports Commission (1994) *Olympic Athlete Program*, Canberra, pp.1-28.

29 Ibid., pp.1-21.

30 Ibid., p.1.

31 Australian Sports Commission (1993-94) *Annual Report*, Canberra, p.17.

32 Australian Sports Commission (1994) op. cit., Canberra, pp.1-28.

33 Ibid., p.17.

34 Australian Sports Commission (1994-95) *Annual Report*, Canberra, p.iii.

35 Ferguson, J. (2001) op. cit.

36 Australian Sports Commission (1986) *Strategic Plan 1986-87 to 1988-89*, Canberra, p.21. See Appendix G.

37 Australian Sports Commission (1987) *Annual Outcomes Report 1986-87*, Australian Government Publishing Service, Canberra, September.

38 Australian Sports Commission (1995) *Evaluation of the Australian Sports Commission's Impact on Sports Performances and Participation in Australia — 1994*, Canberra. See Appendix G.

39 Ibid., pp.192-221.

40 Sport 2000 Task Force — R. Oakley, Chair (1999) *Shaping Up: A Review of Commonwealth Involvement in Sport and Recreation in Australia*, Commonwealth of Australia, Canberra.

41 Sports Education Material, published by the Australian Sports Commission. See Appendix G.

42 Australian Sports Commission (1996-97) *Annual Report*, Canberra, pp.6-7.

43 Ibid., p.7.

44 Ibid., p.8.

45 Bryson, B. (2000) *Down Under*, Doubleday, Sydney, p.113.

46 Ferguson, J. (2002) Curriculum Vitae, Canberra.

CHAPTER FIVE
HOW GOVERNMENTS ASSIST SPORT

1 Coles, A. (1975) *Report of the Australian Sports Institute Study Group*, Department of Tourism and Recreation, Australian Government Publishing Service, Canberra, p.178.

2 Australian Coaching Council (1986/87) *First Annual Report*, Canberra, pp.2-3.

3 Australian Sports Commission (2001) Personal communication with G. Schembri and H. Pru.

4 Woodman, L. (2002) Curriculum Vitae, Melbourne.

5 Brown, J. (1983) *Sport and Recreation: Australia on the Move*, Australian Government Publishing Service, Canberra, December, pp.1-29.

6 Interim Committee for the Australian Sports Commission (1984) *Report to the Minister for Sport, Recreation and Tourism*, Australian Government Publishing Service, Canberra, March, pp.40-41.

7 Australian Sports Commission (1990-91) *Annual Report*, Canberra, p.41.

8 Ibid., p.43.

9 Ibid., pp.43-44.

10 Sport 2000 Task Force – R. Oakley, Chair (1999) Shaping Up, A Review of Commonwealth Involvement in Sport and Recreation in Australia, Commonwealth of Australia, Canberra, pp.81-82.

11 Bloomfield, J. and Thompson, G. (1990) *Current Developments in Sport and Human Movement*, Course Notes for HM684, The University of Western Australia.

12 Australian Sports Commission (1985-86) *Annual Report*, Canberra, pp.35-42.

13 Australian Sports Commission (1995-96) *Annual Report*, Canberra, p.31.

14 Australian Sports Commission (1995) *Evaluation of the Australian Sports Commission's Impact on Sports Performances and Participation in Australia – 1994*, Canberra, p.219.

15 Australian Sports Commission (1999) *Young People in Sport*, Canberra, pp.1-3. See Appendix G.

16 Ibid., p.3.

17 Ibid., pp.1-3.

18 Sport 2000 Task Force – R. Oakley, Chair (1999) op. cit., pp.83-84.

19 Ibid.

20 Capp. G. (2001) Fewer Drug Tests in Sport, *The West Australian*, Perth, 5 June.

21 Masters, R. (2002) Curriculum Vitae, Sydney.

22 Western Australian Institute of Sport (2002) Profile of Rechelle Hawkes, Perth.

23 Brown, J. (1983) op. cit., p.24.

24 Australian Sports Commission (1984-85) *Annual Report*, Canberra, p.45.

25 Australian Sports Commission (1986) *Strategic Plan 1986-87 to 1988-89*, Canberra, p.25.

26 Australian Sports Commission (1988) *Women's Sport Promotion Unit* (Brochure), Canberra. See Appendix G.

27 Australian Sports Commission (1990-91) *Annual Report*, pp.71-72.

28 Sport 2000 Task Force – R. Oakley, Chair (1999) op. cit., pp.94-95.

29 Ibid.

30 Department of Sport, Recreation and Tourism – Australian Sports Commission (1985) *Australian Sport: A Profile*, Australian Government Publishing Service, Canberra, pp.169-188.

31 Brown, J. (1983) op. cit., pp.16-17.

32 Lockwood, R. (1983) *Development of Sport and Recreation for Disabled People in Western Australia*, The Government of Western Australia – Ministry for Youth, Sport and Recreation, October.

33 Australian Sports Commission (1989-90) *Annual Report*, Canberra, pp.11-12.

34 Fitz-Gerald, S. (2002) Career History, http://www.sarahfitz-gerald.com/career.asp

35 Fitz-Gerald, S. (2002), Career Biography, http://www.sarahfitz-gerald.com/bio/asp

36 Fitz-Gerald, S., (2002) Profile, http://www.squash.org.au/fitzgerald_s.htm
37 Australian Sports Commission (1990-91) op. cit., pp.59-60.
38 Australian Sports Commission (1999) *Disability Education Program*, Canberra, pp.1-2. See Appendix G.
39 Sport 2000 Task Force — R. Oakley, Chair (1999) op. cit., pp.92-93.
40 Sauvage, L. (2002) Career Highlights, Sydney.
41 Bloomfield, J., Ackland, T. and Elliott, B. (1994) *Applied Anatomy and Biomechanics in Sport*, Blackwell Scientific Publications, Melbourne, p.267.
42 Bloomfield, J. and Blanksby, B. (1973) Profiles of National Level Oarsmen, *British Journal of Sports Medicine*, Vol VII, 3 and 4.
43 Bloomfield, J., Blanksby, B. and Ackland, T. (1983) Anatomical Profiles of Australian Junior Swimmers, *Australian Journal of Sports Medicine*, 3:2.
44 Hahn, A. (1990) Identification and Selection of Talent in Australian Rowing, *Excel* 6, pp.5-11.
45 Gulbin, J. (2001) From Novice to National Champion, *Sports Coach*, Vol. 24, No.1, pp.24-26.
46 Ibid.
47 Ibid.
48 Jeffrey, N. (1999) Tatiana Clears Final Hurdle, *The Australian*, Sydney, 11 February, p.16.
49 Nankervis, D. (1999) Tatiana: My Aussie Dream, *Sunday Mail*, Adelaide, 21 November, pp.55-56.
50 Wilson, C. (2000) Tatiana's Leap: To Turn Silver to Gold, *The Age*, Melbourne, 28 October, pp.1-2.
51 Epplett, N. (2001) The Making of a World Champion, *The Edge*, No. 2, December, pp.18-21.
52 Lawrence, S. (2002), Personal communication with the author.
53 Epplett, N. (2002) New Kid on the Block, *The Edge*, No. 3, April, pp.11-13.
54 Lawrence, S. (2002) op. cit.
55 Australian Sports Commission (2000-2001) *Annual Report*, Canberra, p.35.
56 Australian Sports Commission (1999) *Active Australia*, Canberra, pp.1-2.
57 Sport 2000 Task Force — R. Oakley, Chair (1999), op. cit., pp.86-88.
58 Ibid.
59 Jenkinson, M. (1985) Social Impact. In Department of Sport, Recreation and Tourism — Australian Sports Commission. *Australian Sport: A Profile*, Australian Government Publishing Service,Canberra, p.24.
60 Darlison, L. (1985) Equality. In Department of Sport, Recreation and Tourism, Australian Sports Commission, op. cit., p. 103.
61 Ibid.
62 Australian Sports Commission (1999) *Indigenous Australians in Sport*, Canberra, p.1.
63 Ibid., pp.1-2.
64 Ibid.
65 Australian Sports Commission (1999) *Athlete Career and Education*, Canberra, p.1.
66 Australian Sports Commission (1999) *International Assistance*, Canberra, p.1.
67 Australian Sports Commission (1999) *International Training Centres*, Canberra, p.1.
68 Athletics Australia (2002) Catherine Freeman, Athletic Profiles, Sydney.
69 Australian Sports Commission (1999) *Management and Sports Education Brochures*, Canberra, p.1.
70 Australian Sports Commission (1999) *Management Improvement*, Canberra, p.1.
71 Bloomfield, J. (1969-2002) op. cit.

72 National Elite Sports Council (1993) *Strategic Plan of the National Elite Sports Council of Australia 2001-2006*, NESC, pp.2-3.

73 Sport 2000 Task Force – R. Oakley, Chair (1999) op. cit., p.67.

74 Pyke, F. (2002) Curriculum Vitae, Melbourne.

75 Treble, G. (2002) Personal communication with the author.

76 Wood, D. (2002) Personal communication with the author.

77 Sport 2000 Task Force – R. Oakley, Chair (1999) op. cit., p.67.

78 Parker, T. (2002) Personal communication with the author.

79 Boultbee, J. (2001) Personal communication with the author.

80 Pyke, F. and Norris, K. (2001) Australia from Montreal to Sydney: The Evolution of a Model. Presented at the Second International Forum on Elite sport, Barcelona, Spain, 21 Sept., p.6.

CHAPTER SIX
COMMUNITY SUPPORT FOR SPORT

1 Bloomfield, J. (1985) Sports Science. In Department of Sport, Recreation and Tourism and the Australian Sports Commission, *Australian Sport: A Profile*, Australian Government Publishing Service, Canberra, p.75.

2 Ibid.

3 Carlile, F. (1963) *Forbes Carlile on Swimming*, Pelham Books Ltd, London.

4 Bloomfield, J. (1969-2002) Personal Sport Archives, Perth.

5 Ibid.

6 Ibid.

7 Australian Institute of Sport (1981) *First Annual Report*, Canberra, pp.25-26.

8 Australian Institute of Sport (1982-83) *Second Annual Report*, Canberra, pp.19-25.

9 Australian Institute of Sport (1983-84) op. cit., pp.21-23.

10 Hahn, A. (1990) Identification and Selection of Talent in Australian Rowing, *Excel* 6, pp.5-11.

11 Bloomfield, J. (1995) Talent Identification and Profiling. In Bloomfield, J., Fricker, P. and Fitch, K., *Science and Medicine in Sport*, 2nd Edn, Blackwell Science, Melbourne, p. 220.

12 Australian Sports Commission (1990-91) op. cit., pp.44-46.

13 Australian Sports Commission (1999-2000) *Annual Report*, Canberra, pp.47-48.

14 Hahn, A. (2002) Curriculum Vitae, Canberra.

15 Parker, T. (2002) Personal communication with the author.

16 Bloomfield, J. (1969-2002) op. cit.

17 Elliott, B. (2001) *Report to IOC Medical Commission* (Biomechanics Sub-Commission), Salt Lake City.

18 Australian Sports Commission (1999-2000) op. cit., p.110.

19 Hahn, A. (2001) Personal communication with the author.

20 Mitchell, S. (2001) Tiny Sensors Will Be Key to Success on Sports Field, *The Australian IT*, *The Australian*, Sydney, 2 October, p.31.

21 Anderson, J. (2001), Personal communication with the author.

22 Bloomfield, J. (1969-2002), op. cit.

23 Ibid.

24 Gill, E. (1985) Coaching. In Department of Sport and Recreation and Tourism and the Australian Sports Commission, op. cit., p.83.

25 Ellicott, R. (2001) Personal communication with the author.

26 Carlile, F. (2002) Curriculum Vitae, Sydney.

27 Daly, J. (1991) op. cit., pp.23-74.

28 Vamplew, W. (1989) *A Healthy Body: The Australian Sports Medicine Federation 1963-1988*, Australian Sports Medicine Federation Ltd., Canberra, p.3.

29 Ibid., pp. 3-15.

30 Cohen, B. (1972) MP: More Sport in Politics, *The West Australian*, 6 September.

31 Bloomfield, J. (1973) *The Role, Scope and Development of Recreation in Australia*, (White Paper), Report to the Commonwealth Government of Australia, p.26.

32 Australian Institute of Sport (1982-83) op. cit., pp. 19-20.

33 Vamplew, W. (1989) op. cit., p.15.

34 Fitch, K. (2002) Curriculum Vitae, Perth.

35 Vamplew, W. et al.(1997) *The Oxford Companion to Australian Sport*, 2nd edn, Oxford University Press, Melbourne, p.42.

36 Cashman, R. (2002) Personal communication with the author.

37 Sport 2000 Task Force — R. Oakley, Chair (1999) *Shaping Up: A Review of Commonwealth Involvement in Sport and Recreation in Australia*, Commonwealth of Australia, Canberra, pp.84-86.

38 Ibid., pp.113-114.

39 Growden, G. (2002) Kiwis Losing the Numbers' Game As Well, *Sydney Morning Herald*, Sydney, 5 April, p.36.

40 Robillard, W. (2001) Personal communication with the author.

41 Harris, B. (2002) Cup Opens a World of Opportunity, *The Australian*, 3 June, p.22.

42 Robillard, W. (1998) *Coach Education*, ARU Sydney, pp.1-4.

43 Australian Rugby Union (2000) op. cit., pp.4-5.

44 Surf Life Saving Australia (1999) *The History of Surf Lifesaving Australia*, Brighton Le Sands, pp.1-2.

45 Ibid.

46 Nance, G. (2001) Personal communication with the author.

47 ACT Brumbies (2002) Player Profile of George Gregan, Canberra.

48 Danzey, R. (2002) George Gregan, David Campese Management Group, Sydney.

49 Surf Life Saving Australia (1999) *Championships*, Brighton Le Sands, pp.1-2.

50 Maxwell, C. (1949) *Surf: Australians Against the Sea*, Angus and Robertson, Sydney, pp.283-286.

51 De Groot, C. with Webster, J. (1991) *Pro Golf: Out of the Rough*, Professional Golfers' Association of Australia, Cattai, pp.21-22.

52 Professional Golfers' Association of Australia (2001) Professional Development Program.

53 Professional Golfers' Association of Australia (2000) *A Career in Professional Golf*, PGA of Australia, pp.2-29.

54 Professional Golfers' Association of Australia and Griffith University (2000) *Bachelor of Business with Certificate of Golf Management*, Crows Nest, pp.1-5.

55 Professional Golfers' Association of Australia (2001) *Corporate Profile*, Crows Nest, p.1.

56 Stephens, T. (2000) Championing a Pool of Dreams, *Sydney Morning Herald*, Sydney, 30 August.

57 NSW Institute of Sport (2002) Ian Thorpe. Profile courtesy of Grand Slam International, Sydney.

58 NSW Institute of Sport (2001) Athlete of the Year, Ian Thorpe, OAM, *The Summit*, March.

59 Sport 2000 Task force — R. Oakley, Chair (1999) op. cit., p.113.

60 Niesche, C. (2001) Aussies Tough Out Kiwi Challenge, *The Australian*, 29 October.

61 Rate, Y. (2002) Personal communication with the author.

62 Australian Sports Commission (2000-2001) *Annual Report*, Canberra, pp.35-36.

63 Brown, S. (1998) *The Rise of National Leagues: Sport and Organizational Change in Australia*, Ph.D. Thesis, The University of Western Australia, Abstract.

64 Vamplew, W. (1994) Australians and Sport. In Vamplew, W. and Stoddart, B. (eds) (1994) *Sport in Australia: A Social History*, Cambridge University Press, Melbourne, pp.8-9.

65 Ibid., pp.9-10.

66 Cashman, R. (2002) Personal communication with the author.

67 Rose, R. (2002) Rabbitohs Bounce Back, *The West Australian*, Perth, 25 May.

68 Brown, S. (1998) op. cit., Abstract.

69 Bloomfield, J. and Thomson, G. (1990) *Current Developments in Sport and Human Movement*, Course Notes for HM 684, The University of Western Australia.

70 Confederation of Australian Sport (1980) *Master Plan for Sport*, Melbourne, March.

71 Hartung, G. (1988) *Sport and Politics*, Ph.D. Proposal, Australian National University, February, pp.49-52.

72 Australian Sports Commission (1985) *Legislation and Parliamentary Debates*, The Australian Sports Commission Bill 1985, Second Reading Debate − Senate, Senator Jack Evans, 31 May.

73 Hartung, G. (2001) Personal communication with the author.

74 Gordon, H. (1994) *Australia and the Olympic Games*, University of Queensland Press, St. Lucia, p.xx.

75 Ibid., p.xxv.

76 *The Australian* (2000) Australians at the Games, Sydney, 3 October, p.20.

77 Gordon, H. (1994) op. cit., p.461.

78 Ibid., pp.429-439.

79 Gosper, R. and Bloomfield, J. (1987) *Olympic Co-operation Agreement Between the Australian Olympic Federation Inc. and the Australian Institute of Sport*, Melbourne, August.

80 Commonwealth Games Association − Australia (1998) *Australia at the Commonwealth Games 1911-1998*, Sydney, pp.8-9.

81 Ibid., pp.64-78.

82 Crosswhite, P. (2001) Personal communication with the author.

83 Gray, R. (1979) *The First Forty Years: The National Fitness and Community Recreation Councils of Western Australia*, 1939-1978, Department of Youth, Sport and Recreation, Perth, pp.35-47.

84 Ibid., pp.95-97.

85 Ibid., p.127.

86 Welch, R. (2001) Personal communication with the author.

87 Sport 2000 Task Force − R. Oakley, Chair (1999) op. cit., p.89.

CHAPTER SEVEN
A PROFESSIONAL SPORTS SYSTEM IN PLACE

1 Coates, J. (2002) Curriculum Vitae, Sydney.

2 Coates, J. (2002) Personal communication with the author.

3 Commonwealth Games Association − Australia (1998) *Australia at the Commonwealth Games 1911-1998*, Sydney, p.78.

4 Australian Sports Commission (1999) *Annual Report 1998-99*, Canberra, p.4.

5 McAsey, J. (1999) A Tale of Two Sporting Years, *The Australian*, 8 December, p.23.

6 Guinness, R. (2000) Australia Takes Centre Stage, 1999 Year of the Champions, *The Australian*, 1 January, p.55

7 Ferguson, J. (2000) *Centreline*, Australian Sports Commission, Canberra, September, p.2.

8   The Olympics (2000) A World Show Stopper Scene by Scene, *The Weekend Australian*, Sydney, 16-17 September, pp.6-7.

9   Megalogenis, G. (2000) A Cast of Thousands, *The Weekend Australian*, Sydney, 6-17 September, p.8.

10   Strickland, K. (2000) Arts Sector Puts Best Face Forward, *The Australian*, Sydney, September, p.9.

11   SOCOG (2000) *The Games of the XXVII Olympiad, Opening Ceremony*, Sydney, 15 September, p.13.

12   *Sydney Morning Herald* (2000) Olympics — Medal Tally, 2 October, p.22.

13   Ferguson, J. (2000) op. cit., December, pp.3-5.

14   *The Australian* (2000) *Simply the Best, Closing Ceremony Souvenir*, 2 October, p.1.

15   Ibid., pp.1-8.

16   *The Weekend Australian* (2000) *Olympics Edition (Torch Relay)*, 16-17 September, pp.10-12.

17   Moore, M. (2000) A Moving Experience, *Sydney Morning Herald*, Sydney, 23 September, p.25.

18   Masters, R. (2000) The Games of Hope, *Sydney Morning Herald* — *Olympics*, Sydney, 2 October, p.21.

19   Cram, S, (2000) http://news.bbc.co.uk/sport/hi/english/olympics2000/athletics-track/newsid_ 937000/ 937427.stm

20   Coe, S. (2000) http://www.telegraph.co.uk/et?ac=002359381548908&rtmo=QxOSeSmR&atmo=99999999&pg=/et/00/9/27/spmott27.html

21   Channel 7 (2000) Olympic Wind Up — Reflections, 1 October.

22   Toler. M. (2000) Marion's Mum Gives Thanks, *Sydney Morning Herald* — *Olympics*, Sydney, 2 October, p. 21.

23   Editorial, (2000) Paralympics Set for Success, *The West Australian*, Perth, 17 October.

24   Gare, S. (2000) The Fire Within, Paralympics, *The Australian*, Sydney, 19 October, p.13.

25   Gare, S. (2000) Unforgettable Fire, *The Australian*, Sydney, 30 October, p.15.

26   Ibid., pp.17-21.

27   Ibid., p.15.

28   Tedmanson, S. and Harris, T. (2000) Games Leave a Legacy of Understanding, *The Australian*, Sydney, 30 October, p.17.

29   Editorial (2000) Paralympics Stir Our Pride, *The West Australian*, 31 October.

30   Kelly, P. (2000) Psyched Up for the Big Letdown, *Sydney Morning Herald*, Sydney, 29 September, p.3.

31   Editor (2000) Australia Asserts Its Identity, *The West Australian*, Perth, 3 October.

32   Ellis, B. (2000) The Miracle We Had to Have, *The Australian*, Sydney, 5 October, p.43.

33   Barrass, T. (2000) Glorious Games a Sign of Our Nationhood, *The West Australian*, Perth, 2 October.

34   Editor (2000) op. cit.

35   Malouf, D. (2000) Here We Are, Against the Plan and Against the Odds, Centenary of Federation Commemoration, *The Australian*, Sydney, 1 January, pp.2-13.

36   Garvin, M. (1987) *Us Aussies*, Hayzon, Sale, p.38.

37   Carr, B. (2000) Nation Can Take a Bow, *The Weekend Australian*, Sydney, 14-15 October, p.21.

38   Manne, R. (2000) Cultural Cringe Pushed to the Fringe, *Sydney Morning Herald*, Sydney, 2 October, p.10.

39   Gunn, M. (2000) Nursing That Public Spirit: Sydney Dropped Its Guard ..., Lessons

from the Olympics, Part 4, Social Capital, *The Australian*, Sydney, 18 October, p.15. See Appendix G.

40 Stewart-Weeks, M. (2000) Nursing That Public Spirit: A Sense of Community is a Fragile Commodity, *The Australian*, Sydney, 18 October, p.15.

CHAPTER EIGHT
THE FUTURE – WHERE TO FROM HERE?

1   Jeffery, N. (2001) Report Suggests Slump in Athens, *The Australian*, Sydney, 11 December, p.16.

2   Magnay, J. (2001) Winners and Losers: Swimmers Beat Olympic Blues, *The Age*. In *The West Australian*, Perth, 17 September, p.43.

3   Coates, J. (2002) Personal communication with the author.

4   Australian Sports Commission (1999) *The Australian Sports Commission – Beyond 2000*, Canberra, p.1.

5   Sport 2000 Task Force – R. Oakley, Chair (1999) *Shaping Up: A Review of Commonwealth Involvement in Sport and Recreation in Australia*, Commonwealth of Australia, Canberra.

6   Australian Olympic Committee (2000) *2004 Olympic Medal Plan: A submission to Federal Government for Olympic athlete development funding for the period 1 January 2001 - 30 June 2005*, Sydney, November.

7   Bartels, P. (2000) It's Time to Get Active and Change, Sport in the 21st Century: The Australian Sports Commission, *The Australian*, Sydney, 17 November, p.1. See Appendix G.

8   Australian Sports Commission (2002) *2002-2005 Strategic Plan*, Australian Sports Commission, Canberra, pp.1-15.

9   *The Weekend Australian* (2001) World Beaters: What we won in 2001, Sydney, 24-25 November, p.55.

10   McDonald, M. and Daff, A. (2001) The Year in Sport: 2001, *The Weekend Australian*, Sydney, 29-30 December, p.32.

11   *The Sunday Times* (2001) ICC Championship, Perth, 30 December, p.73.

12   Conn, M. (2001) Waugh's Men Rack Up Sweet 16, *The Australian*, Sydney, 2 March, p.20.

13   Australian Sports Commission (2001) *Annual Report 2000-2001*, Canberra, pp.132-33.

14   Australian Associated Press (2001) Taxman Wins at Goodwill Games, *The West Australian*, Perth, 10 September, p.56.

15   Coates, J. (2002) op. cit.

16   Jeffery, N. (2001) op. cit., p.16.

17   Australian Olympic Committee (2000) op. cit., p.5.

18   Masters, R. (2002) Alisa Soars as her Rival Recuperates, *smh.com.au – Sport*, pp.1-3.

19   Pells, E. (2002) Camplin Delivers Another Wonder From Down Under, *Yahoo Sports: Olympics*. pp.1-3.

20   Sims, G. (2002) Great Leaps, *Inside Sport*, St Leonards, pp. 59-65.

21   The Australian (2002) Commonwealth Games 2002: Australia's Roll of Honour, 6 August, p.14.

22   *Sydney Morning Herald* (2002) Commonwealth Games – Honour Roll, Sydney, 6 August, p.34.

23   Schlink, L. and Reed. R. (2002) Coaches Plot Clean Sweep to Perfection, *The Australian*, 5 August, p.19.

24 Magnay, J. (2002) O'Grady and Co Toy with the Field, *Sydney Morning Herald*, Sydney, 5 August, p.24.

25 Magnay, (2002) Seventeen Seconds Clear and Just 14 km To Go, Fall Denies Hemsley, *Sydney Morning Herald*, Sydney, 5 August, p.24.

26 Huxley, J. (2002) Saville Walks Back to Happiness in Aussie Double, *The West Australian*, Perth, 30 July, p.58.

27 Hughes, D. (2002) Road Warrior, *The West Australian*, 6 August, p.50.

28 McGregor, A. (2002) Marathon Mamas, *The Australian*, Sydney, 30 July, p.9.

29 Johnson, L. (2002) Australians In Last-Gasp Win After Facing Sudden Death, *Sydney Morning Herald*, Sydney, 6 August, p.35.

30 Schlink, L. (2002) Road Team Fired Up By Track World Record, *The Weekend Australian*, 3-4 August, p.49.

31 Magnay, J. (2002) op.cit., p.24.

32 Jeffery, N. (2002) Girl Power To Rival Men's Team, *The Australian*, 7 March, p.17.

33 Casella, N. (2002) The Making of a Young Champion, *The Sunday Times*, Perth, 11 August, p.6.

34 Smith, T. (2002) New Wave of Hot Talent, *The Sunday Times*, 6 January, p.76.

35 Ibid., p.77.

36 Ibid.

37 Mc Asey, J. (2002) Pittman Emerges From Wilderness and Clears Path To Top, *The Weekend Australian*, Sydney, 10-11 August, p.5.

38 Australian Associated Press (2001) op. cit.

39 Smith, T. (2002) op. cit., p.76.

40 Daff, D. (2002) Athens Target for Precocious Talent, *The Australian*, Sydney, 18 April, p.15.

41 Hefford, C. (2002) Hollie in Limelight at AIS, *Launceston Examiner*, Launceston, 29 September, p.29.

42 Press Release (2002) Philippe Rizzo Wins Commonwealth Games Gold and Bronze Medals, *AIS Media and Public Relations*, 29 July, p.4.

43 Kershler. R. (2001) Aussie Gymnast Breaks Through, *Daily Telegraph*, Sydney, 6 November, p.77.

44 McGee, B. (2002) Biographical Information, www.bradleymcgee.com/Bradmcgee/pages/bio.htm

45 Schlink, L. (2002) McGee Pursues Team Dream, *The Australian*, 2 August, p.30.

46 Denholm, M. (2000) British Sport The Australian Way, *Centreline*, June, p.4.

47 Ibid.

48 Downes, S. (2002) The Poms' Revenge, *Inside Sport*, Sydney, September. p.51.

49 Denholm, M. (2000) op. cit., p.4.

50 Jeffery, N. and Kogoy, P. (2000) Our Bloodless Coup of Britain May Be Just The Beginning, *The Australian*, Sydney, 9 November (Sport Section).

51 Hughes, D. (2001) Wake-Up Call, *The West Australian*, Perth, p.116.

52 Guinness, R. and McAsey, J. (2001) English Cash to Test Our Medal Mettle, *The Australian*, Sydney, 17 May, p.18.

53 Harris, B. (2001) Marsh Switches Allegiance to Old Foe, *The Australian*, Sydney, 30 July, p.21.

54 Downes, S. (2002) op. cit. p.50.

55 Guinness, R. and McAsey, J. (2001) op. cit.

56 Bloomfield, J. et al. (1994) *Applied Anatomy and Biomechanics in Sport*, Blackwell Scientific Publications, Melbourne, pp.104, 88-91.

57 Jeffery, N. (2001) op. cit.

58 Jeffery, N. and Kogoy, P. (2000) op. cit.

59 Coates, J. (2002) Personal communication with the author.

60 Peters, M. (2001) Personal communication with the author.

61 Dortch, E. (2002) Sporting Groups Battle On With Fewer Helpers, *The West Australian*, Perth, 18 January, p.9.

62 McGuire, M. (2001) Insurance Crisis Hits Grassroots, *The West Australian*, Sydney, 12 October, p.25.

63 Peters, M. (2002) op. cit.

64 Coates, J. (2002) op. cit.

65 United States Department of Health and Human Services (1996) *Physical Activity and Health: A Report of the Surgeon General*, US Department of Health Services, Centre for Disease Control and Prevention, Atlanta.

66 Sport 2000 Task Force – R. Oakley, Chair (1999) op. cit., p.67.

67 Australian Sports Commission (2000) op. cit.

68 Ibid.

69 Krupka, P. (2002) It's No Racket as Taxpayers Court Success for Obese Children, *The Australian*, Sydney, 24 May, p.37.

70 Dortch, E. (2002) op. cit.

71 McGuire, M. (2001) op. cit.

72 Dortch, E. (2001), op. cit.

73 Bradley, M. (2001) Bulldog's Bash-and-Dash Puts Girls in a League of Their Own, *Sydney Morning Herald – Weekend Edition*, Sydney, 25-26 August, p.5.

74 North, S. (2001) Hero Worship, *Sydney Morning Herald – Weekend Sport*, 25-26 August, p.69.

75 Associated Press (2002) Moffett: Britain Tied by Red Tape, *The Australian*, Sydney, 21 October, p.22.

76 Stewart-Weeks, M. (2002) Personal communication with the author.

Appendices

Appendix A
Letter of request for a ministry

Australian Sports Medicine Federation

*A Request To The Federal Government Of Australia To Establish A
Ministry For Recreation And Sport*

The Australian Sports Medicine Federation has become increasingly concerned with the reluctance of the Commonwealth Government to follow the example of many nations throughout the world in establishing a Ministry for Recreation and Sport.

The establishment of the Commonwealth National Fitness Council in 1941 appeared to be a forward step for that time and the Council fulfilled its intended role in the forties. However, when one compares the performance of this body in the 1970s with that of many other countries, it is painfully evident that we are not catering for the activity needs of the nation.

In an age when cardiovascular disease is increasing and the fitness level of our youth appears to be declining, no really positive steps have been taken to counteract these trends.

The above problems have mainly occurred because of the increasing urbanisation and automation of our daily life. Man, by changing the physical world to meet the needs of an urban society, has interfered with his biological adaptation, which was achieved through a very long process of natural evolution. Previously man has been forced to have physical activity in order to stay alive. In our present living situation, an unnatural one for a body which is biochemically animal, artificial means must be created to again involve man in physical activity. It would appear that lifelong sports and physical recreation activities are the most appropriate means of ensuring that people continue to have physical activity throughout their life.

This Federation requests, then, that the Commonwealth Government consider as a matter of urgency the establishment of a Ministry for Recreation and Sport which is aimed at fostering good health in all age groups through physical activity. The Australian Sports Medicine Federation believes that it is vital that all Australians are encouraged to maintain at least a basic level of physical fitness in order to cope effectively with the problems of living in a Western society.

John Bloomfield   K.D. Fitch
President   Secretary

20/10/72

Appendix B
Australia's sports performances in 1991–92

The following results were obtained by Australian sportsmen and sportswomen in international events over a period of two years in 1991 and 1992:

- Australia was ranked as the number two nation in *rowing* after several national teams won individual events in the world championships.

- The Australian women's *squash* team won the world team championships.

- Michelle Martin was ranked as the number one women's *squash* player in the world.

- The Australian men's *squash* team won the world team championships.

- Rodney Martin won the men's world *squash* championships.

- Australia won both the *rugby union* and *rugby league* World Cups.

- Michellie Jones won the women's world *triathlon* championships.

- Miles Stewart won the men's world *triathlon* championships.

- Australia won the world amateur *surfing* championships.

- Lyn MacKenzie won the women's world amateur *surfing* championship.

- Grant Frost won the men's world amateur *surfing* championship.

- Simon Fairweather won the world *target archery* championship.

- Australia won the world team *field archery* championship.

- Australia won five senior world *sailing* championships.

- Charlene Machin won the women's lightweight world *karate* championship.

- Brian Peakall won the men's heavyweight world *karate* championship.

- Karen Neville won the women's world *water ski* championship.

- Australia was runner-up in the women's singles world *bowling* championships.

- Australia won the Bianchi Cup (world title) at the world *action shooting* championships.

- Dewie Hazeltine won the women's individual event at the world *action shooting* championships.

- Brian Kilpatrick won the men's individual event at the world *action shooting* championships.

- Australia was runner-up in the Challenger Cup (the top eight *softball* teams in the world compete in this championship).

- Kieren Perkins held three world freestyle *swimming* records — 400m, 800m and 1500m.

- Paul Robertson won the world w*ater ski* racing championship.

- Australia won the women's Champions Trophy hockey tournament.

- Australia was runner-up in the world men's *hockey* championship.

- Michael Diamond was runner-up in the world *trap-shooting* championship.

- Todd Woodbridge and Mark Woodforde were ranked as the number one doubles pair in world *tennis*.

- Australia won the world *netball* championships.

SOURCE The above results were obtained from the 1991–1992 and 1992–1993 *Annual Reports* of the Australian Sports Commission.

Appendix C
Australia's sports performances in 1999

The following results were obtained by Australian sportsmen and sportswomen in international events in 1999:

Team events — Australia won the following:

- the *rugby union* World Cup
- the *netball* world championships
- the *rugby league* World Cup
- the *cricket* World Cup
- the women's *cricket* World Cup
- the women's *hockey* world championship
- the Davis Cup *tennis* championship
- the women's four at the *lawn bowls* world championship
- the world coxless pair *men's rowing* championship
- the world women's *K2 canoeing* championship
- the men's 4 x 100m medley world *swimming* championship
- the men's 4 x 200m freestyle world *swimming* championship

Individual events:

- Grant Hackett — world 1500m freestyle *swimming* champion
- Cathy Freeman — world 400m a*thletics* champion
- Ian Thorpe — world 400m freestyle *swimming* champion
- Loretta Harrop — world *triathlon* champion
- Michael Klim — world 100m butterfly *swimming* champion
- Zali Steggal — world *slalom skiing* champion
- Susie O'Neill — world 100m butterfly *swimming* champion
- Jacqui Cooper — world *freestyle skiing* champion

- Mark Occhilupo — world men's *surfing* champion
- Layne Beachley — world women's *surfing* champion
- Amanda Bradley — world *ten-pin* bowling champion
- Kostya Tszyu — world welterweight professional *boxing* champion
- Karrie Webb — world women's *golf* champion
- Kerry Thomas — *ironwoman* world champion
- Nathan Meyer — *ironman* world champion
- Lars Kleppich — world *board sailing* champion
- Chris Nicholson — world *sailing* champion
- Sarah Fitz-Gerald — world women's *squash* champion
- Michael Diamond — world *trap shooting* champion
- Emma Sheers — world *water ski jumping* champion
- Quinten Hann — world *eight-ball pool* champion

SOURCES   Guinness, R. (2000) 'Australia Takes Centre Stage — 1999, Year of the Champions', *The Australian*, 1 January, p.55.

McAsey, J. (1999) 'A Tale of Two Sporting Years', *The Australian*, 8 December, p.23.

Appendix D
Article by NSW Premier Bob Carr

NATION CAN TAKE A BOW

A Beaming Bob Carr Says We Have the Skills, Savvy and Social Cohesion to Tackle the World

Months before the Olympics, I found myself rehearsing lines in my head: These Olympics will be a once-in-a-lifetime sporting festival. They have advantages for tourism. They will not be a transforming spiritual event. Don't lift your expectations too high, Australia.

I also found myself rehearsing other lines in case something – transport, say – seized up. A voice in my head kept saying these Olympics are a huge undertaking, too huge for any one city or nation. We have bitten off a great deal. Something had to go wrong.

But, in the end, no excuses or talking down were required. The planning had been exacting, the preparation detailed. Our Government knew the rest of Australia was looking to us to deliver. Yet who could have anticipated the extent of the national achievement and pride that would flow from it?

These Games set a new standard of excellence. The Tokyo Olympics of 1964 gave credibility to the words 'Made in Japan'. I sense the Sydney Olympics have lifted the value, the image, of the brand 'Made in Australia'.

We're seen as splendid organisers. We showed ourselves as a socially co-operative society, as a competitive, can-do place. No longer is Australian potential thwarted by the 'she'll be right, mate' approach, long lunches of sluggish managers or bitter industrial fights.

NSW Treasurer Michael Egan was in Dubai this week on a trade mission. He took the lift to the hotel gym wearing a T-shirt emblazoned with the Sydney 2000 logo and took half an hour to get there. Every person he met – American, Indian, Emirati, Pakistani, German and British – asked him excitedly whether he had been in Sydney for the Games. He was able to tell them that not only had he been at the Games, he had written the cheques. Everyone wanted to talk about the Olympics – and to say how brilliantly Australia had done it.

A huge re-skilling of the population was needed to make these Games a success. A highlight of my Olympics was the day I visited Central Station and saw the rail workers full of pride as I praised them for an extraordinary effort. Staff from non-English-speaking backgrounds wore badges to show they spoke Arabic or Greek. Here were migrants, in the new homeland, proud of their cultural heritage and proud of their adopted country's achievement.

TAFE trained all 47 000 volunteers in customer service, venue management, crowd control and emergency procedures. We gained new skills in information technology and security, and bringing in big projects on time and within budget.

The Olympics success story could not have happened without an underlying social cohesion. In the old Australia of entrenched class conflict, we used to admire how West Germany or Switzerland managed things, with the social partners (employers and unions) working together, thinking of the good of the whole, minimising class conflict.

The Games showed that negotiated, co-operative partnerships can work. That a unionised workforce can deliver. That public transport can move large numbers of people with efficiency and comfort. That big crowds can be safely managed. That Aborigines, migrants and descendants of First Fleeters alike are committed to the Australian experiment in nation-building.

Through the Olympics, we showed the world and reminded ourselves what we are made of. As a nation we can and should go forward more confidently now. We have the skills to tackle the big tasks: restoring our degraded environment, lifting the quality of education, making Australia competitive in the world economy. We have the competence, the skills, the cohesion. We showed it.

Bob Carr is the Premier of New South Wales

SOURCE   Carr, B. (2000) 'Nation Can Take a Bow', *The Weekend Australian,* 14–15 October, p.21.

Appendix E
Article by Martin Stewart-Weeks

NURSING THAT PUBLIC SPIRIT

A Sense Of Community Is A Fragile Commodity

by Martin Stewart-Weeks

As much as the sport itself, the display of community spirit across Australia in the lead-up to and during the Olympic Games has left us a memorable legacy and some interesting questions to ponder. Although it shouldn't have, the community response to the Games seems to have caught us by surprise.

Whether it was the response to the torch relay or the contribution of the 47 000 volunteers or the friendliness that broke out on all fronts, that social or community dimension of the Games has rightly captured the public imagination here and around the world.

In tones that stretch from appreciation to amazement, punters and pundits alike wonder at the sustained scale and energy of our collective response to the Games. For many, this was proof that Australia's civil society — our capacity and skills for voluntary association and working together for a common cause — was in better shape than we thought.

We were being given practical demonstrations, on a daily basis, of what social scientists and political commentators call social capital. We saw people working together, we saw trust and respect, and we saw that sense of shared purpose and common focus which is what community is. And we liked it.

The community dividend might turn out to be one of the most valuable we reap from the Games experience — but it might also turn out to be the most fragile.

Australia's history is rich in the tradition of voluntary association. Surf lifesaving, fighting bush fires or battling floods, organising to look after the poor and sick, educating our children, building the physical, social and cultural infrastructure of our farms, towns and cities — none would have happened without the spirit of volunteering backed by a selfless, imaginative but always practical commitment to serve a common cause.

What we saw, and delighted in, as the Games progressed was a marvelous outbreak of a deep instinct at the heart of the Australian achievement.

But our celebration was smudged by a lurking sense of regret that it couldn't last. That ambivalence suggested a tradition in crisis.

The Olympic Games reinforced some of the things we already know about volunteering. People respond to a clear task, to training and leadership, to having the proper resources to be effective and to get good feedback. They are willing to commit their time and skills if they know what they have to achieve and get a sense of the larger result to which they are contributing. But too often, we expect volunteers to work without a clear focus. We don't give them enough resources, we don't train them or help them learn skills, and we expect them to work long and hard for little thanks.

Are our stocks of social capital robust enough to extend that spirit of trust and co-operation for a common cause in which we took such delight for three weeks?

The spirit of Australian pride, co-operation and openness that was abroad during the Games — our sense of community — is going to be as important to our future as any of the business and economic spin-offs. In this networked, e-literate, life-at-the-speed-of-thought world, that spirit of community is going to be crucial. It's a social world after all. That means it's about relationships, which means it's about trust.

As we search for ways to respond to the instinct for voluntary association that fits contemporary values and conditions, we often feel stranded between hope and expectation. The biggest fear is that we are losing our capacity for community even as we work out that we need it now more than ever. It doesn't have to be that way but we will have to work harder to make sure it doesn't happen.

Martin Stewart-Weeks is principal of the Albany Consulting Group. He researches and consults on issues of civil society and voluntary association.

The Way Ahead

- Australia should build on its strong tradition of volunteering in areas such as lifesaving and firefighting by branching out into other areas that will help in the creation of a strong knowledge-based economy.
- The International Year of the Volunteer should be used as a springboard to improve support for volunteering, including internet access, providing greater training for volunteer managers and addressing the issue of WorkCover.
- Governments should recognise the economic contribution of volunteers, perhaps by adding it as a supplementary item to state and national accounts.
- We should seek other ways to harness the experience and skills of older people.
- Community groups must recruit, retain, and reward volunteers far more effectively.

SOURCE Stewart-Weeks, M. (2000) 'Nursing That Public Spirit: A Sense of Community is a Fragile Commodity', *The Australian*, Sydney, 18 October, p.15.

Appendix F
Australia's sports performances in 2001

The following results were obtained by Australian sportsmen and sportswomen in international events in 2001.

Team events – Australia won the following:

- the world Test *cricket* championship
- the world record with 16 consecutive *cricket* Test victories
- the International *Rugby (Union)* Board team of the year award
- the number one world ranking in *netball*
- the 4 x 100m men's world freestyle *swimming* championship
- the 4 x 200m men's world freestyle *swimming* championship
- the 4 x 100m men's world medley *swimming* championship
- the 4 x 100m women's world medley *swimming* championship
- the men's world *squash* championship
- the women's world eight *rowing* championship
- the women's world coxless four *rowing* championship
- the men's world tornado *sailing* championship
- the number one world team ranking in *swimming*

Individual events:

- Ian Thorpe – men's world 200m/400m/800m freestyle *swimming* champion
- Grant Hackett – men's world 1500m freestyle *swimming* champion
- Petria Thomas – women's world 100m/200m butterfly *swimming* champion
- Geoff Huegill – men's world 50m butterfly *swimming* champion
- Giann Rooney – women's world 200m freestyle *swimming* champion
- Matt Welsh – men's world 100m backstroke *swimming* champion
- Dmitri Markov – men's world *pole vault* champion

- Lleyton Hewitt — ranked world number one in men's *tennis*
- Karrie Webb —world women's *golf* Grand Slam title winner
- Grant Bluett — men's world *orienteering* champion
- Kostya Tszyu — IBF, WBC and WBF world junior welterweight professional *boxing* champion
- Layne Beachley — women's world *surfing* champion
- Sarah Fitz-Gerald — women's world *squash* champion
- David Palmer — ranked world number one men's *squash* player
- Jacqui Cooper — women's World Cup *aerial ski* champion
- Emma Speers — women's world slalom *water skiing* champion
- Ann Procter — women's world *water skiing* champion
- Troy Bayliss — men's world *motorcycling* superbike champion
- Andrew Pitt — men's world *motorcycling* supersport champion
- Peter Robertson — men's world *triathlon* champion
- Chris Hill — men's World Cup *triathlon* champion
- Steve Brewin — men's A class catamaran *sailing* champion
- Mark Thorpe — men's world moth class *sailing* champion

SOURCES   *The Weekend Australian* (2001) 'World Beaters: What we won in 2001', Sydney, 24-25 November, p.55.

McDonald, M. and Daff, A. (2001) 'The Year in Sport: 2001', *The Weekend Australian* , Sydney, 29-30 December, p.32.

The Sunday Times (2001) ICC Championship, Perth, 30 December, p.73.

Conn, M. (2001) 'Waugh's Men Rack Up Sweet 16', *The Australian,* Sydney, 2 March, p.20.

Appendix G
Further references

The articles listed below have been incorporated into this appendix, as they provide additional information on important topics raised in this book. They are available from the National Sport Information Centre, which is housed at the Australian Sports Commission in Canberra, ACT. Australia, 2600.

1   Bloomfield, J. (1971) Letter to R. Healy, 29 January.

2   Healey, R. (1971) Letter to J. Bloomfield, 19 February.

3   Anderson, K. (1971) Creation of a Ministry of Sport. Answer given to Senator G. McLaren, 2 December, to a Question Without Notice. (Reply supplied by the Prime Minister, the Rt Hon. W. McMahon).

4   Bloomfield, J. (1972) Letter to H. Graham, 27 June.

5   Graham, H. (1972) Letter to J. Bloomfield, 13 July.

6   Bloomfield, J. (1972) The Conservation of Man, *Proceedings of the Conference on the Human Consequences of Technological Change,* The University of Sydney, 25 August, pp.8–12.

7   Liberal-Country Party (1972) Youth, Sport, Leisure and Recreation Policy, Canberra.

8   Daly, J. (1976) Courageous Amateurs Must Fail, *The Australian,* 3 August.

9   Australian Institute of Sport (1981) Athlete Code of Ethics, Canberra.

10 Interim Committee for the Australian Sports Commission (1984), *Recommendation on Sports Research.* Australian Government Publishing Service, Canberra, March, p.41.

11 Australian Sports Commission (1985) *Legislation and Parliamentary Debates,* The Australian Sports Commission Bill 1985, Second Reading Debate – Senate, Senator Jack Evans, 31 May.

12 Australian Sports Commission (1986) *Corporate Objectives – Strategic Plan 1986–87 to 1988–89,* Australian Publishing Service, Canberra, p.21.

13 Australian Sports Commission (1986) *Sport Development Policy – Strategic Plan 1986–87 to 1988–89,* Australian Publishing Service, Canberra, pp.25-26.

14 Australian Sports Commission (1988) Women's Sport Promotion Unit, Canberra.

15 Bloomfield, J. and Harris, T. (1988) A Case for Additional Funding to Further

Develop Sport in Australia, Australian Sports Commission and the Australian Institute of Sport, Canberra, August.

16 Australian Sports Commission (1995) *Evaluation of the Australian Sports Commission's Impact on Sports Performances and Participation in Australia — 1994*, Canberra.

17 Australian Sports Commission (1996) *Sports Education Material*, Canberra.

18 Australian Sports Commission (1999) *Disability Education Program*, Canberra.

19 Australian Sports Commission (1999) Junior Sport Program, in *Young People in Sport,* Canberra.

20 Gunn, M. (2000) Nursing That Public Spirit: Sydney Dropped Its Guard ..., Lessons from the Olympics, Part 4, Social Capital, *The Australian,* Sydney, 18 October, p.15.

21 Bartels, P. (2000) It's Time to Get Active and Change, Sport in the 21st Century. *The Australian*, Sydney, 17 November, p.1.

Appendix H
Photo credits

DETAILS OF THE ILLUSTRATIONS FROM THE NATIONAL LIBRARY OF AUSTRALIA ARE LISTED BELOW

Figure 1.3   Pictures Catalogue, C. Hutchins, nla.pic-an6308157

Figure 1.5   Pictures Catalogue, nla.pic-an9778108

Figure 1.6   Pictures Catalogue, W.G. Mason, nla.pic-an8021476

Figure 1.8   Pictures Catalogue, nl 3278

Figure 1.9   Pictures Catalogue, S. Calvert, nla.pic-an10280445

Figure 2.1   Australian Information Service Collection. Details: Frank Stewart, the Australian Minister for Tourism and Recreation, 1974. Photograph c20x2x15.4 cm, cPIC/8055.

Figure 3.1   Australian Information Service Collection. Details: John Brown, the Australian Minister for Sport Recreation and Tourism and Minister Assisting the Minister for Defence, 1983. Photograph c20.6x15.5 cm, cPIC/8054.

Figure 6.8   Pictures Catalogue, nla.pic-an2376907

Index

Page numbers in *italic* refer to photographs.

ABC, *Four Corners*   84, 94
Aboriginal and Torres Strait Islander Commission (ATSIC)   131
Active Australia   128, 130, 143
Aggis, Richard   153
Anderson, Kenneth   35, 36
Applied Sports Research Program   112
Armstrong, Warwick   13
Athlete Career and Education Program (ACE)   132
Athlete Development and Elite Sport Program   132
Atkins, David   184
Atlanta Olympic Games (1996)   104
Auckland Commonwealth Games (1990)   98
Aussie Able   102, 119
Aussie Sport *see* Junior Sport Program
Australia's International Sporting Triumphs (1991–92)   100
Australia's International Sporting Triumphs (1999)   181
Australia's sporting origins   14
Australian Association for Exercise and Sports Science (AAESS)   148
Australian Capital Territory Academy of Sport (ACTAS)   67, 136
Australian Coaching Council (ACC)   49, 109, 110, 111, 153, 171
   Levels 1, 2, 3   109
Australian Commonwealth Games Association (AGCA)   176
   British Empire Games   176
   Crosswhite, Perry   177
Australian Democrats   86
Australian Female Athlete of the Year   119

Australian football   *20*
Australian Institute of Sport (AIS)   *58*, 59, 63, 67, 70, 72, 76, *77*, 82, 84, 88, 92, 94, 95, 96, *99*, 136, 140, 179
   AIS/ASC Merger (1989)   95
   Department of Physiology and Applied Nutrition   148
   Elite Athlete Assistance Scheme   95, 111
   Halls of Residence   77
   National Sports Information Centre   95
   National Sports Program   95, 147
   National Talent Search Program   122
   National Training Centre Program   95, 118
   Sport Talent Encouragement Plan   95
   Sports Information Centre   77
   Sports Science and Medicine Centre   77, 95, 147, 157
   Training Centre Program (NTCP)   64
Australian National University   59
Australian Olympic Committee   175, 179, 180, 181, 215
Australian Olympic medal totals (1956–2000)   105
Australian Paralympic Committee   87, 101
Australian Rowing Council   180
Australian Rugby Union (ARU)   163
   Clark, David   163
   Eales, John   164, 165
   Farr-Jones, Nick   164
   Gregan, George 164, *165*
   Marks, Dick   163
   O'Neill, John   163
   O'Shea, Brian   163
   Robilliard, Warren   163
   Slack, Andrew   164
Australian Sports Commission   71, 82, 85, 86, 87, 88, 92, 95, 96, 97, 100, 102, 103, 104, 106, 108, 110, 115, 136, 137,

138, 141, 182, 199, 200, 212, 216, 217, 221

Australian Sports Drug Agency (ASDA) 114
   Athletes' Code of Ethics 114
   National Drugs in Sport Co-ordinator 114
Australian Sports Medicine Federation (ASMF) 156, 157, 242
Australian Swimming 168

Baker, Reg (Snowy) 27
Barassi, Ron 13
Barcelona Olympic Games (1992) 96, 100
Barcelona Paralympic Games (1992) 100
Barnes, David 207
Barras, Martin 127
Barry, Jim 57
Bartels, Peter 199, 200, 217
Batschi, Rheinhold 153
Bayley, Ryan 126, 127
Beaurepaire, Frank 27
Benson, Daryl 127
Black, John 94
Blanksby, Brian 65, 122, 146
Bloomfield, John 35, 37, 49, 92, 95, 96, 122, 146, 243
Bloomfield Report
   1973 (Aust Govt) 39, 41, 42, 51, 55, 156
   1978 (WA Govt) 53, 65
   1983 (WA Govt) 67
Bolger, Billy 26
Bond, Jeff 147
Borchedt, Katrin 123
Bott, Lloyd 136
Boultbee, John 140
Bowen, Lionel 113
Bowman, Peter 59
boxing 16, 25
Boyle, Raelene 116, 185
Bradbury, Stephen 201
Bradman, Don 13, 25, 26, 134
Brettell, Paul 44, 55, 56, 74, 83, 153
British Challenge 211
British Empire Games see Australian Commonwealth Games Association
British influence 5
Brooks, Norman 26
Brosque, Alex 207

Brown, John vi, 68, 69, 70, 72, 80, 84, 89, 90, 91, 93, 96 97, 107, 111, 117, 118
Bruckner, Peter 158
Bryson, Bill 106
Bundey, W.H. 5, 9
Burke Labor Government (WA) 65, 67, 89

Camplin, Alisa 123, 202, 203
Canberra College of Education 59
Carlile, Forbes 153, 154, 155
   full-time coach 146
   Lecturer in Physiology 146
   research in physiology of training 146
Carlile, Ursula 153, 154, 155
Carr, Bob 197, 248
Cashman, Richard 162
Cavill, Dick 22
Cerutty, Percy 13, 146, 152
Chappell, Ian 13
Charlesworth, Ric 13
Charlton, Andrew (Boy) 27
Cheffers, John 75, 76, 79, 80, 81
Christiakov, Viktor 124
Clark, Belinda 116
Clarke, Nerida 77
Clohessy, Pat 153
Coates, John 83, 95, 101, 107, 179, 180, 182, 183, 199, 214
Coe, Sebastian 190
Cohen, Barry 36, 37, 38, 41, 156
Coles Report 42, 43, 55
Coles, Phil 182
Commonwealth Games (1982), facilities 52
Commonwealth National Fitness Council 243
Community Recreation Centre 51, 52
Community Recreation Council of Western Australia 49
Community Sport Development Program 132
Confederation of Australian Sport 47, 49, 53, 54, 174, 175, 177
   Australian Sports Commission 175
   Australian Sports Commission Bill 174
   Daly, Garry 174
   George, Sir Arthur 174
   Hartung, Greg 175
   Master Plan for Sport 174
   Sports Industry Australia 175

Contribution of Sports Medicine   156
Contribution of Sports Science   144
Cooke, Baden   206
cornstalks   3
Corrigan, Brian   159
Cotton, Professor Frank   153, 154
  Anti-G (gravity) suit   145
  bicycle ergometer   146
  Developed talent identification   146
  Harvard University   145
  New South Wales swimming champion
    145
  Professor of Physiology   145
  rowing ergometer   146
Court, Margaret   116
Cram, Steve   190
Crapp, Lorraine   30
Creighton, Ken   158
Crichton-Browne, Noel   94
cricket   11, 12, 26
Crosswhite, Perry   97, 177
currency   v, 3
currency lads   4, 6, 7
  and lasses   3
Cuthbert, Betty   30, 185

Daly, John   11, 45, 46, 55, 73, 74,
95, 162
Darcy, Les   17
Darlison, Libby   118, 131
Dawn Fraser Australian Athlete of the
  Year   119
de Castella, Robert   97, *98*, 147
De la Hunty Strickland, Shirley   30, 185
Deakes, Nathan   205
Deane, Sir William   184, 185, 191
Dempster, Graham   39, 44, 55, 57, 136
Dennis, Claire   27
Department of Sport, Recreation and
  Tourism   85
Developing Australia's Talent   122
  athlete development pathways   125
  developing the talent   123
  foreign athletes   123
  identifying talent   122
  media call-ups   122
  older athletes   122
  sibling profiling   123
  talent recycling   123
Developments in Sports Studies   161

Australian Society for Sports History
  (ASSH)   161
Australian Sporting Traditions
  Conference   161
National American Society for Sports
  History (NASSH)   161
Devitt, John   169
Disability Education Program   120
Disabled Sports Program   118, 120
Division of Physical Education, University
  of Western Australia   146
Dixon, Brian   41, 42, 53, 66, 88, 89
domestic sport   23
Donaldson, Jack   20
Drug Episode, first   84
Drugs in Sport Committee   95
Drugs in Sport, Interim Report   94
Dubin, Mr Justice   94
Durack, Fanny   22, 27

egalitarianism   v, 9
Elite Sport   220
Ellicott, Bob   54, *55*, 56, 63, 68, 70,
  96, 97
Elliott, Bruce   146, 149
Elliott, Herb   13, 85, 86
English Rugby Union   163
European Championships   99
Evaluating the Sports System   104
Evans, Cadel   206
Evans, Jack   85, 86, 177
Eve, Dick   27
Evonne Goolagong   116

Facility development 1975–80   51
Faulkner, John   101, 107, 115
Federal Department of Sport and
  Recreation   136
federal government expenditure on the
  Australian sports system   105
Fédération Internationale Médicine
  Sportive (FIMS)   156
Ferguson, Jim   97, 102, 108, 182
Ferrier, Jim   26
First Fleet   9
Fisher, Peter   84, 85
Fitch, Ken   37, 146, 158, 159, *160*, 243
Flack, Edwin   20
Flintoff-King, Debbie   185
Foley, Larry   16
Foley, Steve   153

Forbes, Warwick   153
Foreman, Wally   67
Fraser Coalition Government   43, 54, 56, 68, 136
Fraser, Dawn   13, 30, 116, 134, 185
Fraser, Malcolm   45, 46, 56, 57, 81
Fricker, Peter   59, 157, 158, 159
Fuller, Neil   193
funding sources for sport   216
future funding for sport   215, 220

Gallagher, Harry   146, 152
Gathercole, Terry   155, 169
Gaze, Andrew   *183*
George, Sir Arthur   48
Gibson, Jack   13
Gilchrist, Adam   29
Giles, Kelvin   84, 153
Giltinan, James   21
Gocher, W.H.   22
Going for Gold   93
Gold Rush   4
goldfields   4
golf   21, 26, 30
Goodwill Games (2001)   201
Gosper, Kevan   57, *96*
Gould, Shane   116, 185
Graduate Diploma in Elite Sports Coaching   110
Graham, Herb   37
Graham, John   37, 49
Gray, Edgar   27
Great Depression   24
Greene, Maurice   190
Greenwood, Ivor   44
Grigorieva, Tatiana   123, 124,
Grima, Holly   *207*
Grimmett, Clarrie   26
Groom, Ray   53
Gulbin, Jason   122, 123
Guthrie, Frank   146, 152

Hahn, Allan   122, 147, 148
Harris, Ted   86, 92
Harrison, Henry   20
Hartung, Greg   48, 85, 86, 87, 90
Harvey, Ron   81, 82, 83, 94
Hawke Labor Government   vi, 63, 69, 70, 88, 136

Hawke, Bob   73, 85
Hawke–Keating Labor Governments 1988–92   vi, 91, 107, 109
Hawkes, Rechelle   116, 117
Healey, Dick   35
Healy, Cecil   22
Hemsley, Margaret   205
Hendricks, Jon   30
Herford, Sam   146
Hoad, Lew   30
Hobbs, Kevin   159
Holey dollar   2, 3
Holloway, Sandy   182
Homebush racecourse   *18*
Honda, Kazuya   59, 153
Hopman, Harry   13, 26, 152
horse racing   17
Howard Coalition Government   179, 181
Howe, Kym   127, *129*
Howell, Max   162
Hunt, Geoff   153
Hurley, Adrian   59, 60, 61
Hussein, Hussy   206
Hyde Park   5, *17*

Indigenous Australians in Sport   131
   Beetson, Arthur   131
   Ella brothers (Mark, Glen and Garry)   131
   Farmer, Graham (Polly)   131
   Freeman, Cathy   132, 134, *135*, *184*, 185
   Johnson, Patrick   133
   Mundine, Tony   131
   Nicholls, Douglas   131
   Richards, Ron   131
   Rose, Lionel   131
   Sands, Dave   131
   Walford, Ricky   131
Intensive Training Centre (ITC)   94, 102, 142
Intensive Training Programs   102
International Assistance   132
International Olympic Committee (IOC)   83, 94, 101, 136, 175
   Coles, Phil   176
   de Coubertin, Baron Pierre   175
   Gosper, Kevan   176
   Grange, Syd   176
   Samaranch, Juan Antonio   176

Jackson, Marjorie   116
Jaggard, Ed   162
Jobling, Ian   162
Johnson, Ben   94
Jones, Gerry   147
Jones, Liesel   206
Jones, Lyn   59, 153
Jones, Marion   190
Junior Sport Program   113

Keating Labor Government   181
Keating, Paul   101
Kelly, Jackie   103
Kelly, Ros   97, 101
Khmel, Michael   127
Kieran, Barney   22
Kirkwood, Joe   26
Knight, Michael   182
Konrads, Ilsa   116
Kuala Lumpur Commonwealth Games
   (1998)   181
Kulacz, Rick   206

Lafortune, Mario   147
Lane, Freddie   22, 27
Lang, John Dunmore   9
Larsen, Kristina   *125*, 127
Lauren, Sarah   206
Laver, Rod   13, 30
Leaders in Sports Medicine   159
Lindrum, Walter   27
Local Government Sports Services   139
Lockwood, Richard   118, 147
Longley, Luc   82
Los Angeles Olympic Games (1984)   75
Low Fitness - High Obesity   220
Lynch, Phillip   48

MacKay, Heather   13, 153
Mackenzie, Stuart   13
Macquarie, Lachlan   9
Maguire, Ken   156, 157
Maintain the Momentum (1992–96)   100,
   101, 102, 103, 180
Manchester Commonwealth Games (2002)
   127, 204, 210
Marsh, Rodney   28, 153, 211
Martin, Michelle   116
Martin, Stephen   93
Mason, Bruce   147

Master Plan for Sport (1980)   54
Masters, Roy   113, 115
Matthews, Marlene   116
McAuliffe, Ron   37
McCabe, Stan   26
McCann, Kerryn   205
McClatchy, Craig   169
McDonald, Bruce   136
McGee, Brad   206, 209, *210*
McKay, Heather   116
McKenzie, David   47, 48
McLaren, Geoff   35, 36, 37
McMahon, William   36
McVeigh, Tom   63, 64
Mealing, Alecia   27
Medal 'Tally' by AOC (2002)   201
Melbourne Cup   18
Miller, Adam   127, *128*
Miller, Tony   13
Milton, Michael   *202*
Ministries of Sport and Recreation   35
Moffett, David   211, 212
Montgomery, Peter   101, 183
Montreal Olympic Games (1976)   44, 46
Morton, Alan   146, 158
Moscow Olympic Games (1980)   56
Moussambani, Eric   188
Murdoch, Rupert   173
Murphy, Billy   17

Nagle, Kel   30
National Athlete Award Scheme   70,
National Capital Development Commission
   70
National Coaching Accreditation Scheme
   49, 109
National Coaching Scholarship Program
   110
National Elite Sports Council (NESC)   141
National Fitness Council of Western
   Australia   146
National Fitness Councils   34
National Leagues and Sponsorship   172
National Sports Advisory Council   48
National Sports Information Centre,
   Sportscan Data Base   112
National Sports Organisations   162
National Sports Research Centre   112
National Sports Research Program (NSRP)
   110, 111, 112

National Sports Science and Medical
Research Council   151
National Talent Search Co-ordinator   122
National Training Centres (NTC)   142
National Training Manager (AFL)   111
nationalism   v, 6, 196
Nedlands Secondary Teachers' College
147
Netball Australia   171
Teede, Gai   171
New South Wales Combined High Schools
Track and Field Championships   127
New South Wales Institute of Sport
(NSWIS)   67, 119, 121, 125, 127, 128,
136, 137, 210
Newman, Kevin   44, 45, 47, 68
News Limited   87, 173
Next Step, The   93, 96, 97, 103
Non-Government Sports Services   178
Norman, Greg   134
Northern Territory Institute of Sport (NTIS)
67, 136
Nunan, Mike   67, 90

O'Grady, Stuart   206
O'Neill, Nathan   206
O'Neill, Suzie   196
O'Reilly, Bill   26
Oakes, Barry   158
oarsome foursome   17
Oldenhove, Jenny   113
Oldfield, Bert   26
Olympic Athlete Program (OAP) (1994–
2000)   101, 102
Olympic Foundation   47
Olympic Village Polyclinic   158
Opperman, Hubert   27

Pan American Games   99
Parker, Tony   148, 149
Parkin, David   13
Parnov, Alexander   124, 127
Pavy, Len   147
Pearce, 'Bobby'   27
Penrose, Tom   149
Peris, Nova (formerly Nova Peris-
Kneebone)   122, 134, *135*
Perkins, Kieren   134
Peters, Mark   212, 214
Pewtress, Margaret   117

Phillips, J.H.   10
Phillips, Murray   162
Physical Fitness and Obesity   215
Physical Fitness Programs
Fitness Australia   130
Life Be In It   49, *50*, 65, 130, 220
'Norm'   50
Participation   130
Pickworth, Ossie   30
Piggins, George   174
Pittman, Jana   207
Ponsford, Bill   26
Ponting, Ricky   28
Professional Golfers' Association of
Australia (PGA)   167
Garske, Max   168
Johnson, Don   168
Robilliard, Ian   168
Thomson, Peter   168
Wilson, Neville   168
professional running   19
Prosser, Sep   152
Purnell, John   74, 76
Pursley, Dennis   153
Pyke, Frank   62, 136, 137, 138, 146

Queensland University of Technology
140
Centre for Rugby Studies   140

Randwick racecourse   18
Recreation Ministers' Council   51
Refshauge, Jack   159
Refshauge, William   159
Reid, Wayne   48, 53
Resource Kits   113
Richards, Karen   191
Richardson, Graham   91, 92, 93, 94, 95,
97, 98, 99, 107, 137
Ministry   91
Ridder, Jessica   122
Rippon, Steve   127
Rizzo, Philippe   207, *208*
Robertson, Clint   122, 166
Robinson, John   58
Robinson's Baths (Sydney Domain)   168
Robson, Ian   211
Rogers, Michael   206
role of government agencies   109
role of non-government agencies   144

Rose Hill (Parramatta)   9
Rose, Murray   30
Ross, Sandy   16
rowing   15
Royal Melbourne Institute of Technology
    111
Ruffles, Ray   59, 153
rugby league   21
rugby union   21
Rural Fire Service   158

Sadler, Joseph   15
Salt Lake Winter Olympic Games (2002)
    201
Salt Lake Winter Paralympic Games (2002)
    201
Samaranch, Juan Antonio   184
Sandow, Brian   159
Sauvage, Louise   119, *121*, 194
Saville, Jane   123, 205
Scarf, Eddie   27
School of Human Movement and Exercise
    Science, University of Western
    Australia   150
School Sport Australia   138
Scott, Michael   151
Sea Rescue service   158
Senate Drug Inquiry, Black Committee   94
Seoul Olympic Games (1988)   91, 94
Seven Sports Program   96
Shakespear, Wilma   59, 153, 211
Shaping Up - A Review of Commonwealth
    Involvement in Sport and Recreation
    in Australia   103, 112, 130
Sharp, John   84
Sheffield Shield   172
Shoulder, Jimmy   59, 153
Smith, Ross   97
Smith, Warwick   107
soccer   21
social cohesion   v, 9, 197
social dynamics in Australian sport   3
South Australian Sports Institute (SASI)
    67, 136, 140
South Pacific Paralympic Committee   87
South Sydney Rugby League Club   174
Spofforth, Fred   11, *12*
Sports Assistance Scheme   110
Sports Coaching   152
    Australia's success   153

followed British model   152
National Sport Foundation   152
sports high schools   139
Sports Industry Australia   217
Sports Institute/Academy Network   140
Sports Medicine Australia   158
Sports Science and Sports Medicine
    Research in Australia   112
Sports Science
    at Sydney Olympics   149
    in universities, institutes and academies
        149
Sports System Developments
    Europe   32
    North America   32
Stampfl, Frantz   146, 152
Stanton, Krishna   205
State Emergency Services   158
State Government Sports Services   137
State Sporting Organisations   177
Stawell Gift   19
Stewart, Frank   *38*, 39, 41, 43, 107
Stewart-Weeks, Martin   197, 198, 250
Stoddart, Brian   162
Strategic Plans   88, 102, 103, 104
strategies for future sport   217
Super League   214
Surf Life Saving Australia (SLSA)   164
    Australian Surf Lifesaving
        Championships   166
    Bondi Surf Bathers, Lifesaving Club
        164
    Surf Life Saving Association of
        Australia   164
surf lifesaving   23, 26
Sweetenham, Bill   59, 153, 211
swimming   22, 27
Sydney Academy of Sport   127
Sydney Equestrian Centre   *19*
Sydney Olympic Games (2000)
    after the Sydney Olympics   199
    Australia's results   185
    awarded to Sydney (1993)   101
    closing ceremony   185
    lead-up   179
    opening ceremony   184
    reactions to the Olympics   187
    Sport Search Program   102
    Talent Search Advisory Committee   102
    Torch Relay   182

Sydney Paralympic Games (2000)
  awarded to Sydney (1993)   101
  lead-up   191
  Australia's results   192
  closing ceremony   192
  reactions to Games   192
  post-Games assessments   194
Sydney Town   9
Sydney University Football Club (SUFC)
    21

Talbot, Don   13, 146, 152
Talent Search Achievements   124
Target Sports Program   131, 217
Targeted Support Program   142
Tasmanian Institute of Sport (TIS)
    67, 136
Tatz, Colin   162
Taurima, Jai   188, *189*
Telford, Dick   59, 147
tenacity   v, 11
tennis   22, 26
University of Western Australia   111
University of Western Australia,
    Department of Physical Education
    49
Whitlam era (1972–75)   vi, 38
Thompkins, James   17
Thompson, Graham   65, 66
Thompson, Peter   30
Thorpe, Ian   170, 205
  Ian Thorpe Foundation for Youth Trust
    170
  NSW Institute of Sport Scholarship
    170
  World's Most Outstanding Athlete
    Award 2000   170
Tian, Ju-Ping   153
Tighe, Karen   193
Toler, Marion   190
Toyne, Howard   159
Trickett, Edward   15, *16*
Trumper, Victor   21, 26
Tszyu, Kostya   123
Turner, Charles   153

University of Sydney   140, 145
University Sports Services   139
unregistered sport participation   171
Uren, Tom   47

Vamplew, Wray   162
Vanderfield, Geoff   159
Victorian Institute of Sport (VIS)   67,
    136, 137
volunteering   v, 13, 14
Von Nida, Norman   26, 30

Walsh, Charlie   153
Watson, Jeff   147
Watson, Shane   207
Watts, Don   74
Waugh, Steve   13, 28, *29*
Webb, Bill   159
Western Australian Institute of Sport
    (WAIS)   67, 89, 119, 126, 127, 136,
    140, 141
Western Australian Sport Development
    Working Party   89
Western Australian Sports Centre
    (Challenge Stadium)   *141*
Western Australian Sports Council   89
Western Australian Sports Federation
    86
wheelchair rugby   120
white native-born Australians   3
Whitlam Labor Government   41, 43,
    68, 70, 136
Whitlam, Gough   36
Wickham, Alick   22
Wills, Thomas   20
Wilson, Ian   63
Wilson, Keith   89
Wilson, Michael   90
Women in Sport   116
  Active Women, National Policy on etc.
    118
  Task Force for Women's Sport   117
  Women's Sport Promotion Unit (WSPU)
    117
Women's International Squash Players
    Association (WISPA)   119
Woodman, Laurie   110, 111, 153
World Championships won by Australians
    (2001)   200
World Swimming Championships   141
World Trade Fair Brisbane (1987)   90
Wylie, Mina   22, 27

'Young Griffo'   17

FROM SIDELINES TO CENTRE FIELD
A history of sports coaching in Australia
Murray Phillips

From Sidelines to Centre Field is the definitive history of the emergence of sports coaching in Australia. It explores the changing role and techniques of coaching in Australia, from its emergence and growing importance, to its professionalisation. It examines issues such as ethics, sportsmanship, professionalism and amateurism over the past 150 years, and documents the initiation of coaching education in Australia and the development of the Australian Coaching Council. It also discusses issues facing Australian coaches in the 21st century.

Illustrated with more than 70 photographs, this book looks at the contributions made by coaches in a wide range of popular sports and is packed with vital information gleaned from interviews with coaches, including Forbes and Ursula Carlile, Don Talbot, Percy Cerutty, Wayne Bennett and Ric Charlesworth.

 ISBN 0 86840 410 1
Published 2000